"MY FIRST DAUGHTER WAS BORN ON JUNE 1, 1970, IN A SMALL HOSPITAL IN CENTRAL MASSACHUSETTS. . . . I don't know if I was the only woman laboring that morning in that small maternity ward, but I felt as if I were. Everyone involved was warm, cheerful, supportive and focused on helping me have my baby. . . .

Finally, there was my daughter's head—dark hair. And then, in a few more pushes, there she was, in a slippery whoosh at 10:27 A.M. She was quite purple and soon cried, and I looked at her and declared, "She's purple, but she's beautiful!" She was beautiful then and still is. She cried enough to turn herself thoroughly pink and then quieted. Her daddy held her first before they even washed her off, and then I held her close to me and looked into her enormous blue eyes. She was tiny—only six pounds, two ounces, but healthy and very pretty and perfect. Her gaze was full of curiosity. I felt she was asking me questions and I answered her in my heart while I babbled nonsense to her out loud. . . .

This past May I went back to Smith College for my twenty-fifth college reunion and I took Katherine with me. Part of our plan was to visit the places her father and I lived when we were newlyweds and the year after she was born—and, of course, I wanted her to see the country hospital where she actually came into the world. . . . [and know] the delight I felt when my oldest child lay on my arm and looked at me with such grave curiosity in her dark blue eyes. . . .

—from *Having a Baby: Mothers Tell Their Stories*

Having a Baby

MOTHERS TELL THEIR STORIES

Patricia Bernstein

POCKET BOOKS

New York   London   Toronto   Sydney   Tokyo   Singapore

An *Original* publication of Pocket Books

POCKET BOOKS, a division of Simon & Schuster Inc.
1230 Avenue of the Americas, New York, NY 10020

Bernstein, Patricia.
   Having a baby : mothers tell their stories / by Patricia Bernstein.
      p. cm.
   ISBN: 0-671-72614-5 : $10.00
   1. Childbirth—Popular works. 2. Childbirth—United States—Case studies. 3. Childbirth—United States—Miscellanea. I. Title.
RG652.B45   1993
618.4′00973—dc20   92-30243
                                                                            CIP

First Pocket Books trade paperback printing January 1993

10   9   8   7   6   5   4   3   2   1

To Alan, Katherine, Jessica, and Rebecca,
who made birth and all its aftermath very sweet

Acknowledgments

There were many who helped me throughout the preparation of this book. Ellen Bianco, Karen Dufilho, Robyn Newman, Marie Wright, and Mary Zimmerman, my staff at the office, were drafted into assisting and did so with enormous graciousness and patience. Dr. Jean Anderson, Barbara Crotty, Sherley Hollos, Sandra Lemke, Polly Perez, Nadia Stein, Sherri Urban, and JoAnn van Compernolle, all involved professionally in childbirth, were wonderful helpers and inspirations and, in some cases, were sources of stories or referrals to stories.

Others shared their time selflessly to help me locate additional stories or sources. Thanks to Lenwood Johnson and Anna Poulin, I came into contact with the Salvadoran-American woman I call Elena. Anna also helped me interview Elena, helped her with her English, translated her Spanish, and helped me draw out her story of a public hospital birth.

Sherley Hollos referred me to Pauline Jonas and to the two women living together who each had a baby by the same donor through artificial insemination. Frances Hammon put me in touch with Nancy Harrison. Children like Mary Anker, Jo McIntyre, Edith Barr, and Ellen Buchanan helped by being willing to sign releases, find photographs, and give additional background information for mothers who are very elderly or deceased.

Librarians at the Houston Public Library who provided interlibrary loan services and at the Texas Medical Center Library

Acknowledgments

were invaluable. Dr. John Gable of the Theodore Roosevelt Association looked up information and clippings for me on Quentin Roosevelt II and his illustrious wife and daughters. Polly Perez and Kay Johnson offered enormous assistance in reviewing the obstetrical accuracy of the book. Gabrielle Cosgriff gave me generous and helpful editing suggestions.

The mothers themselves, who wrote these stories, gave their time over and over, with nothing in particular to gain from it, to make this book happen.

Most of all, of course, I want to thank my daughters, Katherine Ann, Jessica Elizabeth, and Rebecca Floren, who inspired this book and inspire me daily, and my husband, Alan, who shared and believed in this project with me for so many years.

Contents

———— ♡ ————

Contents

Contents

Author's Note

My first and second daughters were born fifteen years apart, in 1970 and 1985. (My third and last baby girl was born in 1988.)

While I was pregnant with the second daughter, I learned that during the fifteen years between my pregnancies, the process of having a child in an American hospital had changed radically—and not for the better.

Having those two babies so far apart and observing all the changes that had taken place in the birth system in just fifteen years started me wondering about the experiences of other women. I began to be curious about how childbirth in America had changed from year to year and from decade to decade throughout this century.

I wanted to learn what childbirth had been like in the "old days" from the point of view of the mothers themselves—not doctors or sociologists or historians or childbirth educators or writers of fiction or movie directors. I suspected that there were probably a lot of other birth stories that ought to be told besides my own—and that some of the most interesting and valuable tales would be lost forever if they weren't told soon.

We all have a mental image of what birth was like during the eons of time between labor in caves and, say, the founding of the Boston Lying-In Hospital in 1832. It was something like the birth of Melanie's child in *Gone with the Wind,* wasn't it? Hours of sweaty agony hanging on to the bedposts with a rag stuffed in the mother's mouth to stifle screams. Scissors under the bed to "cut" the pain. The midwife—or a local matron—in a rocking chair, knitting and waiting, or calling out for more hot water. "There, there, dear," she whispers, as she mops the brow of the laboring woman with a handkerchief. "It won't be long now."

The alternative image is that of the rugged peasant woman who severs the umbilical cord with her teeth, straps the baby on her back, and goes right on seeding the furrows.

These images may or may not bear much relation to the way it really was. But most of us have no image of what birth was like in the early part of this century—childbirth at home in 1918, for example, with the use of ether or chloroform; or birth in a hospital in 1944 under the influence of scopolamine—known to an earlier generation as "twilight sleep."

We may have heard isolated details from our mothers about our own births, but chances are we never heard the whole story. Of our grandmothers' experiences of childbirth we know little or nothing.

Since 1959 and Marjorie Karmel *(Thank You, Dr. Lamaze: A Mother's Experiences in Painless Childbirth),* it has become fashionable in our own time to tell tales of birth quite openly to anyone who will sit still long enough to listen. We all tell our stories over and over, parents swap stories, fathers "share" their experiences.

Magazines and books these days are filled with birth stories. If a new mother can't get her birth story published somewhere— at least in a local birthing center or La Leche League newsletter—she is forced to live with the suspicion that her baby's birth must have been tediously routine.

But the stories of our mothers and grandmothers have not been heard. In their day new mothers didn't discuss ruptured amniotic sacs, enema-shave "preps," and episiotomies in mixed company. (If these terms are mystifying, see the glossary at the end of this book.)

Women did share birth stories with each other, of course, as they always have. In Dallas, where I grew up, they swapped gynecological gossip in lowered voices over finger sandwiches and avocado salad molds at The S & S Tearoom. But they didn't record their birth tales for posterity.

It was my intention when I began the research for this book to record some of these stories of births, from 1927 and 1930 and 1942, before they disappeared. My reasoning was that we could benefit from the good elements and avoid some of the mistakes of the past. But what is probably more important is that these stories give us special insight into women and birth and the basic workings of humanity.

I began my collection of birth stories by advertising in the classified section of *Ms.* magazine and writing letters to the editors of the Older Women's League newspaper and the *Alumnae Quarterly* of my alma mater, Smith College. Later I wrote to several retirement and senior citizens' magazines. I asked for detailed accounts of childbirth experiences from women who were fifty or older.

In the first few months I received responses from almost two hundred different women. There were letters from women who had just barely turned fifty or weren't quite fifty yet and a letter from a ninety-five-year-old woman in a Philadelphia retirement home. There were letters describing births that took place in the early 1920s and others about births that took place in the early 1970s.

When the letters began to arrive, my middle daughter was only about seven months old and I was still coming home from work every day at lunchtime to nurse her. The mailman often came while we were all having our lunch. My husband, who was taking care of the little one in the morning and working the late shift as a reporter, fell into the habit of reading the latest batch of "birth letters" aloud while we ate.

There were some letters that featured remarkable or unusual or shocking incidents—like the story in which the doctor never arrived for the birth, or the story in which a doctor let a woman labor for hours despite the fact that he knew the baby was crosswise in the womb and could not be born normally, or the story in which a woman managed to have a fifth baby despite the pill, an IUD, and a tubal ligation! (She was already pregnant, without knowing it, when she had her tubes tied.)

There were tragic tales of babies who died or were damaged and joyful tales of women who finally bore healthy babies after years of effort or who sought and demanded and finally created the kind of birth they wanted. There were also humorous stories, written by women with a wry perspective that never failed them, despite labor pains and doctors and nurses who insisted on enemas, shaves, stirrups, and straps.

We even got one letter from a man—dear John Todd—eighty-five, who wrote because he knew his wife would have wanted to write me if she were still alive. "I would like to think that all knowledge is not vanity," he said.

But none of the letters, even those without exceptional dramatic incident, were ordinary. For all of these women, birth was one of the most intense experiences of a lifetime—so intense that most could remember the words of a nurse or doctor, spoken casually fifty or sixty years ago. They could remember the color of the curtains in a semiprivate room, what they had for dinner the night before the baby was born, and the measurements for ingredients in formula given to a baby who is now fifty-three years old.

I found myself crying over babies who died many years ago, getting angry at doctors and nurses who are probably long retired or deceased, and smiling at the image of a tiny daughter born in 1938, tucked into bed with her mother with the covers "right up to her chin." (Of course, no sooner did the mother put the baby in bed with her than a nurse came along and removed the baby, declaring in outrage that the mother might "contaminate" her own child.)

After some months of working with these stories from women over fifty, I decided to go ahead and complete the picture of birth in this century by adding contemporary birth stories. My contemporary stories were gathered from women who are currently in the process of creating their families—from friends, sources referred by friends, childbirth educators and midwives, from childbirth-related newsletters, and from more ads and letters placed in various publications.

I added these contemporary stories partly because I knew from my own experience that hospital birth has changed radically in the last twenty years. I wanted to provide stories that would be helpful to women having babies now and give them some idea of what birthing might be like for them.

It wasn't until I began to pull all these stories together in very rough chronological order, as they appear here, that I realized I had, in this collection, childbearing stories covering one hundred years of American history—from Sarah Meyers in the first story, who began having babies in the 1880s, to Elise Gunst, whose second child was born on June 3, 1991, as described near the end of this book, and Elizabeth de Forest, whose baby was born on June 21, 1991.

In some ways childbirth has changed as much as transportation in the last one hundred years. Could Sarah Meyers have imagined seeing an image on a screen of her fetus dancing in her womb when it was only one inch long? Or having a fetus operated on while it was still in the womb? Effie Glass's mother had triplets born three months early in 1912. They died the same day. Triplets born three months early today might live. Susan Vano's quadruplets were born ten weeks early in 1987 and all four survived.

In other ways we have come full circle. Mothers are having babies at home again but with less fear, better health, better nutrition, better training and knowledge, and a more optimistic attitude than in the 1880s. Compare Sarah Meyers's story again to the stories of home birth in the 1980s and '90s by Barbara Crotty and Liz de Forest.

Other basic themes recur in this collection of stories. Many, many women define their own experiences by comparing them to that of a mother, a grandmother, an aunt, a daughter, or a daughter-in-law. Some stories are a compendium of "birth in my family." A number of women used the opportunity of writing to me to record their birth stories for their families.

One of the most consistent themes in the tales of many of these women is a strong protest against being left to labor in total isolation or accompanied only by other groaning, laboring women. Women also complain of having been given no information about what to expect, of being shackled in stirrups and wrist straps, of the callousness of doctors and nurses who treated women giving birth like "meat," and of the monumental absurdity and rigidity of hospital rules.

Some women had their babies over a period of eight or ten or twenty years, as I did, and watched hospital rules flip-flop as times changed. One mother tells of having her first child in 1943 and being told that she absolutely could not get out of bed for ten days, which meant no baths other than sponge baths in bed. By the time she had her last child, in 1954, she was told "the shower's down the hall" and was expected to get there herself the day after the birth.

Undoubtedly, the most dramatic change in hospital birth in the last decade or two (and one reason that I decided to include contemporary births) is the prevalence of the cesarean section. The C-section, or the threat of a C-section, haunts hospital births today like the Phantom of the Opera. (See the chapter on the history of childbirth.)

Women having babies today, however, still have a lot in common with women having babies one hundred years ago. Their stories are not sentimental. They have none of the pastel, sugary colors of a Mother's Day card. Birth is an immense natural phenomenon that takes place on an intimate, personal scale—like a hurricane in a living room.

Birth, every particular aspect of it, cannot be forgotten by the women who live it. The bitterness or disappointment or frustration or joy or ecstasy of the birth—or all of the above—is relived over and over again in the mother's mind as the child grows and matures and leaves home and has children of his or her own. The birth memory stays.

All birthing mothers also feel, I think, consciously or half-consciously, that we are part of a great continuum of birthing women stretching both backward and forward in time, and it's a good feeling. We feel that we are not alone. We feel that we are here for a reason, that this is supposed to happen—the birth, that is, not always the circumstances surrounding it.

To draw any other conclusions at this point would be to second-guess these mothers who speak so well for themselves. Unfortunately, all of my correspondents could not be included, so I have tried to offer a representative sampling of experiences.

What follows is a brief history of childbirth in the United States in this century, just to provide some helpful background notes. Then I will leave you to enjoy these stories and to draw your own conclusions about birth in America. By way of contrast and comparison, I have also included a few tales of births in other countries. My own feelings about what these stories tell us are summarized at the end of the book.

History

*Midwife to Doctor, Home to Hospital—and Back
Again?: A Brief History of Childbirth in America
in the Twentieth Century*

The story of childbirth in America in the first half of this
century was characterized by a massive transition, from midwife
to doctor, from home to hospital, and, finally, from general prac-
titioner to obstetrical specialist. As we near the end of the century we are beginning to observe a much smaller but significant
and intriguing shift from doctor back to midwife and even from
hospital back to home.

But through all these changes, certain sad facts of American
childbirth have remained tragically persistent. More than in
many other industrialized nations, the kind of care available to
well-off women having babies in the United States today is very
different from the kind of care available to poor women. In that
respect, things haven't changed much since 1900.

As late as 1910, more than half the births in the United States
were still attended by midwives. But the midwife attended primarily the births of lower-income women, women who lived in
rural areas and immigrant women. Most middle- and upper-class
American women, beginning as early as the late 1700s, had already made the shift to male doctors, even though they were
still having their babies at home. They turned to doctors in the
hope of benefiting from the doctors' supposed skill in the use
of special instruments like the forceps and in the desire for pain
relief through the use of ether or chloroform.

In other industrialized countries, midwives were eventually

organized and educated and today play an important or even dominant role in the care of women having normal labors and deliveries. (See Suzanne Bancel's story on birth in Norway in the 1980s, for example.) But American doctors saw the midwives as unskilled and dangerous competitors and organized to eliminate them.

By 1930 only 15 percent of the children born in America were delivered by midwives. The midwives were defeated by their inability to obtain education or to counterpropagandize effectively and by the restriction of immigration in the 1920s and the sustained lowering of the birthrate between 1921 and 1930. They were also defeated by the massive movement from home to hospital between 1910 and 1950.

This movement, which changed the hospital from a nineteenth-century refuge for poor women who had nowhere else to go to have their babies to an early-twentieth-century private retreat for the upper and middle classes, was not entirely led and driven by physicians. Nor was it entirely engineered by the popular press, which, for several decades, incessantly promoted the hospital as the only safe place to have a baby.

To some degree, women began to go to the hospital to have babies because *other women* had promised them that in the hospital they could find not only safety and cleanliness and a respite from household chores but also pain relief and, indeed, total oblivion, permitting them to "skip" consciousness of the childbearing experience entirely. The demand for pain relief combined with forgetfulness was embodied in the "twilight sleep" movement, spearheaded by a group of well-to-do American society women in the second decade of this century.

A few of these women even traveled across the Atlantic in search of a better way to have their babies, making a special pilgrimage to the Frauenklinik in Freiburg, Germany, before and during World War I. At the Frauenklinik, Dr. Bernhard Kronig carefully supervised each labor and birth personally with the precise administration of a little morphine when labor was well established, followed by regular doses of scopolamine at intervals throughout labor. (Scopolamine is not a painkiller but an amnesic drug that causes the labor experience to be forgotten.) The combination of the two was called *Dammerschlaf* or twilight sleep. Those women who had positive experiences in Freiburg came back to America determined to introduce twilight sleep in this country.

In understanding their passionate pursuit of temporary oblivion, it helps to remember that around the turn of the century, approximately one mother died for every 154 living births. A method of childbirth that promised not only pain relief but relief from the awareness of childbirth as it occurred was a powerful antidote to the fear that must have gripped many women as they anticipated each new confinement.

Complex combinations of drugs obviously could be safely administered only in some sort of hospital setting. So women came to the hospital in droves seeking the magic of twilight sleep. American doctors initially expressed misgivings about the safety of the drugs but gradually acceded to the popular demand for some form of anesthesia. Over the next few decades a wide variety of drugs were administered to laboring women. In fact, giving powerful drugs to cause forgetfulness and relieve pain became fairly standard hospital procedure.

Experimentation continued because no perfect drug or combination of drugs was ever found (or has been found to this day) that would relieve pain, allow labor to continue normally, and be free of possibly dangerous consequences for mother and/or infant.

In addition, in American hospitals the painstaking personal attendance of a Dr. Kronig was generally lacking. Because of the elimination of the midwife and the heavy patient load carried by most obstetricians, obstetrical procedures were not accepted in America unless they could be thoroughly routinized so that the presence of the doctor was not actually needed until the moment of "delivery." The result was the standardized, "knocked-out" birth where the mother was given drugs when she arrived at the hospital or at some point during labor and "awoke" after the baby was born.

These drugged laboring mothers, however, were not actually asleep. Drugs that would have eliminated pain entirely and put them to sleep would also have disrupted labor. Dr. Robert A. Bradley, who later founded the husband-coached natural childbirth movement, first began practicing obstetrics in 1947. He was strongly affected by the sight of laboring women confined to large "cribs" with bars, their heads encased in football helmets to keep them from injuring themselves as they thrashed about in a nightmare of pain and panic. They were feeling pain intensely, but the drugs had robbed them of the ability to understand their pain, to control their response, or to remember either the pain or their reaction later on.

Of course, in some hospitals amnesic and painkilling drugs were still considered suspect or too expensive or the staff was spread too thin to provide even minimal supervision of drugged women. In these cases, the alternative scenario was to monitor women sporadically as they labored—essentially leaving them alone hour after hour in wards full of other laboring women, with no one at hand to offer any sustained support or comfort. At the very end, when the ordeal was almost over, they might be given a bit of ether, chloroform, nitrous oxide, or some other chemical to see them through the actual moment of birth.

Nevertheless, in 1900 less than 5 percent of American women had their babies in hospitals; by 1939, 50 percent of all American women and 75 percent of all urban women were giving birth in hospitals. By 1950, 88 percent of all American babies were born in hospitals; by 1962 the figure was 97 percent—99 percent for white women.

Unfortunately, the switch to the hospital did not at once improve infant and maternal mortality rates, as was part of the promise. Not until the 1930s and 1940s, with the introduction of new antibiotics and blood banks, the use of oxytocin to counter the effects of anesthesia, the introduction of conduction or nerve-block anesthesia in place of general anesthesia, and the increasing use of C-sections instead of risky mid- and high-forceps deliveries, did mortality rates finally begin to improve.

Better nutrition, better hygiene, and a lower rate of childbearing also played a part in strengthening American women so that they could undergo childbirth more successfully. But in some countries where midwives officiated at most births and many children were still born at home, maternal and infant death rates continued to be lower than in the United States.

As maternal mortality rates improved and women began to be less afraid that they would die having their children, they began slowly to demand more of birth than simply that they and their babies should survive and that they should experience as little as possible of the actual process. Women were responsive to the opportunity to be conscious and aware once more when they gave birth, as soon as they began to gain confidence that the pain they felt would not result in death.

Wartime exigencies during the 1940s and the overcrowded maternity wards of the 1950s also contributed to increasing demands for a change in the way mothers were treated when babies were born. In 1940, 2.4 million babies were born in the United States. Between 1954 and 1964 more than 4 million babies were born each year. The pressure on maternity wards must have been overwhelming.

In a May 1958 article in *Ladies Home Journal* entitled "Journal Mothers Report on Cruelty in the Maternity Wards," women complained of everything from verbal abuse to callous actions, indifference, or negligence that could actually threaten the life or health of a mother or a newborn baby. Many of these reports are confirmed by stories in this book. Among the most common complaints: nurses holding the mother's legs together or holding the baby's head in to keep the baby from being born until the doctor arrived (see the stories by Pauline Plimpton, Lou Bulebosh, and Effie Glass, among others) and being left ignored and uncared for during labor for hours at a stretch. (See stories by Marilyn Bartick, Florine Bond, and others.)

In response to hospital birth procedures that were usually

routinized and impersonal at best, some women began to long for the restoration of elements that had been lost when the home birth was abandoned. They wanted closeness to family and friends and the birth attendant; a warm, supportive, *personalized* environment; and some knowledge of and control over what was happening. Women also began to protest against the unpleasant side effects and aftereffects of medicated birth—for mother and child.

In 1944 Dr. Grantly Dick Read's first American book, *Childbirth Without Fear: The Principles and Practices of Natural Childbirth,* was published. Many of the mothers in this book, including Dorothy Mullenneaux, Mary Garland, Beth McDonald, and Martha McIntyre, who actually corresponded with Dr. Read,[1] were strongly influenced by Dr. Read's description of how women could overcome fear and tension with knowledge and learn to give birth without unbearable pain.

In 1959 came Marjorie Karmel's *Thank You, Dr. Lamaze: A Mother's Experiences in Painless Childbirth,* which rapidly went through seven printings. And in 1965 Dr. Robert A. Bradley published the first edition of *Husband-Coached Childbirth,* introducing the "Bradley method" of natural childbirth in which the husband is trained to coach the mother through labor and delivery.

Of course, the same era, with its massive resurgence of childbearing and female domesticity, also resulted in the revival of breastfeeding, the "womanly art" abandoned by the newly liberated suffragette or 'flapper'' in the early decades of the 1900s. La Leche League was established in 1956.

Initially, women and men demanded more control over birth in the hospital—insisting particularly on the right of the father to be present at the birth of his child. In the 1970s, as birthrates fell once more and hospitals were having to compete for business, this movement began to make headway.

Gradually, the picture of birth in the hospital began to change in other ways as well. Now in many American hospitals other family members, friends, siblings, and women companions or trained birth assistants hired by the parents are allowed to be present at birth and delivery. (See "doula" and "monitrice" in the glossary.)

Attractive birthing suites provide a homelike setting where women can labor and give birth in the same room. In many hospitals, the infamous "prep" (enema and shave) is no longer forced on every laboring woman. Women are allowed to give birth in positions other than the flat-on-the-back, legs-up-in-stirrups lithotomy position. And most women are conscious, if not unanesthetized, when they have their babies. Some hospitals have even developed in-hospital birthing centers staffed by certified nurse-midwives who are trained to handle uncomplicated births.

But scratch the surface of this cheery picture and one wonders if we have moved two steps forward or four steps back. In many ways, hospitals have acceded to insistent consumer demands without really giving up any control over the birthing process. Control has been reestablished through the hardware-laden, high-tech birth.

Laboring women may find they are quickly transferred from the cozy birthing suite or in-hospital birthing center to an old-fashioned, stark labor cubicle if labor doesn't proceed "quickly enough" and Pitocin—or even an epidural—is administered. The whole process is hedged around with arbitrary hourly limits and rules: You must give birth within twenty-four hours of rupture of the amniotic sac, you must dilate at least one centimeter an hour, and so on. The consequence is that trying to give birth in a hospital without interference is like negotiating a minefield.

The hardware is everywhere: the electronic fetal monitor, routine use of an IV throughout labor, routine artificial rupture of the amniotic sac, the use of Pitocin to speed up labor, the use of the epidural, and, of course, the ultimate violation of the natural process, the cesarean section, now occurring in about 24 percent of all American births, up from 4.5 percent in 1965!

Some mothers and fathers have become so disgusted with hospital birth—C-sections and all the rest of it—that they have chosen to have their babies at home or at a freestanding birthing center, in addition to (or instead of) the in-hospital birthing center. (See the stories of Barbara Crotty, Robbie Davis-Floyd, Elizabeth de Forest, and others.) This new interest in home and birthing center births has resulted in the rebirth of the American midwife.

The American College of Nurse-Midwives was founded in 1955. According to Judy Litoff in *American Midwives: 1860 to the Present,* there were 1,256 certified nurse-midwives in the United States in 1971. Today, twenty years later, the American College of Nurse-Midwives has almost 3,800 members. There are about 4,800 certified nurse-midwives throughout the country. There are also about 130 freestanding birthing centers operating in the United States today and about 50 new ones under development.

The number of births taking place out of the hospital is not yet substantial enough to show up significantly in national statistics. In 1988, the most recent year for which we have complete figures, out-of-hospital births were still less than 1 percent of the total, or about 36,400. But births attended by midwives rather than physicians *in* the hospital have shown a very steady increase, from 0.6 percent in 1975 to about 3 percent in 1988. Midwives attended only 19,696 hospital births in 1975; in 1988 they attended 115,886.

But, while some American women are avoiding the hospital partly to reduce the risk of an unnecessary cesarean (a cesarean is much more likely if one is a private-pay patient than if one is a public patient, according to a January 2, 1991, article in the *Journal of the American Medical Association*), other women are not receiving the bare minimum of *necessary* care. Compare, for example, the treatment of Elena in a public hospital when she began to have contractions two months before her baby was due to the treatment of Elise Gunst, a private-pay patient with a similar problem.

Preliminary figures for the twelve months ending November 1990 indicate that the infant mortality rate in the United States has once more dropped slightly, to 9.1 infants per 1,000 births versus 9.7 for the previous twelve-month period—a 6 percent decrease in mortality. However, a number of other industrialized nations, including Japan (where the death rate is *5 per 1,000*), Finland, Sweden, Norway, Switzerland, Canada, and others, still have lower infant mortality rates.

And the infant mortality rates in the United States for nonwhites, especially blacks, still tend to be far higher than the death rates for white babies. The rate of infant mortality for blacks nationally was 17.6 per 1,000 in 1990, almost double the rate of 9.1 for the population as a whole.

Apparently all the new birth hardware and the ongoing struggle for control of the birth process have not solved the problems of women who are poor and uneducated, who may be bearing babies without a partner (in 1989 in Houston, 12.6 percent of white births, 22 percent of Hispanic births, and *57.6 percent of black births* were to unmarried women), who receive little or no prebirth or postbirth care, suffer from poor nutrition and poor health habits, may have serious illnesses or addictions, and, finally, bear low-birthweight babies with a much-reduced chance of survival.

Efforts to reduce the national cesarean rate and to enhance the control of parents over the births of their own children, important as these are, should ideally go hand in hand with efforts to provide good birth care for *all* of America's mothers, not just for those who can choose and pay for the care they prefer.

Dr. S. Josephine Baker, director of the New York City Bureau of Child Hygiene, as she waged her war to improve the health of children over eighty years ago, was fond of saying that she thought she would succeed eventually because "People didn't really like to see children die." That should be at least as true now as it was back in 1908. We all have an obligation to do what we can to improve birth for all mothers and babies and give every baby the best possible chance to live and to thrive.

Laura Dawson
Los Altos, California

♡ *The following are two letters submitted by Laura Dawson,
covering three generations of birth experiences in her family.
First is a letter from Sarah Meyers, Laura Dawson's grandmother, written to Laura McLaughlin (Laura Dawson's mother)
on October 28, 1938. The occasion for the letter, the birth of
Laura McLaughlin's last child, sets Sarah Meyers to reminisc-
ing about her own birth experiences.*

*Sarah Meyers bore nine children by two different husbands
between about 1886 and 1899. (There was a third marriage much
later in Sarah's life. She outlived that husband, too.) Sarah
describes the births of her children with patient resignation and
acceptance. She recognizes the difficulties of her life, but "we
seemed to get along all right," she says.*

*Laura Dawson told me in another letter that, after the sudden
death of Sarah's second husband in 1899, Sarah was so destitute she was forced to put her older children in an orphanage.
She then paid for foster care for her younger children and her
own upkeep by selling pots and pans door to door.*

*The death of both of her own parents before she was four
years old, the untimely deaths of three husbands, trying to support her children alone with no life insurance and no job—these
were just a few of the many terrible hardships Sarah Meyers
faced in her life. Yet, says Laura Dawson, "I never heard her*

say an unkind word or complain about her hard life. She just accepted what came."

My Dear Little Girl,

Received your letter today. I am so glad you are doing so nicely. I wish I could be there to see the little darling *right now*, and I am also glad the family are all right, too.

You ask me how I had my babies, if I suffered any pain. From first to last, I suffered absolute torture, from sixteen hours to four months. The first I suffered till I could not suffer anymore. Then, they gave me ether and took him. The next two were not quite so bad.

And then Marguerite. She weighed three pounds, but she did not want to be born. They had to help her. Then you. They made me walk the floor all night, the doctor and nurse holding me up till it was time to help you.

And then Jim. I had pain four months. A calf butted me in the abdomen when I was five months with him. I went to the hospital thinking he would come right away, but the doctors put me to bed and, in the end, they had to break the membranes before he came. The doctor said that tough membranes was what saved his life. I was in the hospital from December till May. He was born 27 April.

Walter was born at home. I was about sixteen hours with him. Willie was also born at home. He came the night before I had planned to go to the hospital. (The doctor wanted me always to go to the hospital a week or so before [because] I lived too far away from Philadelphia.) They were nearly all night finding a doctor. So Willie came without a doctor. He weighed twelve pounds, or so the doctor said when he got there.

I near died with childbed fever after that and had to go to the hospital afterward to get sewed up, and get cured of blood poisoning, for I was completely torn open. I was there three months that time. The last to be born alive was Alvin and with him all the sewing up was torn out again and I nearly went out, too. I was unconscious for several hours.

All the rest were miscarriages because I had no strength to carry them while I worked on the farm helping out just like Maud does, and I had to carry all the water I used from the barn to the house.

You see we did not go to a doctor before we engaged him. A woman (not even a nurse) took care of us and the other children and the house, too. We paid the woman the munificent sum of five dollars a week and the doctor the same. And, if there were any children old enough, about eleven or twelve, we only kept the woman one week.

I wonder now how any of us got over it, but we seemed to get along all right. The woman I had when Walter was born could not put a diaper on him, but she was good to the rest of you children. The doctor washed Walter the first time and a neighbor came and tended to me and Walter, and her fourteen-year-old daughter came and did the rest so I let my "nurse" go.

I seem a little more comfortable this week.

Love,
Mother

P.S. I baked a cake for the church supper and sent flowers as my share in the work.

This second letter from the Dawson family was written by Laura Dawson herself and tells the stories of the birth experiences of her mother, Laura McLaughlin (1928–38), and the births of Laura Dawson's own three sons in 1953, 1956, and 1959. By the time we get to Laura Dawson's story we are no longer hearing the voice of patient resignation. With her first birth Laura had plenty to complain about; by contrast, she had

*much to praise when her last two children were born in a very
different kind of hospital setting.*

I do remember [my mother] telling me that I was born in the
hospital bed. There was no labor room. She had just been admitted and my father was present. He became very upset, saying,
"Don't strain so hard." The nurse went into a panic and ran to
find the doctor, but it was all over by the time he got to the
room.

Mom stayed in the hospital ten days. The doctor charged $50,
if I remember correctly. The hospital bill was quite low . . .
something like $1 a day for me and a bit more for my mother.
Mom says she never felt any real pain—just cramps that were
mild. Because she tore, they had to sew her up. This happened
(apparently) *with all five* of us. Perhaps that's how they did
things then. She stayed ten days in the hospital.

In 1936, when one of my little sisters was born, I remember
being allowed to visit my mother in her hospital room. The
nurse brought in the baby for us to see. I vividly remember
commenting that "she looks awfully red," and asking why.
They answered that her skin was thin and that she would look
just fine soon. The nurse unwrapped the baby and showed us
her "tiny toes."

John, my firstborn [in 1953], started with labor "pains" about
ten minutes apart. Within about an hour, they were down to
five minutes. We went to the hospital at that time. My doctor
refused to come because he swore up and down that he never
had heard of a baby being born (first baby, that is) in less than
twelve hours.

I was sure, long before I went into labor, that it would be
short. I told him so, that my mother had had short labors, that
I was born in the hospital bed. My doctor still didn't see fit to
rush over.

Labor progressed too fast, and it did become very uncomfortable, and I started calling for the nurse. She was horrified and
started yelling to bring the cart, et cetera.

They got me to the delivery room, where a resident took charge. They strapped me down, all four limbs, at two places on each limb.[2] It was very upsetting, as I was fully in control of myself. Then they said, "There's his head."

There was a big mirror on the ceiling and I wanted to look, but they slapped a mask over my face and put me out, despite the fact that I was protesting. They used nitrous oxide (laughing gas). I was as angry as heck about the way they did it.

They claimed they had to put me out so they could do an episiotomy. (Yet, with my second child, they used a needle and Novocain.) They used forceps on John, which left a couple of huge bruises on his head.

I should state that I knew full well what the stages of labor were, all the physical aspects, in advance. I had been promised that anesthetic would only be used on *my* demand, not at *their* demand. I was not afraid of anything connected with childbirth.

I didn't get to see John right away. I could hear him screaming his head off when I awoke from the anesthetic, but it seemed like ages before they even told me it was a boy.

My husband was required to wait in the waiting room. When he finally got to John, it was through a glass window. When we went home, the moment we were in the car (it was October and cold), he, in a thrilled sort of gesture, pulled the blankets away from around the baby's face and shoulders and gazed at him, with a "finally" sort of look! I could tell he was proud!

I was in the hospital five days, I think. On the day my milk came in, I suffered a high fever, and they refused to let me have John. I was, after that, unable to get him to nurse. I gather they kept feeding him in the nursery, and the net result was that my milk dried up.

There was no support given to those of us who wished to try [to nurse], though they didn't refuse to cooperate, generally, except that they did feed the babies in the nursery. They had one of the firm schedules. They brought the babies at 10, 2, and 6, and 10 again. Every four hours. The babies were left with us for only a half hour.

I felt like I wasn't treated like a human being, strapped down like that. The doctor should have listened to me when I told him it would be a short labor, or at least left instructions. I believe he really had no intention of carrying out my wishes, when you come right down to it . . . just said he would honor my wishes to humor me.

Now, as to my second child, also a boy, born in 1956. His name is Eugene. He was born in a university town with an educated population. I chose the university hospital for my "confinement" this time. In order to have a baby there, one had to be a clinic patient. . . . That meant no specified doctor. I felt it couldn't be any worse than my previous experience!

The accommodations were very nice. They had "semi rooming in," which meant that there was a nursery between each two rooms. There was a large window between the room and the nursery. Access to the nursery was total, and it was "mother's choice" as to how involved she might be. If one wanted privacy, then one only had to pull down the curtain over the view window. They actively encouraged breastfeeding but didn't force it on the mothers.[3]

The doctors were young and conscientious, mostly residents but not inexperienced. They had on call, and often present, the profs of the medical school to assist and instruct, et cetera.

Labor went as expected. By the time we reached the hospital, labor pains were five minutes apart. They placed me in a private labor room (all of them were private, I should say). My husband was allowed to stay with me.

When the time came to deliver, they took me to the delivery room and my husband was not allowed to be with me for the birth (that concept was just too radical for the times). I was not strapped down. They had some very (relatively) comfortable sort of slings to position me for the delivery.

All went well. I did have an episiotomy this time, also, but with Novocain or some such . . . I think they said Xylocaine, actually. As to inhalant anesthetic, they allowed me to have a little Trilene but not enough to put me out.

They said, "You have a lovely little boy." Then they gave him to me to see, though they didn't let me hold him, as he was still slippery. I got to hold him as soon as they cleaned him off.

All in all, it was a very positive experience. I chose not to breastfeed, as I was afraid that I might have a repeat of the fever.

My third child was Wayne. He was born in 1959. Labor for him started in the early evening. I told the doctor that it would be a fast birth like the others, but he insisted that wasn't possible, since I wasn't sufficiently dilated.

Needless to say, he was wrong. Wayne was born in the labor room. They were able to give me a little Trilene to slow things down. (The doctor called for the nurse to bring it.) I did have some tearing, which he had to repair.

Wayne is truly the only one of my children whom I saw born, as there were no drapes or anything. Wayne was yelling his head off before he was all the way out!

It was still positive. One was treated with kindness and consideration.

I might say, however, that my husband felt sort of left out—kicked out, really. They encouraged him to leave and get some sleep, since the labor pains had been so inconsistent as to time between contractions, and it seemed that I was not in any real hurry to deliver.

They called him back soon enough, but by the time he got there, Wayne had been born. They put Wayne and me in one of the labor rooms and brought him in for our "private moments" together before taking me to my room. That was nice, I thought.

Ruth Whitney
Winnetka, Illinois

♡ *With her own distinctively sweet, dry wit, Ruth Whitney recalls the birth of her younger brother at home in 1909, the reaction of well-bred young women of the 1920s upon hearing of the facts of life, and some of the humorous aspects of the births of her own sons in 1938 and 1941.*

Unfortunately, I cannot remember my own birth, as I believe Leonardo da Vinci did, having a snake come into his cradle. All I know is that I was born at home, like most of my generation.

In the 1920s my mother-in-law-to-be and a group of her friends dug the first spadefuls of earth for the Chicago Lying-In Hospital—now a part of the great group of the University of Chicago Hospitals. These ladies were called the Mothers' Aid of the Chicago Lying-In Hospital.

It was the impetus of Ida DeLee Newman, the sister of Dr. Joseph Bolivar DeLee, a famous obstetrician here in Chicago. (Women came to Chicago to have Dr. DeLee deliver their babies.) An aunt of my husband was his head nurse for many years.

The Mothers' Aid operated and still operates a gift shop at the hospital and in one of the North Shore suburbs, and publishes a baby book called *Our Baby's First Seven Years*—all very profitable for the hospital.

While I do not recall my own beginnings, I do remember

vividly the birth of my brother in 1909, also at home. One day I was told that if I would put a lump of sugar on the windowsill, the stork would bring me a baby brother. How did they know in 1909 it would be a boy? Well, hope springs eternal, I guess.

So I put a lump of sugar on the windowsill. The next morning the lump of sugar was gone. Looking out the window, I saw a black electric automobile stop in front of the home. Out stepped a man carrying a little black bag. Stork?

In due course, I was told I had a baby brother. I had not heard a sound.

As for myself, I was a freshman at college before I knew where babies came from or how, believe it or not. Girls fainted in John M. Greene Hall when they heard the news. My mother evidently could not bring herself to tell me. She was always providentially called to the telephone as she was starting to do so.

My own experiences in 1938 and 1941 at birthing were comparatively uneventful. I did have to spend some weeks in bed with the first child to avoid a miscarriage.

When the time was near, I had a permanent wave one afternoon. About five o'clock the pains started, but we were having an extra good dinner that night, so I didn't tell my husband until it was over.

We went to the hospital. I had the baby about eight in the morning. I went back to my room and ate a hearty breakfast! In fact, I have rarely missed a meal in my life!

With the second child, the water broke in bed at night after we had been to a lecture at the University of Chicago. This was in September 1941, and a Japanese diplomat, a classmate of my husband at the University who was the lecturer, made me so angry by what he said about our relations with Japan, that it must have upset the baby, too.

At that time, one stayed in the hospital ten days. After one week the legs could be hung over the bed. A nurse always accompanied one home. One's legs were very weak and re-

accompanied one home. One's legs were very weak and remained so for a while.

When we arrived home, my little boy, age two and a half, met us at the door. I said, "Danny, this is your new little brother!" And Danny patted my stomach and said, "And is this your new little tummy?"

Effie Glass
Brandon, Florida

♡ *Effie Glass begins her childbirth stories with the tale of her mother's premature triplets, born in an outhouse in 1912—the sad beginning of twenty-three years of almost uninterrupted childbearing. Then, after stating proudly that she was "not so young" (and, she implies, not so naive) as her mother when she married, Effie follows with a matter-of-fact account of the births of her own* nine *children between 1934 and 1951 (eighteen years of childbearing).*

I was born in Brooks County, Georgia, six miles east of Pavo in the community of Tallokas in a house my father built, with the help of his father. It only had two rooms, the kitchen and the living room–bedroom. As the family grew, my father built on two more rooms.

My parents were married at Pavo, Georgia, April 9, 1911. My father went to Quitman, the county seat of Brooks County, to get the license, and they drove to Pavo in a horse and buggy. I don't know where they spent their first night together.

My mother's first pregnancy ended in a miscarriage. She said it must have been two or three months along. Then shortly after that she became pregnant again. This one resulted in triplets.

Women didn't go to doctors back then when they were going to give birth. You prepared for the occasion the best you could,

11

and, when the time came, you engaged a midwife and you had a baby.

Actually, about all a midwife could do was cut and tie the umbilical cord on the baby. They would also clean up the mess.

My mother was young (twenty years old) and inexperienced, and didn't know for sure what was going on. In those days a toilet in the house was unheard of, especially in the back parts of the country.

When she was about six months pregnant with the triplets, she went to the outhouse and two of those babies were born in there. The best I can recall, she was alone. She made it into the house somehow, and the third one was born in the house. They were born in 1912-and died the same day.

It's almost impossible to comprehend what all this was about, unless you have been through it. There was no known method of birth control, only abstinence, which virtually no one practiced. It seems today that people, especially young people, discovered sex, but I've got news for them. You did what had to be done, and if pregnancy occurred, you just had a baby.

By July 28, 1913, I was born. I was the first one to live, so I kinda saw the scenario as it unfolded.

It seems like all my mother did was get pregnant and have babies. All in all, for twenty-three years she bore children. Eleven lived past infancy. But, with all of her time that she spent having her babies, she managed to feed her family, sewed their clothes, washed, ironed, scrubbed floors, and sometimes worked in the field.

It might seem that Daddy was a man who didn't consider the trials a woman has, or have any feelings about all of this. But he was a good man, hardworking and devoted to his family. The relationship he had with his wife was about all of the diversion he had.

Now for my experiences in raising my family.

I was not so young when I got married. I was twenty and my husband was also twenty. We were married August 26, 1933.

We had $50 to start housekeeping. We bought enough bed ticking to make a mattress and two pillows, then picked scattering cotton (that's cotton left over after it's been picked), took it to the gin, and made our bedding.

When we married, it was in the depths of the Depression. The largest percent of the people in south Georgia were sharecroppers. We (my husband and I) were sharecroppers for six years while we lived in Georgia. The last year we were there, my husband worked for the landlord for 75 cents a day. The day was from see to not see (daylight to dark). In 1939 we also had a tobacco crop, about three acres, which we did on shares.

The same year, in August, we came to Florida. I had lived here before and I thought it was heaven here. When we first married, a very feeble attempt at birth control practice was made, but it wasn't foolproof, so, after eleven months of marriage, our first child was born. Preparations were made to give birth at home. I had a doctor when he was born.

That was an easy one. He was born before I thought I was in trouble. There were six or seven women there to help out. My mother was there, and she was also pregnant. So she left the scene shortly before my baby was born.

When he was nine months old, I was pregnant again. I was nursing him and he got sick, so I had to wean him, which broke my heart. During this pregnancy I contracted malaria fever. I was sick for three months. You could not take anything but quinine for it, and, if you were pregnant, that was a no-no!

Also, you could not afford to go to the doctor. If you had a doctor for the actual birth, you didn't see him until the day of the birth.

Anyway, my legs swelled up four times as large as they ought to be. On the day she was born, I woke up about four A.M. with pains. My husband went after the doctor. He came and said it was not time. But he did give me some medication to take the swelling out of my legs.

Later on, the pains became worse and my husband walked two miles to a telephone (they were few and far between then).

When he got there, the line was down. He came back to the house and surveyed the situation and ran across the road to the landlord's house. A worker went in a car to fetch the doctor.

By the time the doctor got there, the baby was thirty minutes old. That was a very scary time for us because of my condition, but the baby was fine and I snapped back quickly.

Twenty months later, I had another baby. This time I decided to try a midwife. It seems between midnight and day is the best time for the birthing process to start. So this time was no different. My husband went to get her.

She came about four o'clock, and she didn't know as much as I did. She started off by having me bear down hard with every pain. About two P.M., when the real bearing down was necessary, I was so exhausted I almost didn't make it.

Let me say right here that it was necessary to have a midwife because there was not money to pay a doctor. We lived on a farm and you paid midwives with meal, syrup, a bushel of corn, or whatever you had. I recall the doctor's fee was $25 or maybe $35 and it was hard to scrape together that much.

With the next one, which was number four, I also had a midwife. This time, thinking about the last one, I kinda knew what to do and it worked out fine.

Then we moved to Florida and with my fifth one, I went to the hospital. This was the first time I was put to sleep. All of the rest, there was nothing to help the pain. They put me to sleep and held my legs together so she wouldn't be born before the doctor got there. She was okay but this same hospital had a reputation for doing that and caused some damage to some mothers and babies. The next one, number six, was also born in this same hospital. This time I was wide awake.

Number seven was born in 1945. The doctor I went to had a place over his office where he delivered babies. You could stay twenty-four hours. The price for this delivery was $35, and you rode home in an ambulance.

When I was ready to come home, the ambulance was in use

and they brought us home in a hearse. The funeral homes also operated the ambulances then.

I became pregnant for the eighth time. It seemed to me from the start that this one was different. I just had that feeling. At five months and one week it died. For seven weeks I waited and worried. I had no idea what would happen. I had already felt the quickening, so I knew when it didn't move anymore. At seven months it was born. I did not see it.

At thirty-eight years old, I found myself pregnant for the ninth time. Again, I went to a doctor who had a room over his office or the drugstore. This was my last child. After losing one, I quit worrying about being pregnant and menopause came and went at age forty. So I guess, all things considered, I didn't have it too bad.

My husband was a truck driver for years. When my last child was in school, I went to night school and got my high school diploma, of which I am very proud. It took me two years of classes, two nights a week. I was forty-five years of age at the time. I never had to show my diploma in any of the things I worked at, but it gives me a great satisfaction to know I have it.

Three of my daughters have had children. The first one to have a baby was my third child, second daughter. She was able to see the doctor regularly. Everything was all right during the pregnancy. But the birth was breech, which was very traumatic. As it turned out, she had four and every one was breech. They all lived and are doing well.

When *her* daughter was ready to have her first one, her husband equipped himself with a camera and made all kinds of neat pictures. There's a world of difference in four generations of childbearing.

Charlana Cook
Kansas City, Missouri

♡ *Charlana Cook tells another multigenerational story of births as experienced by her great-aunt in 1914, her mother (1924–31), herself (1951–55), and two of her nieces (1978–84 and 1981–89).*

My mother was born on March 24, 1905, in Burnside, Kentucky, and I have only a handwritten birth certificate indicating her birth. She was ten years old when her Aunt Eddie (who was about nineteen or twenty years old at the time) gave birth to her first child, and she told me about that.

Aunt Eddie Roberts was my grandmother's sister, and her husband was a riverboat captain traveling out of Burnside, Kentucky, because that was the way they shipped products then.

I gather Aunt Eddie gave birth to her first child around 1914.

Mother said the baby was stillborn but beautiful, like a doll. She can remember Uncle Walter taking her down into the living room where they had put the baby in a box on the library table. Aunt Eddie had made beautiful embroidered garments for the baby. [My mother] has remarked to me that she thought it was kind of Uncle Walter to show her the baby.

The second baby born to this same aunt also died, but her third child lived. Both the stillborn children are buried on the farm. (I'm not sure if the "farm" as such exists today as I understand that area is now a very popular resort area.)

As to her memory of herself . . . she only remembers [being told] that her mother could not breastfeed her and that they milked a cow in the morning and her grandmother would "spoon feed" her, sometimes dipping her finger in the milk.

As a side remark, my mother sucked her forefinger for almost thirty-five years and, in her comments to me, she feels this might have played a part because of this early feeding. She said that, after feeding her, they would "stick my finger in my mouth." My grandmother's three births were also "at home" deliveries.

Eventually my mother ended up in Kansas City, Missouri, and was married at age eighteen, giving birth to me at age nineteen. I was born April 10, 1924. Mother feels she married early because of the difficult home life she had. Times were hard and money was scarce. My grandmother had to go out and work, despite the fact that she was married twice. It was during the dissolving of the last marriage that my mother felt it might be better to just get out, which she did.

My mother's marriage didn't work out either and she left my father before she knew she was pregnant and moved back in with my grandmother, so that when I was born, she was separated. She did go to court and fight to keep me, which she did.

I was born in a breech presentation. My mother had no prior care, so to say, to determine if the baby would be a so-called normal delivery. She was of the era that just figured you had a baby.

She can remember that it was a very difficult delivery. They didn't realize it was a breech delivery until the baby was on its way, I suppose, and the doctor ripped her vagina to get me out. She recalls all the nurses and other people were standing around watching, as a breech birth was considered unusual.

They thought she might die if they moved her so they left her all night lying on the operating table. She said the actual delivery took four hours. She was in the hospital in the morning and I was born around midnight.

She remembered the flowers in the room, the long night on the operating table with the blood running even into her hair, and the one and only near-death experience she's ever had. She remembers seeing a bright light and her family standing around her. She was linked somehow to me (her new baby), her mother, et cetera. She suddenly felt she "knew everything" and it was all so wonderful.

When I was about three years old, my mother married again. She had three sons by him, each born at home, and he was with her through all three births. She was going then to clinics—free in this area for women—and getting the proper advice. Her sons came two years apart and she had all her children before she was thirty.

The doctor would come for the birth (at home) and she told me that in one instance, during the birth of my brother Jess, the doctor came sooner than the baby, so he just stayed on there until she gave birth.

There were women (brought by the doctor) who stayed and tended to her afterward. Of course, there were neighbor women who were supportive. She recalls going in and staying with her friend until the baby came and helping afterward.

I still have the handmade baby dresses my mother made for me. She told of buying the material by the yard and cutting and putting on lace and embroidery "as that is what we did in those days."

She recalls boiling diapers (birds-eye material) to be sure they were clean. To this day, whenever she hears of a baby having diaper rash, she says, "Boil the diapers." Today, of course, there are disposables, but even these cause the rash.

I asked about anesthesia. This is a gray area, as she can just recall getting "whiffs of something." I [assume] it was ether. When I was born, they gave it to her off and on for four hours. With the boys, however, they only gave her a bit near the end.

She says that in the home deliveries they had a vial they broke, usually over a mask (probably gauze) on the woman's nose. She recalls that she went to help out a neighbor and the doctor had *her* administering this ether, and she thinks now, in retrospect, that this was a dangerous thing she was doing. It was strong enough to sort of knock one out, but not completely, so as to take the woman over the hardest pains.

I married when I was twenty-six, giving birth to three children at twenty-seven, twenty-nine, and thirty-one. In the light of today I feel I did not have the information and knowledge I should have had, which is my own fault. I was working and felt the baby would just come naturally.

My doctor was provided through the company where my husband worked and it was very casual. When my time came for delivery [August 11, 1951], my doctor was out of town and my baby was delivered by a doctor I'd never seen. I was in a good hospital but was very sick afterward.

It was a difficult delivery (forceps) and, for some reason, when I didn't get better afterward, I refused to go back to either the first doctor or the one who delivered the baby. I had the name of one of the best OB doctors in town (Wichita, Kansas). I was lucky this doctor took me, I suppose. Anyway, he delivered my other two children.

My second and third children were fine. At the birth of my last child, my husband had gone home when I woke up and so they just knocked me out for another eight hours or so, which I felt was unnecessary, but more for the convenience of the nurses in the hospital.

Today I have heard of experiences my nieces have been through and I wonder how far we have really progressed, except that most children born today do live. One niece and her husband (who have three children) have used the method where they are together and it is natural without any anesthesia, and they also are allowed to bring in their children to see the baby.

Another niece had to endure labor all day and then the doctor found they couldn't get the baby out, as she was too small, and so did a cesarean! Why they didn't do any measuring prior, I don't know.

Edith McConnell
Philadelphia, Pennsylvania

♡ *Edith McConnell describes the home birth of her first child in 1918. Her understated tone is very characteristic of the era. Unlike many of the later stories in this collection, she does not dramatize herself or the experience. But her courage and love for the baby are apparent, nonetheless.*

Edith, a former schoolteacher and librarian who kept journals of her trips away from home for forty-eight years, wrote the following letter to me on October 28, 1986, at the age of ninety-five.

You will not get many accounts like mine because I cannot see what I am writing, but it is worth guessing at. My first baby was a girl who arrived on my twenty-seventh birthday.

My husband and I lived in a small home on the outskirts of Philadelphia. It stood alone. When I knew the baby was on her way, I went to our family doctor, who said,

"Have you any idea when this child will be born?"

Me: "Yes, I have."

When I thought perhaps I was going to have a baby, I told my mother. She gave me a book called *Tokology,* which she read before I was born. It was a modest book with pictures of an unborn baby in an envelope, modestly put in the back of the book. The book said how many days should pass from the supposed conception day. I told the doctor.[4]

So he said, "Come back in three months. I want to talk to you."

Back I went. The doctor said, "Fine. Come back again three months from now."

So I did. He then said, "Edith, you are a sensible girl. Do you want me to deliver your baby or go to a hospital?"

I said, "No hospital. I'm afraid they might mix up the babies."

He said, "Okay. Some of these days I want you to make two thick bed pads made out of newspapers. Make them as thick as you can get your needle through. Also, if possible, have a piece of oilcloth handy. Also a twenty-five-cent bottle of chloroform on hand. You think the baby will arrive on February 21. So come see me a week or so before that and we will be ready— if you have found an experienced woman to help me."

Early, about five A.M., I woke Will and said, "Okay, the baby is showing signs of coming."

He said, "What do I do?"

I said, "Call the doctor," who said, "Call the nurse."

He did. She said, "I don't know how to get there. Will you come for me?"

My husband said he would and said [to me], "Oh, I hope you are safe till we get here."

In the meantime (before the pains were getting pretty awful), I was reading a book called *Johnny Appleseed*—a very good book in which the death of a woman giving birth to a baby (which also died) did not scare me. I had faith in the coming baby.

It began to snow when my dear baby arrived at eleven A.M.— on my twenty-seventh birthday. It was a hard birth. The doctor turned me in bed with my legs far apart. (Before that, the nurse had wrapped up the baby and put her in the bassinet, which I made from a clothes basket, covering it with dotted Swiss. It lasted for many babies—two more of mine and various nieces and nephews.)

The doctor knelt on the floor. My husband held my right leg. The nurse held my left leg.

The doctor said, "I need a lady's handkerchief right away quick."

The nurse was nervous and couldn't find one.

So I told her, "Get one of Will's from that drawer over there."

The doctor yelled, "I said a *lady's* handkerchief. Hell! Do you want me to kill Edith?"[5]

Poor nurse. She said, "Oh, I have one."

So the doctor dumped some chloroform on the hankie and put it under my nose. I glanced at Will and he looked very white and very sick.

He said, "Oh, Edith, this is awful. No more babies."

I faintly recalled saying, "Oh, yes we will, since children must have a brother or sister."

The only light in that bedroom was from a single yellow gas flame. But the doctor knew what he had to sew up.

When I came to, my aunt was sitting near me.

She said, "Oh, you are awake now. Are you in much pain?"

I said, "No, I just want to see the baby."

She was a dear—who now holds a good job with the Louisiana N.W. University [Northwestern State University of Louisiana] as chief archivist and cryptologist. She has six children of her own.

Because my three daughters are working, I live here in a too-large but very pleasant retirement home. I need lots of stamps, for my now-large family scattered all over the world. So I hate to use this stamp on you, but think you will not have too many records of an event taking place nearly sixty-nine years ago.

John Todd
Delta, Ontario, Canada

♡ *This letter from John Todd was the only one I received from a father. John was eighty-five when he wrote to me in 1986. He died in 1990. He writes here on behalf of his deceased wife, who, he is sure, would have wished to respond to my request for birth stories.*

The story John tells is sweet and simple—a father's perspective on the birth of his first child back in 1926, in Port Glasgow, Scotland.

I find myself taking an unusual interest in your ad in Ms. magazine. For several reasons I keep mulling it over and I think you should have our story. Here it is.

Married in 1925, my wife found herself pregnant in springtime 1926. Being beginners and thinking ourselves up to date and able to handle anything, we procured two handbooks on the subject and both said contact your doctor early, within three months of confirming pregnancy.

She went to see her family doctor one evening and I waited at home. She got home, came in, and sat down opposite me. I could see that she was confused, so I asked what happened.

She replied, "I told him I was going to have a baby and I came to see what I should do next. The doctor asked who I was and, when he discovered that he knew me, he said, 'Go home to your granny. She knows more about it than I do.'

23

"As I turned to go home, he said, 'Of course, you are married?' "

Now, in our circle, sex was never discussed, nor even hinted at in any way with one's parents. Nevertheless, during our engagement my mother-in-law let her daughter understand that there was to be no nonsense "absolutely."

Now, my wife's grandmother lived with her mother, so she went to her mother tearfully and said, "I am going to have a baby."

Her mother put her arms around her and said, "That's all right. You are married now."

Right there a corner was turned, and a new phase of relationship began joyfully. A midwife was contacted and everything was left to her, and everything went along without a hitch.

My wife went to her mother's house and stayed there and the baby was born there. Describing the birth, my mother-in-law said everything went well. After the baby was born and attended to, the midwife spread a sheet of paper on the floor. Then the afterbirth was placed on it and the midwife got down on her hands and knees and spread it out and pieced it together to make sure that none of it was missing [that none was left inside the woman who had just given birth].

When it came time for my wife to come home, her brother's wife and I went to fetch her. We were standing shoulder to shoulder as Mother-in-Law came forward to place the baby in our arms.

Looking at the baby as she lowered him into our arms, she said, "Now no more for six weeks. Three weeks it takes to get back into place and three weeks more to return to normal."

That boy will be sixty years old this year, 1986.

I would like to add a little more and explain. I am writing because my wife died last year, aged eighty-one, and I know she would have written to you. Wherever we found someone doing what you are doing, or compiling data, conducting surveys, getting at the truth or learning or educating, we find a kindred spirit.

I would like to think that all knowledge is not vanity.

Dorothy Conard
La Selva Beach, California

♡ *Dorothy Conard writes of four daughters, two born at home in 1926 and 1928 and two in a hospital in 1929 and 1932. I like the succinctness of her account of eating "two poached eggs on toast" at two A.M. after the birth of her second child.*

I was also intrigued by the husband who remained in the next room during the birth—a practice that must have been perceived as discreet and delicate and a natural division of the genders in a long-ago era. Not all husbands maintained this discreet distance, however. Many, like Edith McConnell's, stayed at their wife's side throughout labor and birth at home.

I was living in a small town in North Dakota when my first two children were born and had them at home, with a trained nurse and a doctor. The second two were born in a hospital in Fargo, North Dakota, where we had moved between second and third babies.

I had the first two at home because there had been some deaths in the only hospital in town, which disturbed me and many others, and I was afraid it might not have been sanitary. I grew up in a germ-conscious family and studied public health after college.

My first baby was born in 1926 and I had a trained nurse to see that everything was done right. My parents sent me a Johnson & Johnson package of all the necessities, to be sure everything was sterile. I had sent for a U.S. Health Department Bulletin on infants, et cetera, and followed it to the letter.

After labor pains all day, I called the nurse that it was time to come (about six P.M.), and she set everything up ready for the doctor, as she said doctors didn't like to deliver babies in the home. He was pleased at the Johnson & Johnson supplies.

The nurse called the doctor when the right time came, and she had me pushing more and more. When it got so bad that I felt the top of my head would be pushed off, and that I didn't care anymore, the doctor had the nurse put something over my face.

It seemed like only a minute or two, and then I heard the baby's cry, and said, "I wish my husband could hear the baby's first little cry." She assured me that he was in the next room.

Not long after, the baby was placed on my bed next to my head, all wrapped in her blankets, and I was aware and surprised that her eyes were opened and she seemed to be trying to look around.

A few minutes later, the doctor left and I asked the nurse, "Did he put the drops in her little eyes?" I had read the importance of it in the Public Health bulletin.[6]

The nurse called after the doctor as he went downstairs, and he told her the drops were in his bag he had left there—and he was on his way back to the bridge party I had interrupted. This all happened—doctor's arrival and departure—between nine and nine-fifteen P.M.

My second baby was born twenty months later, at home. All the same preparations were made, but the actual birth was different, and I feel it must have been because the baby was of smaller build and, especially, smaller head.

As I felt that the baby was starting to come, the nurse looked and realized it was so, and went downstairs to call the doctor. When she got back to my room, the baby was there, kicking and crying and sounding healthy and all right.

It all happened so quickly and easily. I was able to raise myself up and look at her and see that it was a girl.

The doctor came and finished it up and everything went fine and, after two poached eggs on toast, I and all the household went to sleep at two A.M.

I'm glad I had my first two at home. My third and fourth daughters were born in a hospital. We had moved to Fargo, with a choice of at least two fine hospitals. I arrived at the hospital and was put to bed in the maternity room, holding the *Time* magazine I was reading (same each time, but different date), and woke up a few hours later, to be told I had a baby girl.

I preferred the home births when I had them because of the circumstances, but preferred the hospital births when we got to a "big city." I realize that I was very fortunate in taking the chance, because a friend in another small town had her first baby at home, and it turned out to be a difficult birth and ended in the death of the baby. She had a doctor, but I don't know if she had a nurse.

Nowadays, my grandchildren are having the fathers in with them for the whole thing. I'm sure my husband wouldn't have been interested. He was happy to be in the next room, at home, hearing all the talk, et cetera, and the first cry.

Times have changed. I wonder if the fathers will continue to be in on the whole thing.

Pauline Plimpton
New York, New York

♡ *Pauline Plimpton grew up in Boston and at her family's country home, Borderland, in North Easton, Massachusetts. She met her future husband, Francis T. P. Plimpton, traveling home from Europe on a Cunard ocean liner. Francis Plimpton later became a prominent attorney who also served on the Council of Foreign Relations and as Adlai Stevenson's number-two man at the United Nations.*

Below, Pauline tells of the births of her four children between 1927 and 1936, with the enthusiasm and wit that she has passed on to her famous son George, author and perpetual "dilettante extraordinary."

What fun it is to talk about the horrors of childbirth! I was married in June of 1926 and had four children, the first born in March of 1927. As I remember, we counted the time between pains and went to the hospital when they were close enough.

But I must have had at least thirty-six hours of labor after I got there, with the most excruciating pain at the birth. I had no medication to slow down or speed up but a whiff of something at the end.

Of course, I knew what was going on but had been given no idea how painful it would be. The baby boy weighed eight and a half pounds, had a large head, and I had been very athletic, which, in those days, was supposed to make childbirth harder.

The only prenatal advice I remember was about weight and that golf would be better than tennis.

I was kept in the hospital for three weeks and hardly allowed to put my legs over the side of the bed. This was usual. My mother came down from Boston and was horrified. She got an exercise woman and a Victrola and had me take exercises in bed to try to keep me in shape, and insisted that I nurse the baby.

She fought with the doctor about breastfeeding. He was against it, I think, because they felt they could control the baby's health through the milk formula. I was never conscious of any social climate about it, but it took a lot of courage to resist the doctors' advice that they could do better with a formula.

I only saw the baby when it came to nurse. I was fortunate to have a nurse for six weeks. She knew just how to get the baby to breastfeed. I nursed it for four or so months with one supplemental bottle a day, so that I would be freer. I would not do that if I were doing it again.

The baby was fed every four hours. No nonsense about picking him up and nursing him when he cried. By the time the nurse left at the end of six weeks, she was supposed to have the baby off the two A.M. feeding and to have started to train the baby on its potty.

I know how people feel about that now, but I never sensed that it did any harm—in a manner, the baby was more loved. I shall never forget that sacred hour of ten o'clock when we had to be on the spot to pick the baby up, so that it could go dry through the night.

Then disaster struck. This doctor had given me a suppository for birth control, which didn't work, and, while I was still nursing, I was pregnant again. I almost didn't survive. At six to seven months, my kidneys became solid with sugar. (I don't know the technical terms [toxemia?].) I was sick and my face swollen.

They rushed me to the hospital and "took" the baby by blowing a bag up inside to induce labor.[7] Although I don't remember my husband being present for the first birth, at this one he was holding my hand. His mother had died in childbirth of the same thing when he was born.

The nurse thought he was making me feel sorry for myself and sent him out. I was so furious I gave a tremendous push— the head nurse tried to hold the little head in, as the doctor was not there—and I was struggling against her.

The doctor finally came. He seemed to bounce in at the end with the nurse handling everything in the beginning. He was a fashionable, esteemed doctor. I did not use him again. His last words as he left: "It won't make any difference with the next one!"

They brought mother's milk, worked on me with a breast pump until my milk came in and the baby was strong enough to nurse, and I continued to nurse for six months.

By then I was interested in Planned Parenthood and I spaced my next two pregnancies with no adverse problems, except for an early miscarriage between the third and the fourth. I suppose they were not so spartan about anesthesia by then, and I enjoyed the third one especially and was delighted with the fourth, a daughter after three sons, both born in the thirties.

I was basically positive about having children as it had always been my ambition to have four children, as I was one of four. All the above started, of course, over sixty years ago.

The first baby, whose birth I describe, was named George Ames Plimpton and is George Plimpton, whose books you may have read and whom you see on TV.

Jewel Baker
Nederland, Texas

♡ *Jewel Baker's first child was premature. He was born weighing only two and a half pounds, in a small town in Texas in 1930. The doctor said the baby would not live, but Jewel and her aunt, who "knew a lot about babies," proved him wrong.*

I had finished high school at Douglass, Texas, at an unaffiliated school in Nacogdoches County. I then had to take a checking course in all subjects to receive a diploma. I did this at Stephen F. Austin in Nacogdoches.

It was in 1928, during the deep Depression. We were farmers with no market for what we grew, like tomatoes, beans. We also grew cane for syrup, potatoes, corn, and cotton. We had plenty to eat but no money.

I married June 1, 1929. I had no mother. She had died when I was two years old, when my sister was born. She had what the country people called "childbed fever." It was really an infection. Many mothers died with it.[8]

I knew nothing of birth control. My grandmother, who reared us, had ten children. I'm sure she did not know. We never discussed it. I finished my period the week before I married. I became pregnant the next week.

I was nauseated constantly. I could keep no food or water on my stomach. I went to my doctor. He told me I was pregnant. There was nothing he could do about the sickness.

31

My mother-in-law cooked good meals—fried chicken, crowder peas, other nice vegetables—but I just could not stand to smell food.

Finally, we were invited to visit a friend who lived in town. She had three children and knew how sick I was. I shall never forget that meal. She cooked macaroni and tomatoes, made fried salmon patties, but, best of all, she had iced tea. Nothing was ever so good.

After we ate, she insisted I go lie down for a while. I lay down while she did the dishes. I did not vomit. It was the first food I had held on my stomach in weeks. After that, I began to get better.

I visited the doctor once every six weeks with a urine specimen.

My labor began about three or four o'clock in the morning of my seventh month. My aunt and uncle had come for a visit from Port Arthur. I had worked hard that day getting ready for them.

I woke up with an urge to urinate. I got up several times and my aunt woke up. She got up and I told her how I felt. She said, "I think you are in labor."

Then my husband and uncle got up. We had no phone, so they drove to the doctor's house. They could not wake him. By this time it was daylight and we knew he would go to his office at seven. After seven, the doctor came. He examined me. He said I was dilated the size of a dime. The baby would come, but it would be a long time.

He went back to his office. I stayed in bed. I did doze quite a bit between times.

The doctor came back after noon and examined me again. He helped with the delivery. So did my aunt and a friend. He broke my water just before the baby was born. We named the baby Roger. He weighed nearly two and a half pounds.

The doctor told me there was no way he could live. I prayed and prayed. The snow was over the ground. It was January 13, 1930. My aunt knew a lot about babies. She heated the old black irons in the fireplace, wrapped them in cloth, and put them on the other side of the baby. He was in my bed with me.

He slept almost all the time. My aunt took the fluid from my breast and fed it to the baby for three days. After that, he learned to nurse. All mothers nursed their babies. This was a natural birth.

I carried him to the doctor one month later when I went for my checkup. The doctor could not believe how much he had grown.

Florine Bond
Inkster, Michigan

♡ *Florine Bond started having her thirteen babies early in the Great Depression (1932) and was still having them well into the baby-boom years following World War II (her last child was born in 1954). Yet she is cheerful and philosophical about her many labors, the hard ones as well as the easy ones—including two less-than-ideal hospital births. Florine today has 26 grandchildren and 20 great-grandchildren.*

So you want the history of my childbearing years, which wasn't so bad. I was a young lady, had just turned twenty, and was married in the summer. Our first baby was born in February at home with the midwife in attendance.

I never asked anyone anything concerning childbirth. I married, I ordered a pregnancy book, I learned quite a bit from it. I also bought a bottle of Mother's Friend[9] and rubbed with it and continued to use it during my childbearing years, and I do not have a stretch mark. You may check me out!

We both lived on a farm. My husband gathered his crop and went to a big farm to pick cotton for hire. He was a good picker. He sent for me and I went. I didn't work. After I got married, I never worked in the field. I had to cook and baby-sit. My husband said, "No field."

When the cotton ran out, he went into a plant and worked for a while and decided that we should come home. We came home February 13. Our first baby (Lloyd) was born on Valentine's Day, February 14, 1932.

He was a smart baby. He was looking around in the room when he was a week old. He started crying. I sang a sweet little song to him and he was listening with his eyes, just rolling them around.

When he could talk, we tried to teach him to say "Mother dear," and he would say, "Maya," and that went well with the rest of the children—mine and some of those in the neighborhood. Some of those grown children still say "Maya" now.

My husband was a good provider and did love to feed his children and buy good clothing. Whatever they wanted, he would get it. We never owned a car, but he bought a car for several of the boys when they asked for it.

We lived as good as any of our friends. I sewed for myself and some of my friends. We didn't smoke, chew, dip, and drink or play cards or numbers. My husband stayed on the job here [in Inkster] for seventeen or eighteen years. We never had any difficulties.

My husband would go to Sunday school and take the larger children with him and come back and go to bed till dinner. He had to go to work at midnight. I never wanted for anything. The Lord always blesses those who trust Him.

Voss was my second son. The nurse came early and it wasn't too long before the baby came. He was a nice baby, over eight pounds.

The third one came in June, Everett. I had gone out to dig some white potatoes early. I could feel myself getting sick. My baby sister came up on her way to the field. I told her my trouble and she stayed with me and I went to bed.

It wasn't long before the baby came, and I moved him to the side, and my husband came for dinner but had to go and get the nurse nearby. I was waiting for her.

I breastfed all my babies and had more milk than I could handle. I would draw it out with a breast pump and pour it in the fire to dry up some of the milk.

I always got up and took care of my babies. I wasn't ever ill, just slow for a few weeks, but was pretending—to let the time pass. Young mothers was told to not let their husband go to bed with them, which was a big job, until their month was up. So sometimes we pretended we felt bad.

I really did want my times spaced, but my husband always obeyed his father. He wouldn't use what I had bought for him and only did what someone had told him at home—a home remedy, just sometimes.

The next was a boy, Charlie. He came soon. That was good.

So came my first girl, Vivian. I waited a little while for the nurse. I told her I wanted to use the potty, so she stayed right with me. As I started to get on the pot, out popped the baby, and she caught her before she fell into the slop jar. She said she had had that luck once before.

I had another girl, Evelyn. Everything was good and quick.

Willie, the seventh child, was born in the hospital. One of the doctors in the clinic suggested that I go there for the delivery. My water broke early that morning before I left home. I was getting my family's breakfast. I got ready to go to the hospital. We had a neighbor waiting.

In the hospital a doctor came and checked me out and said, "Are you ready?"

I said, "Yes, I am ready," and he said, "Yes, in about three hours."

A nurse came right on and checked me and yelled.

"I told the doctor," I say. "I *should* know."

The baby was coming. She grabbed the stretcher and started running down one ramp and up the other one into a ward. The baby came so fast, she couldn't even prepare me. She was so excited, she patted my face, she kissed my jaw, saying, "You'll be all right. Don't worry." They had to prepare me and put me to bed after the baby came.

One day a nurse brought me the wrong baby.

I said, "That's not my baby."

She say, "Yes, it is."

So I insisted, I said, "Well, you check the band out on the baby's wrist, and if it has 'Bond' on it, that's my baby."

She checked it out and found my baby. He had a fair complexion and the other baby was red-faced.

The next was Louis and everything was fine.

With the next pregnancy, Jimmy, I just knew I wouldn't be able to give birth, so I would pray and talk to the Lord. I knew I couldn't, so I put my trust in Him. So, when my pains stopped, I told Him I couldn't have the baby. He would have to take over.

When my pain stopped, the nurse had called the doctor already but I didn't know it. The baby tried and couldn't. They asked my husband and I what to do. We said to take the baby and leave me here with my other children. So they did.

The baby lived two days and passed. They told me that he wouldn't make it. They told me he might be afflicted.

I had four more, two of which were hard and long. The other two were short and easy.

Lydia was the next one. She was born in the winter—snow everywhere. I got sick after going to bed. My husband got up and went for the doctor who had his office nearby, but he had gone home to Detroit, miles away.

I couldn't wait. I started my pains. My pains stopped and all I could feel of the baby was one leg, so I talked to the Lord, "Just please give me my strength and I will finish the job." He gave me my strength and I had the baby, sat up, and lay her off to the side.

I was almost asleep when the doctor and my husband arrived. They didn't believe me, but it's true as gospel. She weighed more than eleven pounds.

The next one was Florine, a girl. It was early in the morning. I went to bed. A friend of ours were over there and she kept calling the doctor and finally he was in the office. He came right on. That was an easy, short time. He came back twice and gave me my okay.

Essie was the next girl and everything was okay with her.

And then came Valerie, the last baby. I was going to a doctor and he told me when I feel a pain, to come right in. I had a few light ones that didn't last very long.

So, a month later, I felt them frequently all night. I had cooked Thanksgiving dinner, didn't feel like eating, and I got up early on the next morning, and went on to the hospital. I was in before six o'clock, but my doctor had gone on vacation.

A new doctor and nurse were there. They met me, she put me to bed, and both left the room. Finally, she came back, raised the sheet. At that time my water broke and flew out. Some hit her uniform. She scolded me and left. Now, you know that was crazy.

They all stayed away so long, I asked about an ambulance so I could go to another hospital. They came and carried me to another room and left again. The nurse came back, checked, and left.

Then she came again and tried to tie my hands down, but I told her that she couldn't do that. I had to have my freedom.

I kept my eyes on the clock, so, about two or two-thirty, she came and checked me again and saw the baby coming and ran and got the doctor, and, by three-thirty, everything was over, thank God.

I didn't know they had lost a woman up there at childbirth just recently, and I imagine they were afraid—that was why they kept eluding me.

I did have a hard time with some of my births. But the Lord is so wonderful. Don't let anyone tell you that there isn't a Supreme Being. All you have to do is believe on Him. And He sent the help I needed.

Alice Henry
Penney Farms, Florida

♡ *Alice Henry's story is one of several I received from women who accompanied missionary husbands to faraway places and subsequently bore babies under very difficult conditions.*

After spending one year in the Kennedy School of Missions of Hartford Seminary, I went over to the Belgian Congo to be married to my fiancé, Robin Cobble. It was during the Depression. He was to have come back to the U.S. to get married, but, when the Depression hit, there was no way—no funds!

Not wanting to "lose" my man, I persuaded the Disciples of Christ Missionary Society to be allowed to go out to Congo, on my own, to be married in Congo. (I was to pay my own way and was not allowed to speak for funds in any of the churches, et cetera, but the Society did agree that, when and if we got married, Robin would be put on a married man's salary—the magnificent sum of $1,000 a year.)

We were married in August 1932 in the Congo.

In 1933 I found that I could not expect a baby and trek long hours in the tropics by bicycle with my husband—the two were just not compatible!! (Morning sickness and fatigue.) So I came back to the mission station alone, in a dugout canoe with one African paddler—a matter of six to eight hours—while my husband continued the two-month stint of visiting schools, churches, et cetera, in the back country by himself.

39

It was so very lonesome. Oh, yes, there were six other missionaries on the station, but they were "in their awful forties" and I was in my mid-twenties. There were no other white people for miles, and I did not know the African dialect to any great extent then. Everyone was very cordial but everyone was very busy, too.

I wrote my mother immediately to ask her to send out some baby clothes, et cetera. She also sent some pamphlets from, I believe, the state of Michigan, even though we lived in Massachusetts. Those pamphlets were "lessons" on what to do for your baby month by month for the first year and were invaluable to me later on. It took four months for these to arrive.

We had a doctor on the station—no nurse except some African men who had been trained by the doctor. The hospital was very primitive. It was decided that I should have the baby at home—that a couple of the women missionaries would be there "to help" and, of course, my husband.

The doctor's wife, who was then in her mid-forties, remembered the long, painful time she had in childbirth and asked her husband if there wasn't something that he would be prepared to give me to help relieve the pain. I did not know it at the time, but he decided to use what I believe was called "twilight sleep"—something which he pumped up into the vagina. Later I found it was a kind of gas which could have been fatal to the baby. [This was not authentic "twilight sleep."]

Well, anyway, the doctor told us that when I began to have "pains," to let him know. We weren't quite sure just when to call him when they began, so we decided to see if there were any mice out in the storeroom, just to pass some time.

We found one, which scurried up the wall, and my husband had a bow and arrow and shot the thing as it went up the wall—a little distraction for me, but by that time we felt we should call the doctor.

He and his wife came, and I was in our big double bed under a mosquito net which we had hung from a frame which my husband had made so that it formed a kind of room, instead of having to be tucked under the mattress. You see, we had some mosquitoes which could infect us with malaria!

This was now about midnight, but nothing really was happening. They all sort of dozed. Then at six A.M. one of the single ladies came to relieve the doctor's wife so she could go to school. I don't really remember just how long it went on, but I suppose around ten o'clock the pains were such that the doctor blew in some "twilight sleep" with some kind of rubber pump inserted into the vagina. It helped but did not take away all pain.

My husband was right there. I don't remember any real surgical gowns. I just remember that, when the baby finally came, my husband told me later that he thought he heard my bones cracking. But they didn't. In fact, I had no broken bones or even any lacerations. It *was* pretty strenuous, to say the least.

The single lady was then commissioned to wash the baby. I remember Betty (the baby) was just a little over five pounds—no extra fat but very strong and lusty.

We had a little tin tub on a table—high enough so I would not have to bend down to bathe the baby later. Miss Batemen was lathering the baby, who slipped right out of her hands and fell plop into the little tub—facedown!

Everyone laughed as they fished Betty out and dried her off. Then she was wrapped in a little blanket and put into the basket we had prepared beside our bed. I remember then that everyone went home, and I remember looking at the baby, sleeping peacefully in that basket—and I looked at my husband and said, "What if she cries! What will we do?" It was a very scary feeling!

Betty is a grandmother now. Four grandchildren for her!

Maurice Talley
Hacienda Heights, California

♡ *This is one of my favorite stories of all, partly because Maurice Talley conveys such a vivid sense of the era in which her son was born. We've heard so much about the babies born after World War II, but much less about the millions of American couples who had babies* during *the war—with no money and under conditions of terrible uncertainty.*

My son was born in 1942, my daughter in 1948. I'll tell you about the first. My husband and I were married in July 1941, in Albuquerque, New Mexico. After a disastrous chasing a rainbow to get wealthy in the prewar construction boom, we settled down in Phoenix, Arizona, very much in debt. This bothered me greatly, but my husband was the eternal optimist—it bothered him not a whit.

I soon found work as a payroll clerk for $25 a week. My husband was making $27.50 a week. We lived in a furnished apartment. We owned one set of Woolworth dishes, two towels, two sheets, and two pillowcases.

Although I suggested we pay our bills, we spent all our money. I mention this because it was a value disagreement for the first fifteen years of our marriage. I'm sure you can read between the lines that I was the traditional subservient wife. Perhaps even more so because I came from a broken home where my mother was the dominant partner.

Having a Baby

In February 1942, I became pregnant. It wasn't planned. We had been out dancing; I was tired and a little drunk. My husband was very drunk and I didn't put in the diaphragm.

I was very unhappy and fearful. I had never been around babies. I didn't know how my husband felt about the pregnancy. I had absolutely no knowledge of prenatal care—or childbirth except for *Gone with the Wind*.

At this time my husband was trying very hard to get into the Marines. I was far from home, had made only a few friends. Since we had been drinking, I was fearful for the baby's development.

After several months I went to the doctor to confirm pregnancy. I was very ill with morning sickness, very despondent, didn't want to and couldn't share my feelings.

I believe we loved each other dearly, but, in all twenty-nine years of marriage, we seldom truly communicated. I didn't want to upset him or burden him.

In May, Walter was transferred to Florence, Arizona, population 1,000, with a new prisoner-of-war camp. I couldn't find work or an apartment there, so remained in Phoenix, mainly to work. I moved to a rented room owned by a family who loved garlic and other pungent spices. I was miserable and sick. Occasionally, Walter would come to Phoenix to visit. Since he had our one car, I didn't go there.

In July I became angry, quit my job, took the bus to Florence, found an abandoned adobe house on the edge of town—then called my husband, who had been having a wonderful time being single again.

Temperatures reached 125 degrees. We had what was called a "swamp cooler"; it leaked and was eroding the adobe. It wasn't much good. I kept the refrigerator door open quite a bit of the time.

My mother sent me one maternity dress. We bought another one in October. There were two grocery stores in town—one for the town people and rich ranchers, the other for the Mexican population. The town people wouldn't talk with the army people, and neither the town people or the army people would talk to the civilian employees. So, again, no friends, no money, and rotten food. Walter was still chasing rainbows and went to school at night to learn to be a welder.

At this time there was only one doctor in Pinal County. It seemed that I'd go to one and then he was drafted. Literally, I had four doctors. The doctor who delivered my son had seen me only once. During the war doctors were overworked, so I got all my prenatal and child-rearing information from two U.S. Government Printing Office books, *Prenatal Care* and *Your Child from Birth to Six Years of Age*.

After the morning sickness was over, I became very happy about the baby. I walked a great deal, knitted, cleaned the house—which involved sweeping snakes out after the August thunderstorms, killing scorpions. I wrote poetry and many letters to my family and friends. I made two good friends.

One week before the baby was due, Walter decided we needed the extra money (which we did), so he took two weeks' vacation to work in the shipyards of San Francisco. He left me $6 or $7.

I practiced, timed the different ways to walk to the hospital. The shortest, fastest way was by an irrigation canal, but if the pains came at night, I couldn't see and there was a big dog at one house.

All of this wasn't necessary because Walter came back before the event. It was part of my development and conflict in my life—to be a good wife and mother, putting husband first, then children—and yet with the determination that I would never be dependent on anyone and I would never, and my children would never, go hungry or be poor.

The first pains began about seven P.M., when the landlord came to collect the rent and inspect the house. He stayed to visit. It wouldn't be polite to let them know how I felt. I was fearful that we'd be evicted because I wasn't the best house-keeper and the adobe was crumbling under the cooler. He left about eight o'clock.

So that I wouldn't upset my husband, I timed the pains myself and then told him at nine o'clock. As represented in the movies as comedy, he did go off and leave.

They wouldn't admit us to the hospital until we paid something. Walter had a small paycheck. He showed it, they admitted me, he left to go to the bar to cash it. He came back, but I didn't want him around to see me cry, so I sent him back for a drink and cigarettes.

The nurse said it would be five or six more hours. After an hour I asked for something for the pain. The nurse said, no, I'd appreciate it more later. I believed her, kept quiet, didn't want to disturb anyone.

I concentrated on what was best for the child and to deliver with dignity. So when the nurse would pop in from time to time, I'd say, no problem, just fine.

About midnight she decided to have a look. The head was showing. She yelled for me to pant; she asked someone to call the doctor, another for a gurney. I was in the delivery room before the doctor arrived.

They covered my eyes. I asked to see and they said no. I peeked as best I could. I may have been given a whiff of ether when the doctor cut, but I recall the relief and the feel when the head plopped out, the shoulders, the body. Plop, plop, plop.

An assistant said, "Shall we give her ether now?" The doctor uttered an oath. I didn't get ether *for* or after the birth. The doctor and nurse chattered about my beautiful baby boy, but wouldn't take the cover from my eyes. I don't know whether they tied my hands down or not.

I was cleaned up, taken back to my room, just in time to greet my husband bringing in our son. I was never so happy in my life. I immediately forgot the pain. I can recall it now only in relation to the birth of our second child.

How did I feel? Challenged to do it right, curious about what I was doing, proud that I did it without embarrassing myself or others, but, most of all, love for my husband first, my son second.

My husband has been dead seventeen years and I can recall that instant as if it were yesterday. Standing in the door, cigarette in hand, awkwardly holding this bundle, face aglow and saying, "Jesus!"

Dorothy Mullenneaux
Fairfield, Iowa

♡ *Below, Dorothy Mullenneaux tells the story of her mother's births (four children between 1920 and 1929), her own six birth experiences (1944 to 1959), and those of her daughter-in-law (five children born between 1971 and 1985)—all tending to illustrate Dorothy's belief that the natural way of birthing babies is the best way. Dorothy is one of several women in this book who read Grantly Dick Read's* Childbirth Without Fear, *became determined to have babies without drugs, and achieved her goal.*

My mother was a college graduate of New York State Teachers College, class of 1918. My father attended Colgate, volunteered for the army; they married after his discharge.

They had four children between 1920 and 1929. We lived in the modest city of Albany. All of us were born in the hospital with Albany's "best" obstetrician. The normal routine was to walk until labor was too strong, then to be anesthetized and in the hospital for two weeks *in bed*. It was not necessary to breastfeed so she didn't. "I trusted my doctor completely," she would say. Father saw the babies in the hospital nursery.

My experiences: I left Smith College after one year to marry my fiancé, who was going into the Air Force. We had six children between 1944 and 1959.

At the time of the first birth I was very ignorant. I trusted my obstetrician. I had a long, normal labor, about twenty-eight hours, and was given many kinds of anesthesia—Demerol, scopolamine, rectal ether, et cetera. I was out for the delivery. I came to, hours later.

Mother said, "You had a little girl."

Me: "Oh." (groggy)

My husband was in England flying a B-17. I was sure he'd survive. They had reduced the hospital stay to seven to ten days because of the war. I was in bed the whole time.

The baby was dopey from drugs. I believe forceps were used, as she had red marks on the sides of her head. She was brought in every four hours. It was routine to breastfeed but we were given no instruction. I had difficulty waking her, and I never had quite enough milk, due to lack of stimulation. She did a lot of crying on that four-hour schedule.

When she was four months, I read *Infant and Child in the Culture of Today* by Gesell and Ilg. I immediately changed to demand feeding. My pediatrician (the same one I had had as a child) said most people couldn't handle this.

With the second child I had a shorter labor, eight hours. I had no more education, but in 1946 doctors were against using too much drugs. Pain! I was in one large room with many laboring ladies and one not-helpful nurse.

I had too much ether on the delivery table. "Breathe, Mrs. Mullenneaux." I came to. It was a normal delivery with an episiotomy again.

I was startled to find most mothers bottle-feeding. I didn't. My husband saw the baby for a few minutes, then departed for a new job. I was in the hospital for five days—in bed.

With the third child, born in 1949, I was determined that this time it would be different. I bought Dr. Read's *Childbirth Without Fear*. Great! I began to understand the mechanics of labor and to practice techniques of relaxation.

I asked my doctor to read it. She read only the first chapter and was disgusted. She said it was going back to the old days when she delivered poor mothers in the South End without anesthesia.

I asked a nurse friend trained in natural childbirth to be with me. They begged me to "take the shot [Demerol] so you won't suffer," then begged me to take the ether cone during delivery. I took nothing. It was great. I had an eight-pound, twelve-ounce boy nicknamed "Happy" all his life. Now I am living with him, his wife, and his five children!

They laid him on my stomach still attached. I watched him turn pink. My husband was allowed in the delivery room after we were cleaned up.

I was in the hospital five days, I think. They did routine episiotomies with every birth, but I had no trouble with the stitches afterward. Bedrest still! I fed the baby on demand so I had lots of milk—partly because drugs inhibit the hormones and I had had no drugs.

The fourth child was born in 1955. I changed to a natural childbirth doctor and had rooming in. Great! It was a normal delivery and the baby was breastfed.

In 1958 I had my fifth. My great doctor had retired. I had a supposedly natural childbirth doctor. They took me to the delivery room too soon. It was long, slow, and uncomfortable. Again, I had rooming in and breastfed the baby.

With the sixth in 1959 I changed doctors. This was better. It was an incredibly easy labor—quick, four hours. I had no severe contractions, possibly because I had had a baby just eighteen months before. I was more in control of the situation.

The doctor I had was such a jolly man, and yet the stresses and pressures of medical training and the pace of his large practice took their toll. At the most wonderful, spiritual, tender moment, when the baby had just emerged, he said, with a disappointed tone,

"Oh. Another split tail." (Our fifth girl.) Incredible! Those were the first words Joanie heard!

I had rooming in, was there for only two days, breastfed the baby. My husband and my sister and her husband were allowed in the room to see us, clad in hospital whites.

My son and his wife have five children, born 1971 to 1985. Their first birth was much like my last three—in the hospital but in a maternity hospital, not a big city one. The baby was in the nursery for twenty-four hours—natural childbirth, no complications, breastfed.

But they were not pleased to be separated, so with the second they had the baby in the hospital but checked out as soon as the baby was pronounced all right. The hospital did everything to keep them from leaving (this was in 1975), but the doctor agreed. This child was born with a shorter labor and was breastfed.

The third child was the first birth at home—our house. It was a fairly long labor for a third baby—strenuous. We had a great doctor, a GP [general practitioner], a saint. We also had a home birth team—husband and three friends. All of us had breakfast together afterward, including the mother with the baby on her lap. The doctor told stories.

The fourth was born at home with a midwife. (The doctor had had his license taken away for doing home births.) The support group was all the meditating family. Meditators seem to have more energy and attention to give, even through a long night.

My daughter, who had had two home births, coached her beautifully. Everything was normal, the baby was breastfed, mother and baby were never separated.

The fifth was also a home birth. It was the first born here in Iowa. We planned to have midwives from Iowa City but a blizzard prevented it. They knew a lot, so Hap caught the baby and Richard, husband of another daughter of mine, lifted her up at the last minute so that Emanuel could slide out. Great!

So that is the way to have babies, I say:

1. Practice transcendental meditation so parents are strong and healthy and unafraid.

2. Know all there is to know (almost) about the subject.
3. Have the baby at home with the closest friends and relatives you trust, and your husband, there at all times.
4. Have expert assistance for the first deliveries.
5. Nurse on demand.
6. Don't be separated at all. Have the baby in your bed.

. . . And you will experience no depression postpartum. And your baby will be a little lamb chop like Emanuel.

Perhaps I could mention that it didn't hurt at all to have Grandmother (me) around for those first few months. My daughter-in-law got all her energy back quickly and did beautifully.

Simple, natural, effortless.

Frances Roosevelt
Oyster Bay, New York

♡ *Frances Roosevelt joined the Motor Corps, part of the Red Cross, and was sent overseas to England in 1942. She met Quentin Roosevelt II, grandson of President Theodore Roosevelt, in October 1943; they were married in April 1944.*

In August 1944, Quentin was transferred back to the United States to join the OSS (Office of Strategic Services, precursor of the CIA). The Roosevelts' first daughter was born in Washington, D.C., in 1945. The two younger daughters were born in 1946 and 1948 while the Roosevelts were living in Cove Neck, Long Island, near the longtime home of the Theodore Roosevelt branch of the Roosevelt family at Oyster Bay.

This very controlled but loving birth story has a sad ending but, I think, a triumphant postscript in the subsequent lives of Frances and the three daughters born of Frances and Quentin (see endnote, pages 268–69), who were raised in a household of nine women.

The birth of my first child (January 1945) began when my amniotic sac burst at six A.M. My husband called a taxi in a snowstorm and roared at the driver when he picked up another passenger. The driver said, "It's her first baby. It won't come for hours." It didn't.

I was given nothing to speed labor. I played Monopoly and chess all day with my husband until six P.M., when he and the doctor went out to dinner! At seven P.M. I felt the real push pains and was moved to the delivery room. I was given some medication but found that a book was a better narcotic.

The other ladies had been taught to scream; I thought this was unattractive. One woman, between screams, asked me in a normal voice, "What are you reading?" Finally I received a spinal shot and was unconscious for the actual delivery. I was told later that the bleeding lasted too long after the birth. Some medication from a South American plant was used which stopped the bleeding.

I had read about and been told about the process of birth. It was more unattractive than I had anticipated. I had an episiotomy which was slow to heal.

My husband saw the baby through the window right after her birth. He wasn't enchanted by her beauty. She had his big head and got quite red on the way out. He had not been present at the birth, of course. It is an unesthetic process and I would *never* have anyone I loved see it. (My daughter does today.)

The procedure after the birth was an old-fashioned system. I could not even get up for one week; I was in the hospital for two weeks. The baby was present for the afternoon, which was nice, but I was too long in the hospital.

I breastfed the baby for six months. I was informed that it was good for the baby. The social climate was that no one cared one way or the other. She always had a bottle in case of a party or other event that would take me away.

All in all, it was neither a trauma or a poem. I could wish for no more two weeks in the hospital. I was pleased by my ugly little baby's bright eyes, but rather insulted when a friend of my father-in-law, General Theodore Roosevelt, Jr., said she looked like him!! Not for long. By three months she was beautiful and still is. I missed a good party that night!

The birth of my second child in May 1946 was almost a disaster. I ate a bad oyster two nights before she was born, *one month* before she was supposed to arrive. I had very bad diarrhea, followed by sudden pains. I called the doctor who met me at the hospital and said to stay.

Then I waited outside a room. The hospital had lost its volunteer Red Cross nurses the day before and was disorganized. I finally got a room and played one brief game; I beat my husband! The rest of the process was so rapid I don't remember much, except that I got a shot in the arm this time instead of in the spine.

The little pet only weighed four pounds but was healthy and 21 inches long, so she was not put in the incubator, even though she went down to three and a half pounds the day after. She was not expected until June.

Her father saw her through the window again and felt gratitude that, though she was one month early, she survived. He had been waiting anxiously!

This time I was only in the hospital four days—hurrah![10] I had more time with the baby. I got a nurse for one month at home. Nursing was difficult in the hospital because of the loss of the Red Cross volunteers. I breastfed briefly. Perhaps because of the early birth the milk was not enough. She wanted to eat every two hours and I could not produce at that rate.

She was astonishingly pale and beautiful because her small size did not produce the battered red face. I was pleased that she survived the oyster. I have learned to smell oysters before putting them in my mouth!

With the third baby (April 1948), labor began during a tea and cocktail party we were having. I had already packed my suitcase for the hospital with former occasions in mind. Since those mild pains go on for a long time, I didn't even tell my husband until later and then, when they got firmer, I called the doctor and he said, "Go!"

My husband drove to the hospital rather rapidly. The nurse examined me and said, "Oh, it won't come for a while." The baby must have heard her because the sac burst and I got to the delivery room with the baby protruding! I had no narcotics except one whiff of ether at the end! I just got there!

The doctor made it on time. "Fathie" (the children's name for Quentin) dressed in the doctor's robes and a mask and got to hold her one hour after the birth because he was going to China right after she was born. He picked her name. This time I stayed in the hospital only two days. I had to get up after I got home to remove my beloved dog from my bed when he wouldn't leave me after 12 hours.

I breastfed this baby for seven months because we went to China on a freighter when she was only two months old (a three-month trip!), and I thought it was safer. The other two girls thought she was their doll.

I was very glad that I got to the hospital just in time. I did wish she had been a boy. One telegram was fun: It said, "Three of a kind. Best wishes for a full hand!"

She is precious, however, and has five children. I wasn't really concerned because we meant to have seven children. Sadly, my husband was killed in China so there were no more."

Beth McDonald
Perryton, Texas

♡ *Beth McDonald tells about a 1946 labor and birth that began on a farm and ended in a small-town hospital, both in rural Oklahoma. She recalls her birth experience very fondly, with much affection for her husband, her family, and the medical people who helped her.*

In December of 1945, when I was eighteen, I married a World War II veteran of the South Pacific campaign, M. C. "Chuck" York. By Christmastime of 1946, we were happily looking forward to the birth of our first baby, scheduled for mid-January.

We were staying with my parents on their Oklahoma Panhandle farm, sixteen miles northwest of Perryton, Texas, the nearest town. My husband's brother, Junior York, who was just six months older than I, had come to spend the holidays with us.

On the 29th of December, Chuck and I went to bed in the cozy, southeast front bedroom. The outside temperature was 20 below zero, though—fortunately—no snow was falling. My husband asked for sex and we had a very gentle intercourse around ten P.M.

Between two and three in the morning of the 30th, I heard the front door blow open. Someone had failed to close it firmly. When I got out of bed to go and shut it, a rather large amount of water ran down my legs and onto the hardwood floor. I was embarrassed, a little scared, and excited.

I was too wet to get back into bed. I woke my husba͞
then my mother, who was sleeping in a bedroom that adjͼ
ours. She was instantly and happily alert, excited, and efficiͼ ..
She explained the sudden rush of water, and I needed to hear
it from her, though I'd thoroughly studied Dr. Grantly Dick
Read's book on natural childbirth. My mother woke my dad and
he called my Perryton, Texas, doctor.

By then my back had begun to ache and the first mild contractions had started. My legs trembled slightly, the same as they
had in the early-morning hours ten years before, when I'd stayed
with relatives while my only sibling, Elvin McDonald, was being
born.

When I tried to talk, my chin quivered in much the way of
someone who is chilled, though my mother had brought me a
Kotex and helped me into dry clothing. I was warm, wrapped
in a blanket and my husband's arms.

I was so absorbed in my own body's actions and sensations,
I barely heard the disturbing news that, since my labor was
early, the Perryton hospital my doctor had intended to use for
my delivery was not completely built. No delivery room was
ready for me there. My doctor advised my dad to take me to
the next nearest hospital in a town in Oklahoma, forty miles
away. So Daddy called our family doctor (not the obstetrician
I had been seeing during my pregnancy) to tell him we were on
our way.

My backache worsened. I was dimly aware that my young
brother-in-law was awake and outside with my dad, that the
pickup had started, and then I didn't hear Daddy's and Junior's
voices anymore for a while.

In memory it seems almost no time elapsed between my getting up to shut the door and the arrival of my dad in a black
1940 Ford in front of the house. My backache had intensified,
and the contractions were stronger, about seven minutes apart.

My husband helped me into the Ford's backseat and tucked
a quilt securely around me, though the car's heater was working
well. He drove and my mother sat beside him in the front seat.

Junior stayed home to look after my brother, who was not quite ten, and to take care of the farm animals. Daddy followed us in the pickup and, especially considering the 20-below cold, I was immensely glad to have a standby means of getting to the hospital.

Chuck kept his speed moderate. The last thing we needed was an accident. Now my backache was so bad I sat rigidly, hanging onto the front seat, trying not to sway with the car's movements. We were at the hospital door about seven A.M., and I was put to bed by smiling nurses, who obviously shared our happy excitement.

I remembered everything Dr. Read's book advised and I cooperated with my body. Contractions were coming four minutes apart and then three. Between them I relaxed so completely that I caught minutes of restful, even blissful, sleep.

Another woman in labor was using that little hospital's only delivery table. The doctor prepared to deliver my baby on the bed. My mother stood on my right and I held her hand. The doctor put his foot up on the bed frame so I could hold onto his leg with my left hand.

He was laughing, "Come on, pull my leg and *push.*" By that time, *push* was exactly what I wanted to do. I worried about the bones in my mother's small hand, because I felt them slip together as I strained, but she was smiling while the doctor kept coaching, "Push." I clamped my teeth together so hard they were sore for a week, and I pushed.

Just before the baby slipped out, a nurse gave me some whiffs of ether, which I did not need or want. Fortunately, it was not enough to keep me from fully experiencing that supremely exultant moment when the doctor held up my new baby girl, who was red and crying strongly.

I was amazed at the enormous red-blue cable that came out with her, hardly a simple cord. It was nine-forty-five A.M., December 30, 1946.

The doctor easily delivered the placenta. I bled little and was very hungry for the meal, topped off with chocolate cake, that was brought to me at eleven-thirty.

Our daughter weighed five pounds and fifteen ounces and we named her Diana after the goddess, Christine after a war buddy of my husband, whose name was Christiansen.

My brother-in-law, Junior, has never tired of telling the story of that night, and, until someone did tell a version of it that was theirs, not mine, I never realized the scare my dad went through. When he'd gone out to start his black 1940 Ford, the motor was too chilled. The battery couldn't turn it.

Junior laughs and laughs as he tells how "J. D. turned white and never looked back to see if I was behind him. He jumped in the pickup; it started and we drove to Charlie Stewart's in nothing flat." Charlie Stewart's place was four miles away.

So the warm, comfortable car in which I rode to the hospital was not my parents' standard '40 Ford but the Stewarts' slightly prettier and larger deluxe black 1940 Ford, and I never realized the difference in the cold and the darkness and the excitement.

I look back on that early morning of December 30, 1946, and marvel at how much emotion and thought can be contained in a single flash of time. For, as Diana was born, I was simultaneously the happiest I'd ever been in my life, but *also* aware that her birth both expanded *and* limited my life radically, *for the rest of my life*. She opened the center of my being, and I could never close it to end that vulnerability.

I haven't mentioned pain in this childbirth story, because, aside from the backache, it was only labor—hard work and enormously satisfying. I was young, healthy, well built for childbearing, educated about the process, and I had total support from my family, plus a doctor and nurses who treated me with understanding and kindness.

Margaret Atlas
Sunrise, Florida

♡ *Margaret Atlas speaks warmly of her sons and grandchildren. "We are indeed blessed," she says. But, in the process of getting those sons, she endured difficulties that would have caused most women to curse their fate and give up. Margaret persevered and finally got what she wanted.*

I will be seventy-seven in December. The history of my pregnancies has always been of interest. There were ten in all. It was a miracle that two have survived.

In April 1938, at the end of a seven-month pregnancy, I gave birth to a lovely boy who died shortly after birth. I was told, since he was premature, he was in an incubator. I kept inquiring and not until the third day was I told. I cried hysterically and was so depressed an aide remained in my room for several days to prevent me from jumping off the balcony outside my room. My parents took care of the burial.

In January 1939, I lost our second baby boy. Again, our parents took care of the burial. In May of 1939, I had a uterine X-ray, which revealed I had a double uterus. My obstetrician suggested I try again.

In April 1940, we lost a baby girl after many injections and an on-and-off stay in bed. Again, there was a burial. I was very persevering and again became pregnant. This time we stored our furniture and went to my parents' home, where I remained

in bed until my sixth month when the doctor suggested I could
get off the bed just to go to the bathroom. The next day, the
end of June, I went into labor and lost another baby girl. It was
1941.

In November 1941, while still taking it easy in my parents'
home, I had a miscarriage. At this point the doctor thought it
was enough. Regretfully, he told me to try another doctor. It
was on Pearl Harbor Day, December 7th, 1941, that I left the
hospital feeling very dejected.

The only thing that kept me from doing something desperate
was the thought that all five babies might not have been normal,
and I so much wanted a normal baby. I come from a big family,
the youngest of seven children, and always wanted many children. Getting pregnant was easy; holding on was my problem.

When I became pregnant again in February 1943, I went to
the clinic at a large hospital, which was highly recommended,
but in May of 1943, I had another miscarriage.

When I became pregnant again in December of 1945 and was
in my third month, I again started staining. I went back to the
hospital. They were impressed with my record and suggested
since it was my seventh pregnancy that I agree to remain in
bed, flat on my back, for the remainder of the pregnancy, get
hormone injections every day, medication, et cetera. I was desperate and agreed. My husband did not like the idea but I insisted. What an experience that was!

My bed was in a large airy room with three other patients
who had heart conditions and were near delivery. I can write
endlessly about the six months I spent there. When I had been
bedridden for only two months, one of the doctors came in and
told me he did not agree with the bed theory and suggested that
I get up, but I stubbornly refused. Each morning the nurse
would come in and say, "Are we getting out of bed today?" I
just shook my head.

I had entered the hospital in February. There was snow on
the ground and I had worn boots when I walked to the subway
that would take me to the hospital. I was working at the time

and that morning had called my office to say I was not feeling well and would be out for a few days. My husband was at work.

When I reached the seventh month in lovely June, I was wheeled in my bed up to the roof by elevator for some sunshine and fresh air. I must have been a trial case. Each day student doctors and others would come to my bed and question me. My morale was great. I was optimistic. I was going to have a baby!

In August 1946, I did reach my ninth month. That wonderful day a nurse raised my bed just a bit (I had been lying flat) and the room swam. The second day they allowed my feet to dangle off the side of the bed. They were just skin and bone. The third day I went into labor and delivered dear little Tommy. Everyone was jubilant. My seventh pregnancy was in our eleventh year of marriage.

In March 1948, I became pregnant again. Since I had my precious baby now I could not stay in the hospital, but they recommended my medication and care, and in November of 1948 I delivered another boy.

In June 1949, I was again pregnant but miscarried a few weeks later. Here I needed a curettage again in the hospital.

The next one was a real tragedy. My baby boy was born alive in April 1950, on the first day of my seventh month, in the hospital. I spent nine days there, both before and after delivery, in agony always, on the delivery floor with all the screaming, et cetera. The baby died and I was advised never to get pregnant again. I have not.

My baby history has been both physically and mentally painful. My husband had a rough time as well. He was always supportive and in July on the 13th we will be married fifty-two years. We have two very fine sons and each is married and has a son and a daughter. We are indeed blessed.

Anonymous

♡ *The writer of this piece has asked to remain anonymous. She had her babies in 1939, 1942, and 1948. A very bad case of postpartum psychosis followed the birth of her last child. (There was a somewhat milder attack following the birth of the second child but no one seems to have anticipated that it might recur.)*

Postpartum depression is a fairly common follow-up to birth that was identified and reported by Hippocrates as far back as 2,400 years ago. Occasionally, postpartum depression takes on the much more severe form of postpartum psychosis. In the case of the woman who speaks here, the psychosis lasted for two years. It was the Lord's Prayer, she says, that finally started her on the path to recovery.

I think these days women think more seriously about the job of having children. I was a "babe-in-arms" myself, and simply plunged into having children. Granted, my children were "planned" by the use of a diaphragm, which at that time was brand new and very hush-hush. I had to go to a doctor in a nearby big city to get one. My mother was incredulous!

My first child was born on January 26, 1939, at 7:31 A.M. My husband took me to the hospital the evening of January 25. I had a long labor. In those days, when you had a baby, anesthetics were administered as a matter of course. Few women used natural childbirth.

My obstetrician presumably used the same medication and technique—Seconal and Nembutal with scopolamine, forceps, median episiotomy—which he used with my other children. I had the same obstetrician for all three children, but his own detailed information was given only in number two's baby book.

I didn't regain consciousness until about eleven A.M. I started breastfeeding the third day; most of my friends did not breastfeed. The only time I saw the baby was at feeding time. My husband saw him hardly at all, certainly never held him until we got home. I stayed in the hospital two full weeks, then had a nurse at home for three weeks.

On March 11 supplementary feeding was started, one bottle a day. By March 24 the baby was completely on the bottle. He was breastfed for two months.

I had a normal recovery and experienced no reactions of any kind.

On June 20, 1942, at one P.M., my second child was born. On June 19, I saw the OB and got a clean bill of health. He said it would be at least two more weeks before the baby was born. There was a full moon that night and I couldn't sleep.

The next morning labor pains started at about six-thirty A.M. My husband was out of town. My father took me to the hospital. Mother stayed with my son.

My daughter was born weighing six pounds, eight and a half ounces. My husband arrived the next day. My milk came in the third day and I started to breastfeed. The baby gained quickly.

I started exercising the fifth day with an exercise called "bottoms up." On the ninth day I sat in a chair for twenty minutes. I was shaky. On the tenth day I was up twice feeling much better. On the twelfth day I was up and walking around. I left the hospital on the thirteenth day. I took a nurse home with me who stayed for three weeks. After four weeks of nursing I started the baby on one bottle a day.

I had been getting shots for hay fever all that spring before the baby was born and then continued them afterward. Sometime during August I got a bad case of athlete's foot, for which

I received X-ray treatment. The infection worsened and spread over my entire body. Our family physician then treated it by covering it with a green dye.

The skin infection plus my nerves continued to get worse until I landed in the hospital, hallucinating. This they called postpartum depression. I had a private nurse around the clock who took me each afternoon into the psychiatric ward of the hospital for hydrotherapy. Gradually, I recovered completely.

Then I had child number three, born on December 8, 1948, at 1:58 A.M. It was an easy pregnancy, filled with happy expectation and a minimum of discomfort. A cooperative husband and an excellent obstetrician helped me sail through the nine months.

Two weeks before the approximated December delivery date, labor pains started and my father took me to the hospital. (My husband was in New York.)

Soon after I arrived, and before going to the delivery room, I was given sedation, then shots. Several hours later, I was strapped to the delivery table, fidgeting in the stirrups and squinting at the overhead lights. The doctor slowly pulled on his rubber gloves.

"Bear down harder," said a nurse at my side. "It won't be much longer."

A spasm of pain clutched at me. I heard the doctor's voice, then the nurse swooped down with a rubber mask. The smell of ether gagged me. I thought I was suffocating.

The next thing I remember, seven hours later, was the doctor's thrilling announcement: "You have a fine baby who wants to see you." I had been unconscious through almost the entire procedure. It was hard to believe the child had actually been born.

I breastfed about the same length of time as with the others and again had a nurse at home. During the next busy weeks I remember thinking how lucky I was to have three healthy children and a fine husband.

On the glacial morning of February 14, 1949, I set about on

a typical day, caring for my children and my house. I have no recollection of blacking out or going to the hospital, but I came to in a psychiatric ward, hallucinating and confused. Doors were locked and windows barred.

I imagined myself in jail and the psychiatrist a warden. A nurse tied me down in bed at night. Twice each week an attendant took me to a large, dismal room to wait in line for shock treatment. After a series of these, my mind cleared and the doctor told me I had suffered from postpartum amnesia, or loss of memory following childbirth.

Soon I had more attacks. As March slush melted into April mud, I was in and out of the hospital. I got the notion that nationwide, scientific experiments were being carried out just on me. I imagined billboards bearing messages in code for me. I visualized my very much alive mother dead of heartbreak caused by my foibles, my infant hideously withering away from neglect. In rational periods I feared permanent insanity. When my father suggested a nearby sanitarium, which had always seemed the jumping-off place, I wanted to die.

Snow flurries returned in May, and the furnace still clicked on in June. About that time my sister recommended a large, renowned hospital located near her, and I was taken there. Once more, those in attendance treated me as a potential suicide, with belts and all sharp instruments removed or allowed only under surveillance.

Yet, sick as I was, I saw a difference from previous hospitalization. The country girl had come to town. There were separate buildings for varying degrees of illness. There were tennis courts, a golf course, a beauty shop, even a chapel.

I found myself in C House, again barred and locked, but somehow lacking the abasement of former confinement. They gave me insulin therapy, which, to me, was more palatable than shock treatment. The whole mess was a slightly less virulent hell, or, by now, I was partially conditioned to my predicament.

The psychiatrist, who was short and taciturn, saw me for half an hour each morning. In a monotone he would ask, "Did you dream last night?"

"I don't remember, you know, I mean . . ." I couldn't carry on the simplest conversation.

I couldn't even talk to Sis. I'll never forget one hot July afternoon when she came to visit and we sat together in my room. My condition had worsened and she soon realized I wasn't tuned in to her cheery anecdotes.

So, pointing to the bed, she said, "Can you tell me what that is?" I just gaped. Then she turned to a table, "I'll bet you know what that is." I couldn't name it. Finally she walked over to the wastebasket, put something in it, and looked over at me quizzically. After long minutes I sputtered, "Wastebasket."

For a while we sat in silence. Even after she left, I sat there staring at the one thing I could recognize—the wastebasket.

Soon, however, I improved sufficiently to be transferred to a less restrictive building with freedom to go about the premises unescorted. One sultry afternoon, while out for a walk on the hospital grounds, I approached the little chapel. No one was around, so I ventured inside the dark, deserted church.

After a period of vacuous gazing, I slid into a rear pew and bowed my head. The blank continued. Before long I felt trapped and hustled outdoors.

It was steamy hot. All the buildings looked alike and seemed to encircle me in a maze. Suddenly distant thunder clapped and I ran back into the chapel, as in childhood I had scampered home at the sign of a storm.

Now I knelt and in a moment heard myself blurting out loud, "Our Father, Who art in Heaven, hallowed be Thy name."

My heart machine-gunned. Perspiration rained down my spine. Here, finally, was something I *remembered*. I said the Lord's Prayer over and over and over.

Then I strode outside and now it was cooler. The impact of my discovery easily transported me to the correct building and my room.

The next weeks were a series of ups and downs but now,

fortified by the Lord's Prayer, I fought to get well. When I couldn't figure out the score in a tennis game, or would lose my way to the occupational therapy room, I'd repeat to myself, "Thy will be done." This proved relaxing and helpful.

Before long, I knew that somehow I'd get better. I deeply sensed that my rediscovery of the Lord's Prayer was the spark of support that, together with that excellent hospital, would see me through. The rankling apprehension of possible permanent disorder was gone.

By the time I was fully recovered, however, my youngest child was two years old. (The second child was nine and the first was twelve.) I've never had a recurrence of any kind. Hypersensitivity to the medication brought all this about.

Today, forty years later, perhaps my illness would have been prevented. When I was nine years old, I developed an intestinal colitis problem and missed half a year of school. It was treated with diet and rest and eventually got better, but that was an early indication of my supersensitive system.

Since then, I've discovered I'm sensitive to many things, including caffeine, alcohol, and Novocain. I'm unable to take stimulants of any kind, including sweets. Today I'm enjoying excellent health and feel great, but I stick to my diet!

Now, before receiving an anesthetic, usually a patient is tested for excessive sensitivity. Further, with the current prevalence of natural childbirth, few, if any, drugs are needed for child delivery.

In retrospect, though I was unlucky with the effects of anesthetics, I'm grateful to have grown up with the Lord's Prayer. Over the years, having recited it daily in school and weekly in church, those words were so ingrained in my memory that they occurred to me during an illness in which I could remember little else. They provided confidence when I needed it most.

Mary Fairfield
Fargo, North Dakota

♡ *Mary and Leslie Fairfield met in 1937 and married in 1940 while working for Episcopal missions in China. They came home on furlough and their first child was born in July 1941. Leslie returned to China alone soon after the birth. He was interned by the Japanese after Pearl Harbor but released in a prisoner-of-war exchange in 1942. The Fairfields, now with three little boys, went back to China again in 1947 to continue their missionary work.*

We were able to return to China in 1947 after the war, when Leslie and Andrew were six and four, and John was six months old. We were stationed in Yangchow in Kiangsu province. It is just north of the Yangtse on the Grand Canal. It was a China full of unrest. Communist troops held much of the countryside but were unable to capture the cities.

Les would travel up the Grand Canal to other cities on business, and would be cut off by guerrilla attacks, but he always got back somehow. However, we were soon transferred to Nanking to begin work there the fall of 1948.

There was a Baptist hospital the other side of the city from us, but, since I expected Tim in early September, we decided to have him at another hospital closer by. Most babies were being delivered at home by midwives, but, in the cities where there were hospitals, it was more and more popular to have babies there.

Missionary boards were seeing the handwriting on the wall at this time, however, and all the hospitals were being put under the direction of native Chinese. Everything was in an upset state.

We arrived in Nanking in blistering hot weather on September 1st. Besides settling the home, my first anxiety was to get a competent "amah" to care for the children.

The day after our arrival I got an appointment with the doctor who was doing the obstetrical work at the hospital. My husband stayed with the children and sent me to the hospital in a rickshaw where I was to find the doctor in the OB clinic.

I think the temperature was near 100 degrees that day. Instead of traveling the main thoroughfares into town, the rickshaw chose less crowded but cobblestoned streets. I stood it for a couple of miles and then paid off the man and walked the last mile. I remember bystanders guffawing at me! My condition and reason for leaving the rickshaw were quite obvious!

At the hospital I read the characters for "OB Clinic" on the second floor of the general clinic building. In the corridor outside the door I found a queue of perhaps twenty women waiting. Through a glass window in the door I could see the doctor moving about from time to time.

Because I stood at the back of the line, I didn't notice at first that all the women held slips of paper with a number. "Where do you get these?" I asked the next woman. She replied, "At the general admission desk downstairs."

I went down. Here was no neat queue. Here were at least thirty people, all crowding and pushing and yelling to get attention. I couldn't cope and sat down on the bottom step and burst into tears!

A young Chinese doctor stopped to inquire. "You don't belong here," he said. "The clinic for foreigners is in the hospital building. When you get there, they will send over for the doctor to come there to examine you."

Ordinarily, I would have resented special treatment, but that day I was just thankful. The waiting room for foreigners had cushioned wicker chairs and an electric fan. I sat down and continued to weep with relief. Other patients were sure I was about to deliver and insisted on getting me attention right away, though I assured them I was able to wait.

The doctor hurried over. I suppose the other poor women stood waiting. He examined me and pronounced, "Not now but soon." It wasn't news to me. I can't really remember the trip home to our house just outside the north gate in the city wall. Our property bordered on the moat. That was September 2nd.

My membrane ruptured just after we got in bed the evening of the 4th. Les got the only other foreigner on the premises, an older maiden lady, to stay with the children and he drove me to the hospital in the mission jeep. Because of the troubles the city gate was closed from midnight until six in the morning, so we had to hurry so Les would be able to get home again. We had trouble getting through a large herd of pigs being driven into the city for market.

Les banged on the hospital gate, and a sleepy gateman called out that patients weren't admitted at this hour of the night. I giggled as I heard Les trying to explain. His obstetrical Chinese wasn't up to it. I had to help out. For most purposes, his Chinese is far better than mine.

I was let in and Les left in a hurry. No one seemed to know what to do with me. There was no one to assign a place. Finally I was taken to the delivery room where there was a young nurse on duty. Though my contractions were just starting, I was put on a delivery table that was made in two sections which kept coming apart when I moved. I knew I should be trying to get some sleep but what could I do?

Hours passed and in the morning a Chinese lady resident turned up. "You shouldn't be here," she scolded. I thoroughly agreed. She left and returned to say that there were no first-class beds available. All they had was third-class.

I was taken to a basement room with a high cellar window.

The bed was a wooden shelf attached to the wall on which was spread straw matting. The ceiling was a maze of heating pipes and there was a single naked light bulb on a cord over the bed. There was also a straight chair. One advantage was that it was blessedly cool.

Ordinarily, patients' families supplied the food in these rooms, but I was able to get liquids, which was all I wanted. At intervals a shy Chinese resident examined me. Twice he hit his head on the overhanging light bulb as he straightened up, and he would laugh in an embarrassed way. He looked frightened of a foreign lady.

I asked to see my doctor, and the resident explained, I wasn't ready to see him yet. He would come to deliver me. I recognized this as very Chinese. In every craft and trade the assistants do all the work and the master comes in for the final touches.

My contractions increased during the day and were stronger as night came on. I worried over the long labor. How was this baby doing? How was Les managing with the children and all that had to be done?

In the afternoon the lady resident appeared again and listened to my woes. She said she would help in the matter of finding an amah to care for my children. She had examined a woman she knew and recommended highly for an embassy family a couple of days earlier, but the family had been sent home and the woman was free. She'd have her come in and see me right away.

The amah arrived shortly—an angel in disguise! I saw a clean, capable-looking, motherly creature, and we took to each other right away. Les arrived while she was there and she arranged to go right home with him if he would stop at her home so she could collect a few things. You can imagine my gratitude!

I was in the basement room through Sunday night, September 5th. Contractions continued but I didn't seem to be making any progress. The giggling doctor checked in at intervals. Otherwise, I was alone.

Monday morning I was moved upstairs to a larger, lighter

room with a hospital bed, a bureau, and an easy chair. The same naked bulb was overhead.

I spent the day feeling at the end of my tether. I had had no sleep for two nights and the pains were beyond anything I had known possible. I'm afraid I lost control of myself and howled.

In the afternoon an American doctor I had known socially years earlier when I was in language school in Nanking dropped in for a visit. I was surprised to see him and he told me that he was letting the Chinese doctors have full responsibility now, and he had confidence in my doctor—whom I still hadn't seen.

At midnight that night two stretcher bearers arrived to move me to the delivery room. I hadn't realized that one bounced up and down on a stretcher!

My doctor awaited me. At each contraction someone held chloroform to my nose and I snuffed it in thankfully. Les, who was standing just outside, heard the doctor keep repeating, "Push, Mrs. Fairfield, push!"

My next memory is being moved back onto my bed from the stretcher. They told me I had a twelve-pound son, and they brought him to me. I thought his head was overlarge, but the doctor said it was within normal limits. (Subsequently, pediatricians told me that there was undoubtedly a prenatal hydrocephalic condition, but since his birth there has been no further abnormal growth.) Tim was born September 7th at two A.M.

Les came in and brought great reports of Chen Ma, the amah we took. He said she had baby John well in hand, and the little boys liked her.

Wednesday night I ran a 103-degree temperature and felt sure I was dying of childbed fever, but Les was able to scare up some sulfa, fairly new then, from army medical friends, and I got better. The lady resident came in to show me exercises to do to get back in shape.

The doctor said I could go home the next Monday and I could scarcely wait. Tim was brought to me in a little padded quilt folded around him like an envelope and kept in place with a cord tied around the middle. Evidently, he was perspiring a lot in the 90-degree heat and was peppered with heat rash. I wanted to get home and do something about it.

Sunday noon, when he was brought, I saw that he was feverish and fretful. I asked about him, but the strange nurse filling in for Sunday didn't know anything and no one else was about to ask, so I waited and worried. In the afternoon the nice lady resident dropped in. I told her about Tim and she promised to check him in the nursery and come back and tell me, but she didn't. The baby wasn't brought to me again that night or the next morning.

About ten A.M. the next morning, my doctor came in. It was the first time I had seen him since the delivery. He said the baby had been diagnosed as having erysipelas.[12] We couldn't go home and were being removed to the section for contagious diseases.

I found Tim had a tremendous abscess in the center of his back from which a scarlet tide swept out over his shoulders and down onto his buttocks. Again, the army came to our rescue with the new penicillin.

It seemed to me someone was doing something to the baby every few minutes, poulticing, giving shots, feeding, examining. At least he was with me now and I could keep watch. I was no longer under my obstetrician and got a crotchety old American doctor who got us a special nurse, an RN who was the wife of a Chinese professor at the university.

When she arrived, Tim's care was reorganized. All treatments and feeding were done at one time. "What that child needs to survive is to sleep," she said. She settled herself in a rocking chair with Tim in her arms and rocked quietly.

"Don't worry, Mrs. Fairfield [literally "put your heart down"]. I will be holding the baby and watching and praying all the time. All my patients get well." It didn't seem like a boast, just a statement of fact.

We both settled down and slept and got better. The red tide stopped spreading and got darker and less fiery. The nurse left after a week, but we were not discharged for another two weeks.

My husband, Les, had had a spring cold, and the cough lingered through the summer. The heat and the packing, which he had done without any help while we were in Shanghai, had gotten him down and, since many of his students at the school were active TB cases, I urged him to see a doctor while we were still in the hospital.

One day he came to the door and told me he had TB, too, and was ordered to bed. It was before the days of drug therapy. It wasn't long before the mission authorities and the State Department told us to get back to the States.

Everyone was pulling out then and no passages were available. We came home courtesy of the U.S. Navy—Les on a Med-Evac plane, and the children and I on a MATS (Military Air Transport Service) bucket-seat prop plane, island hopping and getting bumped here and there . . . Okinawa, Guam, Kwajalein, Johnson Island, Honolulu . . . two babies in diapers and no disposables. It took more than a month to reach Amherst, Massachusetts, but we made it by Christmas. Eighteen months later, my husband was able to leave the sanitarium and rejoin us. A whole new life started.

Timothy is an epileptic with considerable brain damage who lives in supervised housing and works in a sheltered workshop. All my sons (there was one more born in 1951) except Timothy are married and I have eight grandchildren: five of them are *girls!*

Do I feel that Timothy's birth in China was the result of mismanagement? The answer is I don't really know. He most certainly had a prenatal hydrocephalic condition, which naturally caused the extended labor.

In this country I doubt if I would have been left in labor fifty-two hours, but cesarean sections were never done in China at the time, and I am probably lucky they didn't try it.

Timothy seemed to me a normal baby for the first week. My concern started after he had the neonatal infection with high fever. As you see, there are many possibilities. It interests me that among sixty-odd families in the mission, there are three other brain-damaged children. Maybe this is not a large proportion.

I do not think of my China years as years of hardship. (You've heard the worst!) I met my husband out there and a love story runs through those days. I had a marvelous time. It was only after the war when I went back with the children that things were tough. But those days "came to pass"!

Timothy has just been home for a week's visit. His I.Q. is in the mid-50s, but he is, oddly enough, a card shark! He took on all sorts of people and beat them at canasta.

Emma Louie
Los Angeles, California

♡ *Emma Louie is an American of Chinese descent who grew up in San Francisco's Chinatown. "I believe we all have deadwood in our minds when it comes to race relations," she wrote me in one of her letters. "It requires effort to get rid of it."*

Unfortunately, the crystallizing moment of discrimination for Emma occurred in connection with what should have been a completely joyous occasion—the birth of her first child.

The year was 1949. In those days a baby did not stay in the same room with its mother and, at this particular hospital, mothers either stayed in a private room or in a room with two beds, depending upon availability and the arrangements made before the baby's due date.

I recall feeling very fortunate to be able to stay in a room with two beds, which was all we could afford. I was taking a nap on the second day after my son was born, when suddenly a nurse came into the room and started piling all my belongings on my bed and proceeded to move me, bed and all, out of the room. There was no greeting, no explanation.

"Where are you taking me?" I asked.

"To a private room," was the reply. I remember saying I didn't want to be in one because I couldn't afford it.

We were halfway out of the room when I asked her to stop what she was doing and to get the head nurse. When the head

77

nurse came, she said I had to move because the other bed in my room was unoccupied and two women had just given birth.

When I ascertained that they were not related or friends, I asked, "Why can't you put one in the empty bed and the other in the private room? I'm already in this bed." That seemed logical. But the head nurse's reply was that I had to move because neither of the women could afford a private room. That made no sense.

So I said, please call my doctor and I'm calling my husband because I was not going to move. The head nurse thought I was being unreasonable.

Then the director of nurses came, bringing the hospital administrator, who said, "You don't understand, Mrs. Louie. Neither of the new mothers is Chinese or Negro." (The term *black* was not in use at the time.)

Yes, I finally understood. But, for some reason, for the first time in my life, I didn't care to comply. I had accepted several incidents of racial discrimination directed against me as a part of life. But sitting on my bed in the middle of the room, where the first nurse had left me, with the door shut, was a shocking experience. It hurt all the more because the nurses had been so friendly, coming into my room to chat. Then, all of a sudden, they were angry at me. Fortunately, my doctor was very supportive so I was not moved.

The other bed remained vacant during my five days at the hospital, the usual stay at the time. The two new mothers went to the surgery ward. The nurses remained hostile. But my baby was fine among all the white babies; his nurses were very pleasant. What should have been a very happy occasion with the birth of my first child was marred by the ugliness of racial discrimination.

Even the sequel to my childbirth story was illogical. It was during the late 1960s, when Asian-Americans were starting to speak up against racial discrimination, that I got up the nerve to write to the hospital administrator—who, undoubtedly, was not the same person—about my experience, to say, I'm glad hospitals don't have that practice anymore.

His reply was that such a thing could not possibly have happened at his hospital and he was sorry that I had imagined that it did.

Janice Gale
Berkeley, California

♡ *Janice Gale's story of a 1949 birth vividly depicts the contrast between the birth you expect and the birth you actually experience. Janice's actual experience contained moments of disappointment but also moments of amusement and of supreme revelation.*

I was twenty-three years old, healthy, intelligent, self-confident. I had been in Berkeley, California, for a little less than a year and knew very few people. My husband, a World War II veteran, was a student, a sophomore, when we married in August 1948. He was twenty-five when David was born on June 22, 1949.

We lived in a studio apartment on the not-too-posh University Avenue. The "cross street" was the Santa Fe railroad tracks, but it seemed fine to me. I had made some drapes and curtains and built a bookcase. I had made my baby's layette by hand (knit, crochet, and sew). I had worked part-time at a tutoring school until mid–sixth month.

My mother had come to be with me and was staying just up the street three or four blocks. We had never had such a visit—just the two of us—before. Sometimes it seemed as if we really had nothing in common. Other times we felt close and confiding as women, but with the mother-daughter relationship still there.

We also clashed—for the first time that I could remember. I

refused to have the baby christened in the church, or christened at all. There were other minor issues on which I stood my ground. I felt completely grown-up.

I hiked and played tennis throughout my pregnancy, gained fourteen pounds . . . weighing about 139 when I went in for delivery.[13] I was determined not to let a baby dominate my entire life, nor turn me into a "middle-class" housewife. I feared that my interests in study, arts, sports, nature, would be lost to me.

During the pregnancy I gave up sugar, cut coffee to one cup a day. I smoked about five cigarettes a day and quit altogether several times. My husband had been raised in foster homes and was convinced that motherhood was almost "holy." He was helpful and adoring throughout the pregnancy.

I read Grantly Dick Read's book *Childbirth Without Fear* and thought his ideas were wonderful. I practiced the relaxed breathing and stored up information (such as panting to slow labor) for the delivery. I felt childbearing was completely natural and that, while it would hurt, it would soon be over. My mother had always presented childbirth as a wonder of wonders, great happiness, and so on. She remarked—several times—that I had a good pelvic girdle for easy delivery.

I was two weeks late and my doctor suggested I take castor oil, which I did. Ugh—what a taste.[14] The next morning I awoke at about five-thirty A.M., realized I was in labor, timed the pains (about twelve minutes, I think), and got ready to go to the hospital.

My mother and husband were with me. I felt very calm, very unflappable, fully prepared for the event. I had even visited the delivery room beforehand (in those days unusual, I think), so I'd know what to expect. The pains were harder than I had imagined, and I remember thinking how uncomfortable it was and how unnecessary for me to have to stand and wait at the admitting desk. (Sound familiar??)

My husband was not allowed to accompany me, and I remember getting into the elevator to go to the labor room and looking back at my husband. A gulf of gender suddenly separated us. I felt a quick stab of resentment that men get us pregnant but take no responsibility for birth . . . or similar thoughts.

Before the elevator doors opened onto the fifth floor, I felt a thrill of aloneness. The positive aspects of giving birth by myself asserted themselves. My efforts alone would be those that resulted in a smooth, nonstressful birth. I was determined to relax, breathe deeply, let nature do its work with no inhibition, panic, ambivalence from me.

Once I was in a gown in the labor room, I got out my book to read during labor (what a cerebral creature). The book was Marcel Proust's *Remembrance of Things Past*. I read the first (famous) page about twenty-three times, finally giving up the effort altogether.

I was offered various kinds of medication—for the moment and for the actual birth—and declined them. There was a red-haired Scottish nurse, an older woman, who had "worked with Dr. Read." That made me feel very good, very close to Dr. Read's precepts. It also made me feel that I just couldn't "fail" and get frightened or panicky.

After a while my OB man came to examine me internally. It hurt a lot. Then he came back with four interns, each of whom took a turn at feeling the breech birth that was about to take place after the required turning of the baby with forceps. Were a troop of interns to come toward me now—with outstretched forefingers—I would order—not request—them to leave immediately. In 1949, however, I thought it necessary to do "whatever the doctor said or wanted."

At length my doctor told me that I was doing very well, but that he would recommend a saddle block due to the breech birth. I remember agreeing, but feeling defeat. I was given a spinal, became numb from the waist down—or almost numb, and was able to do whatever they said to do—to push, to pant. It was as if I were a delighted observer at my own baby's birth.

I remember no pain for the last half hour and could draw a diagram of the delivery room right now—forty-one years later.

I saw the electric-blue, silvery shiny cord that connected the baby to me. I saw his grayish silver, slithery little body, a flame-red face, black hair, long and low on the neck like a monkey, deep forceps dents, two hematomas [blood blisters]—later, at home, called "twin peaks."

In the moments it took to wash and swaddle him I must have dozed off, because, when the nurse laid him on my upper stomach, I awoke to his dear presence, as if awakening at the precise moment of the dawn of time. (Tears spring to my eyes as I write this. The tears are in recollection of a moment ineffably pristine, unequaled from that time to this.)

My husband came with kisses and flowers. We agreed that David was quite funny looking . . . but wouldn't be, later. My mother talked her way in for a visit. (No one but husbands allowed.)

A woman's baby had been born dead . . . she was put in a room by herself. It was filled with flowers and gloom. So sad.

The babies came to nurse on a cart. They were all squalling, squealing, crying at the same time, in different keys at different intervals. I pretended to know my baby's cry but didn't until the third day. (Or maybe I sort of knew it but wasn't sure.)

The nurse taught me how to hold him for nursing, how to prepare my nipples, and so on. It was a blissful feeling with small, unexpected, sexual thrills.

We went home after five days and coped with one another from then on. I read Proust much later.

Martha McIntyre
Long Beach, California

♡ *Following is the correspondence between Martha McIntyre and Dr. Grantly Dick Read, which took place in 1955. Dr. Read's letter was kept by the McIntyre family and has never been published before. Following the McIntyre-Read correspondence is a story by Elizabeth de Forest, Martha McIntyre's granddaughter, about the home birth of her own first child in 1991.*

Martha McIntyre's letter to Dr. Grantly Dick Read is undated, but was probably written in February or March 1955.

Your secretary, in his letter of February 17, 1955, said that you would like to hear of my experiences with my two "naturally" born children. I shall answer thusly:

I was married in 1937 when I was twenty-two years old. In December of 1939 I gave birth to a daughter. My memory is not too good, but I do remember being strapped down to a table and having ether forced upon me—then nothing.

The next morning I wondered why my ribs hurt—result of artificial respiration. My attending physician told me I had turned completely blue. My baby had been removed by forceps and her forehead was bruised and her head was misshapen. Of course, these conditions were outgrown. Also, I was stitched inside and out, and informed by my doctor that, if he ever deliv-

84

ered any more babies for me, they would be by cesarean section. This all took place in Pittsburgh, Pennsylvania.

Following World War II, in a small town in New Mexico, August 10, 1946, I delivered another daughter. My then-attending physician was not present when I entered the hospital, but the nurse on duty immediately started to give me some kind of shots.

Finally, I was taken to a delivery room where I was once more strapped down and forced to receive ether (the anesthetist, a big, husky man, told me later I was quite a fighter). When I came to, back in my room, the next morning, I asked to see my baby and was delighted. I learned later that she had been born blue and had to have oxygen.

Then, in January 1951, I gave my first "natural" birth! We were still living in New Mexico, but I didn't care to repeat my previous experience, so we went to El Paso, Texas. There a doctor suggested I read your book and encouraged me and instructed me all during my pregnancy.

I was very calm and prepared when I started labor. There were times when I thought I might need some discomfort remover. But then the doctor examined me (after only about three hours' labor) and told me in another hour I would have my baby.

So, with those soothing words *and* his reminder that I'd never forgive myself for not going through with natural, we proceeded. I was wheeled into the delivery room and put on the proverbial table. I was, for the third time, "put up in stirrups," but they were adjusted to my comfort, and, instead of my hands being strapped down, I was given straps to help pull.

There are many heartwarming memories for me in this delivery and, since I think I have you to thank, I feel inclined to tell you them. This was my first baby that only my husband and I were present. I mean none of my family. He was taking his final examinations at college, earning his Bachelor of Science degree in civil engineering, and I had worried about missing his graduation.

The baby was born on January 23 and my husband graduated on January 29, and I was there! And the doctor was not only a competent physician, ordering the nurses, et cetera, but kind to me. All the time he scrubbed, he counted for me—"Push! One, two, three, four, five, six, seven, eight, nine, ten. Take a deep breath!" et cetera. Then he placed a cool cloth on my forehead. And then the baby started to come and he got very busy.

I will never forget the thrill when the doctor held him up for me to see. And as you said, nature does anesthetize the mother. I also remember pushing out my placenta (or, as we refer to it, the *afterbirth*).

The nurses were kind and considerate but not familiar with "natural." Before I went to the delivery room, one of them kept coming into the labor room with a hypodermic needle, and I kept telling her I didn't want it. And in the delivery room another nurse kept offering me "just a whiff of ether." But, after it was all over, I think they were all glad to have participated. I had absolutely NO stitches, as in both previous deliveries.

Another innovation for me was that I could get up and walk twenty-four hours after delivery. In my thank-yous I must include our monthly magazine *Reader's Digest,* which quoted or told of your book and some of your mothers. The doctor received my thanks, and I have told any interested women of your book.

Following my husband's graduation, we left New Mexico and came to California. And, once again, we were expectant parents. And, as was my experience in New Mexico, where I knew no doctors, I inquired of my friends for a good obstetrician.

I tried a few and, when I asked if they'd cooperate in delivering me "naturally," they either gave me a funny look or said that they "did not have the time." Now, can you imagine! They would rather give spinals or whatever else they thought was needed. They did have the time to send the bills. Or, rather, the office sent the bills.

Then I remembered a true *doctor* whom I had met ten years ago in a little town in southern California—San Juan Capistrano—and wrote and asked him if he delivered babies. He said he did and quoted his fee and from then on I was his patient. Upon my first visit I asked him if he'd help me deliver "naturally."

His reply: "I've delivered several thousand babies, breech, sideways, anesthesia, no anesthesia, in houses, trailers, tents, and hospitals." In other words, he treated me as an intelligent woman who knew how she wanted to have her baby and also knew what she was talking about.

My labor lasted a little longer this time—my cervix would not dilate. So the doctor ordered some kind of sedative and told the nurse to take me into the delivery room. And, as soon as he said that, I started to "bear down," and he told me not to work so hard—to wait for a good pain—and I did. I believe he studied under Dr. DeLee of Chicago.

But I was not strapped down, rather informed not to touch the sterile field, and I'll never forget my relief when the doctor told the nurse *not* to put me up in stirrups!

Once again, I refused ether from the nurse. Several times she asked me, and I kept telling her "no" and finally, the doctor said, "She's a good sport. Let's go ahead." So he gently pushed my legs down against my abdomen and from then on I don't remember too much except the nurse saying, "There's the head!"

Then the doctor was awfully busy and told me I had had another boy! I just wish I had thought to ask to have mirrors put up so I could have watched. Once again, no stitches and the doctor said he had never seen such a bloodless delivery. That has been almost a year ago and I still feel awed by the beautiful experience.

How can I ever thank you three [doctors]!

I've had perfect strangers come to my door to ask me to tell them all about my "natural" deliveries and I always recommend your books, and, if they aren't already under a doctor's care, I tell them about my doctor. But they think forty miles is too far to drive. . . . It really took less time than to get a number and sit with a whole bunch of other "cattle" and wait to be called.

And then get an impersonal and fast check, just like a car being run through the assembly line, or a herd being guided through the gates!

I just wish the women would wise up and among us we could wise up the medical profession. After all, we're the ones who have the babies! Just a little education, explanation, and guidance is all we need. I didn't even know where my uterus was until [the doctor in El Paso] showed me.

Dr. Read, you can feel that your books are like pebbles tossed into a pool and I, for one, am helping to increase the size of the circles you have made. I just wish my doctors would have the time to write some books, too.

Yours most gratefully,
Martha McIntyre (Mrs. J. H.)

Dr. Grantly Dick Read's reply,
written at his home in Hampshire County, England
Dated 7 May, 1955

I feel ashamed that your letter should have been in my study for three weeks and not yet replied to, but it is infrequently that I receive a letter that has given me so much pleasure and pride to read.

It really is grand to hear, and happily I do frequently hear, of medical men who have got the humanity and good sense to assist their patients to have their babies without unnecessary interference and what I call meddlesome nonsense, which is so frequently thought to be modern science.

The story of your first two labours, which, unhappily, I hear all too often from the United States, is one which should be published all over the world and then should be followed by your reactions to the second two labours. I think there can be no greater weight of persuasion than the history of the arrival of the family of a woman like yourself. Perhaps that does throw rather a big responsibility on you when I say that, because it is ladies like yourself who definitely can do so much good in the world, even though it is against the modern training of some of the medical schools.

Fortunately, as I expect you realize, this very natural approach to childbirth, although it has got many names in America, is spreading rapidly and I do believe, in good time, the American women will have just exactly what they deserve for their common sense. I might add, by the way, that my wife is half American. Perhaps, that prompts me to write like this.

I do wish you could see a film I took of the last four cases I delivered before I left South Africa. It is the most perfect example of women as they should behave having their babies naturally and the enjoyment, the whole happiness of the proceedings, although three out of four of them could not be described as absolutely normal in some ways. It is worth seeing. I am trying to get the distributors to make it available in America for those who would like to have and show it to women who need the sort of help of which they are so well aware.

All I can say is thank you very much indeed for writing me so fully. I appreciate it a lot, and I hope you won't mind if I use your letter sometimes without using your name. I have got many hundreds of which I have asked that question, and from time to time one or the other seems to be very fitting for the occasion.

I am going to write the doctors because I do like to get in touch with men like that. So many women write and ask me if they can be given the name of a doctor who will help them have their baby as I teach it. My list grows, and I would like to write and ask these two men whether their names can be put on that list.

My best wishes to you and please congratulate your husband on having you for a wife, and I must say I also congratulate your children, particularly the last two without any difference in feeling, but they have been born as I believe the Creator intended they should.

Yours very sincerely,
Grantly Dick Read, M.A., M.D. Cantab.

Elizabeth de Forest
Salt Lake City, Utah

♡ *The following story is a sort of "postscript" to the McIntyre-Read correspondence from Martha McIntyre's granddaughter, Elizabeth de Forest, who had her first child at her own home in Salt Lake City, on June 21, 1991.*

Joshua was born June 21st on the summer solstice. Everything went well, due to the preparation I got through my midwife and the help and support I got from my husband. At each point in labor my midwife helped me to focus my energy productively and keep the pain at a manageable level. I cannot imagine going to the hospital for a birth now.

Joshua never left us and was never tortured with the presence of strangers and bright lights. He didn't even cry for several days. He came out breathing normally and smiling. I know he was happy with the birth.

Kent and I chose home birth because we felt that hospitals create more problems than they solve in *low-risk* deliveries. We read up on all of our options before we made the decision.

I was and am unhappy with the way conventional medicine focuses on problem solving rather than prevention. Even though I went from one centimeter to delivery in three hours, I had no episiotomy and only a minor tear. I also received at-home follow-up care.

I doubt I would have been open to the option of home birth

if I hadn't been taught by my mother to treat childbirth and pregnancy as a normal and natural process. I had also read my grandmother's correspondence with Dr. Grantly Dick Read. Her experiences gave me a fear of intervention and the belief that I would recover best drug-free.

My grandmother touched everyone who knew her very deeply, and I respected what she had to say. She told everyone far and near how wonderful natural childbirth and nursing were. Her contemporaries thought she was nuts. (I get the same reaction to home birth.)

I have difficulty saying much about the whole subject of my own labor. Much of it has already faded in the blissful forgetfulness of motherhood.

Suzanne Wilson
Walnut Creek, California

♡ *Suzanne Wilson's birth experiences were thirteen years apart (1956 and 1969), in two different cities, with two different doctors, but they were remarkably similar—both were disasters. The problem in each case was a doctor who was determined to arrive and to deal with her birth complications at his own convenience.*

I was married in 1950 at age twenty. In the next four years I experienced five miscarriages. My doctor could find no single obvious reason for the spontaneous abortions. In 1954 we adopted a three-month-old baby boy in California.

Then, in February 1956, I found I was pregnant again and this time I went to an OB/GYN man considered the best in his field in San Francisco. He prescribed DES as an aid in deterring a possible miscarriage.[15] My pregnancy was uneventful until ten days before my due date, when I went into labor and gave birth to a son weighing four pounds, six ounces.

Labor began at ten A.M. with a single, sharp pain. Nothing else happened until that evening when I began to feel very uncomfortable and crampy. At midnight I started timing the pains and they were fifteen minutes apart.

My husband took me to the hospital around one A.M. Contractions were ten minutes apart by the time I was prepped and put to bed. My husband bought a Sunday paper and we read and talked.

By seven A.M. the contractions were five minutes apart and getting strong. By nine A.M. contractions were very strong and painful, and coming one minute apart, each one lasting forty-five seconds.

I wondered where the doctor was. (I learned later that he was moving that day. He had told me the week before that this day was moving day for him and that I shouldn't have my baby on this day. Sorry, Doc.)

At this point I was given something called "twilight sleep"— a medication that caused me to forget the previous labor pains as soon as one was finished and be unaware that another was coming soon. Consequently, I fell sound asleep for fifteen seconds between pains.

The baby was in a full breech position (unknown to me at the time), so there was no concern on the part of the nurses about my delivering before the doctor arrived. I have the feeling I was simply left there until it was convenient for the doctor to come.

When he did arrive at noon, he examined me and told me about the breech position. He said he was going to do an instrument delivery and would need another physician to help him turn the baby as it was being delivered. He also called a pediatrician in because the baby was considered premature and might need special care.

By two P.M. these two doctors had arrived and I was given a caudal anesthetic. I fell sound asleep for an hour while the delivery room was being prepared. The caudal anesthetic numbed me from the waist down, but I was wide awake during the delivery. My doctor used forceps while the other doctor pushed and turned the baby—poor baby! Eric was born healthy and normal, but small. I had an episiotomy and that certainly slowed my recovery. I was very sore for two to three weeks.

I was elated to have a live, crying, pink baby, and I sobbed with relief and joy. I credited my doctor with the successful, almost full-term pregnancy, but now, in retrospect, I do think he neglected me at the critical time of birth.

I have no idea where my husband was during all of this. He left when I was given the "twilight sleep," and I didn't see him until I woke up hours after the birth.

My baby was never brought to me. He stayed in the incubator for ten days. I went home after three days. When I had rested and recovered for a couple of days, I went back to the hospital to see my baby, but was never allowed to hold or even touch him.

I finally stopped going—the experience was too painful and frustrating. Finally, when Eric weighed five pounds, we were able to bring him home. By that time he was well established on a formula and I'd given up my plans to nurse him. (My doctor urged me to "forget it," saying it was too complicated.) I was very disappointed since the one thing I felt I had missed with the adoption of my oldest son was the nursing experience.

Also, it was considered rather old-fashioned at that time. We young suburbanites were really moving into the age of technology, with washers, dryers, TVs, and electric sterilizers for our babies' bottles. The sight of a nursing mother only seemed to make everyone uncomfortable.

I felt that I went through that birth experience entirely alone. Not even the nurses seemed to care about the long hours of hard labor I had to endure while waiting for the doctor. I felt that my body was something they were all working on, but my feelings were ignored.

Soon after Eric's birth, my husband became mentally ill and was committed to a state mental institution. Several years later, our marriage ended through divorce, and I continued to raise my two sons alone.

Then at age thirty-seven I remarried. Two years later, I got pregnant and, at age forty, I had Kris. My husband had never been married so he was thrilled and I was absolutely delighted (though a bit embarrassed) to be having another baby. My two teenage sons thought it was wonderful so we were a very happy family.

I was vaguely aware during my pregnancy that women my age sometimes gave birth to children with Down's syndrome, but I shook off the worry and convinced myself this baby would be normal and beautiful (he was and still is today).

At eight and a half months my doctor was examining me and told me the baby was in a transverse position. He said it was unlikely the baby would get into a normal birthing position, so he would probably do a C-section. I assumed he meant as soon as I started labor, and I remember feeling relieved that I wouldn't have to go through a long, hard labor. Wrong.

I went to the hospital at midnight—my neighbor took me because my husband was out of town. I called him in San Francisco and he flew home, arriving at seven A.M. The contractions were coming close together and I was hurting. A nurse had given me a pubic shave and an enema. Apparently, the doctor had not alerted the hospital that this was to be a cesarean delivery.

By ten A.M. I was drowning in pain with no relief between contractions. Still no doctor in sight. My husband was getting frantic. Finally, I was placed on a stretcher and taken to delivery and put on a table with my feet in stirrups. A nasty German nurse stood beside me and said, "Vell, you just better start *pushing.*"

When it finally became obvious that nothing else was going to happen, I was taken back to my room. My poor husband was white with distress. I tried to speak but couldn't. I wanted him to get a priest for me, then get a knife and kill me, but I was in too much pain to speak.

At two P.M. the doctor arrived and examined me. He ordered X-rays so I was rolled and bumped down the hall into the elevator, up and out onto the next floor, when I was lifted, pushed, pulled, and rolled back and forth for the X-rays. After I was returned to my room, the doctor came into the room and announced that he was going to do a C-section (this was news?).

Mary Garland
Hancock, New Hampshire

♡ *Mary Garland was a pioneer with the courage to challenge the status quo and insist on having babies her own way, when her first child was born back in 1956 and through four subsequent births.*

My husband and I had lived in Italy from 1952 to 1954, where we were impressed by the human approach of hospitals toward childbirth: mother and baby sharing a room, husband in a room next door, loving nuns who encouraged celebrations with wine ("good for the production of milk," et cetera)—such a contrast to the sterile atmosphere of the fifties, that we decided we wanted to produce our first child there.

That didn't work out, however, so, in 1956, pregnant and back in this country, I read Grantly Dick Read's book on natural childbirth and decided that was for me.

When I was six months pregnant, we moved to New Hampshire, where I was unable to find any doctor willing to go along with natural childbirth. I found a woman obstetrician in Boston who didn't promote the "Read method," but was willing to go along with my desires.

I would come down to Boston from the boonies for checkups and she was marvelously generous with time, explaining exactly what was going on in my body so there was no sense of mystery and fear. She also told me it was possible to have rooming-in with the baby at the hospital.

A few days before the baby was due, my husband and I went to Boston, took part in the Boston Arts Festival, did a lot of sightseeing (I was piped aboard the USS *Constitution* by some very nervous sailors), and eventually woke up one morning with strong and regular contractions. I remember washing my hair and, around noon, driving to the hospital through the Fens where a thousand million red roses were in bloom.

At the hospital my husband stayed with me in the labor room (unusual in those days) while I did a lot of retching. I had not done any exercises in preparation for childbirth but was so determined not to be "knocked out" or have any medication that the conviction carried me through. About an hour before the baby was born, I went into the labor room, without husband, and went through the indignity of having about a dozen interns come to stare at this funny woman who wanted to be awake for the birth.

My doctor was wonderfully calm and supportive and helped me through the whole procedure. I remember thinking that it was a bit like Nijinsky, lying under a grand piano and raising it to strengthen his leg muscles—hard work! The baby was large—nine pounds—and I had an episiotomy because the doctor felt there would be a lot of tearing, but she explained everything along the way.

By seven o'clock that evening a gorgeous little bundle popped out and was laid on my breast—with red, curly hair. I remember joking about the color, but it turned out to have been blood. It was truly the most ecstatic moment of my life—only dimmed by the fact that my husband wasn't there to share it with me. As I was being sewed up, I had an overwhelming urge to eat some ripe, juicy peaches (weird expressions on the faces of delivery room personnel).

To my fury, hospital regulations said I must spend two hours in a recovery room, which I found outrageous, since I had had no anesthesia. I was wheeled into a room with four or five other women, all knocked out. That was a total downer, as I was brimming over with excitement, and had not even been able to share my joy with my husband.

Every now and then, a woman would come to and slur, "Nurse, nurse, what did I have?" and then pass out again. I was so bummed out by the atmosphere that I asked for something to read, only to be informed that there wasn't anything available.

I noticed that a door was being propped open by a magazine and demanded it. There, after having just done the most exciting thing in my life, I was reading stupid articles about "The Most Unforgettable Character I've Ever Met" in *The Reader's Digest*—instead of beautiful, at least, poetry.

I eventually saw my husband and my doctor came with a bag of delectable peaches. I was given a room with Baby Dear far from the usual activities of the maternity ward, but what the hospital had not explained was that, while they were willing to make an accommodation for rooming-in with the baby—they didn't approve of it. Consequently, I was treated like a leper with minimal help or services for eight days.

I was not allowed to leave my room and could have no visitors, except for my husband, who had to be gowned and masked for his visits. It was totally exhausting but also delicious. I had a chance to get to know my exquisite little daughter—and to get accustomed to doing everything for her, which was fortunate as we brought her right back to New Hampshire where I had no help.

For the next few years the obstetrician stayed in close touch, coming up to the country, asking me to appear with her at natural childbirth and breastfeeding seminars. Since all had gone so well with the first child's birth, I felt I could handle the borning of the others with local GPs and did so (four more in four years).

I made sure they would not snuff me out and *always* took reading material with me. The second child—a hefty twelve-pounder—was born to the battle of Borodino in *War and Peace!*

With number two, the nurses thought breastfeeding a pain they didn't want to be bothered with, so would feed him in the nursery. However, he was such a hungry elephant that he was still hungry when brought to me, so I had no problem continuing to feed him.

Child number three got pneumonia and had to stay in the hospital a week after I returned home, but I brought thick, rich breast milk in wine bottles to the hospital every day and was able to maintain the milk supply when he came home. By that time, the nursing staff was understanding about breastfeeding and indulged me with whatever I wanted, as I was always the only mother breastfeeding her baby in the hospital.

There were distinctly unpleasant experiences at the times of my children's births, but never in connection with me. I spent time in labor rooms with terrified young women whose doctors did nothing to allay their fears and were often utterly brutal in what they said to the women. To this day, I cannot be civil when I see one of the local doctors, who snarled and shouted at a wailing, frightened young woman.

I always felt the stirrups were an indignity and made the pushing much harder than need be. I always complained that there was no mirror in the delivery room, though I remember watching the moon shine over Mt. Monadnock during one birth—and I felt badly that I could only wave through a window to my children when in the hospital.

Needless to say, all that has changed and natural childbirth is no longer considered an aberration. Classes for prospective mothers and fathers, homelike rooms in the hospital where all the family can be present if desired, breastfeeding, et cetera, are all encouraged and supported. I've had the fun of doing the interior design for the local maternity wing—some change!

I was always sorry that my husband could never be with me for any of our children's births. My husband only saw them through the glass of the nursery until they came home—a real loss for him—and, since he was so little a part of things, became less involved with their births. I used to send him home from the hospital because I didn't want to think of him sweating it out—and then would call him from the delivery room to announce the latest production.

I always stayed one week in the hospital (I'd had a wild case of tuberculosis upon returning from Italy and childbirth was considered a particularly vulnerable time for recurrences). I would've loved to have had babies at home, but nobody would go along with that—and, under the circumstances, it didn't seem worth the risk.

I had episiotomies with all babies—and do remember the postpartum shuffle and accompanying discomfort vividly.

In retrospect, I think I had as positive an experience with childbirth as was possible at the time. I had to fight for my rights to do it the way I wanted—but there's no doubt that the whole climate has radically improved, and it would be lovely to have a child under today's circumstances.

On the other hand, if I were having children today, I seriously doubt I would've felt free to drop five children on the face of the planet. So it all evens out.

Lou Bulebosh
Plymouth, Wisconsin

♡ *Lou Bulebosh's story of the doctor who never came to the birth at all was unusual even in 1958.*

My first daughter was born in 1951 in a woman's hospital run by Catholic nuns in Chicago. My baby was four weeks premature and weighed five pounds, four ounces at birth. I received tender, loving care from my doctor and the hospital staff. As it was my first child and premature, my doctor stayed the night at the hospital to check me periodically during my labor. The baby was put in an incubator after birth. I stayed in the hospital three days and took my baby home with me. Her weight had dropped to five pounds, which is not unusual.

My second daughter was born in the same hospital in 1954. She was two weeks early and weighed six pounds, seven ounces at birth. Again, I received loving care in the hospital. Since this hospital had been built in memory of the builder's wife, who had died in childbirth, and was strictly for women, all facilities there were for the patient's comfort. Each labor room was a private room. The staff were efficient and kind.

The birth of my third daughter in 1958 was an entirely different experience. I then lived in a little town in Pennsylvania. This was during a recession period and my husband worked 400 miles away from home and was lucky to have a job at all.

When my labor started, he wasn't there and I had no car.

Having a Baby

The undertaker in town offered a service to expectant mothers by driving them to the hospital if they didn't have any other means of transportation. Therefore, I called the undertaker, who drove me to the hospital in his limousine.

My obstetrician had seen me three days earlier and determined the baby would not arrive for another two weeks. He was going on vacation but would return in time for the birth. If I needed a doctor in this interim, I was to call his associate, who would look after his patients for him in his absence. I therefore phoned this associate to advise him I was leaving for the hospital and to meet me there.

I was prepped at the hospital and put in a labor room. It wasn't exactly a private room but, rather, one large room with partitions, but not soundproof. I could hear the moans and screams of the other women, which was unnerving to me.

The nurses were not gentle or compassionate. They checked me periodically in a rough manner and not sympathetic to my pain . . . telling me not to be such a baby if I moaned when they were handling me.

The doctor had not arrived and I could hear the nurses asking one another where he was and when he was going to get there. I felt the baby's head start its downward movement and called the nurse. She told me to cross my legs to delay the birth until the doctor arrived. I was ready to give birth and not about to delay it and endure further pain. Finally, they frantically rushed me into the delivery room.

One of the nurses delivered the baby. Fortunately for me, it was small, five pounds, four ounces, and did not tear me. Had the baby been bigger, the nurses—not being surgeons—would not have been permitted to cut me, and I might have been seriously torn.

My doctor's associate did not arrive that day or the next day. Therefore, there was no doctor checking my condition or my baby's condition. I asked the nurse if my baby was in an incubator and was told my doctor had not given this order. I asked if she was on a preemie feeding schedule—that is, every four hours, as my first premature baby had been. They said the doctor had not given orders for this feeding schedule because he had not seen the baby yet. I was concerned about the baby and myself because I had no doctor attending us. Up to this point, the nurses had done all his work.

On the third day the doctor came sailing into my room in his golf clothes. He told me my baby had a navel infection and suggested I call in a pediatrician because he did not handle these things. He did not account for his absence at the birth nor apologize. He briefly checked me and left. It was the only time I saw him.

My baby's weight had dropped down to four and a half pounds when I left the hospital on the third day. I was permitted to take her home with me. I felt the care I had received was negligent and that it was ironic that any doctor's name should appear on the birth certificate at all.

When my original doctor returned from his vacation, I went to see him and told him what had transpired. He seemed surprised to hear about it but didn't say anything against his associate. I told him I would pay him for the few prenatal visits I had with him but would not pay a delivery fee because neither he nor his associate had earned it. He said that was fair enough.

I was so young and naive then, but realize now I should have filed a complaint with the American Medical Association about this absentee doctor who was not there to prevent my baby's infection.

Virginia Duncan
Solon, Ohio

♡ *Virginia Duncan's first C-section in 1959 led—unnecessarily by today's standards, but inevitably then—to two more cesareans, in 1962 and 1965. Virginia never got over a sense of having been cheated out of the births she wanted to have. She quotes another mother of the era as saying, "They take our babies from our bodies and tell us we're mothers."*

In the spring of 1958 I was twenty-eight years old and pregnant for the first time. We had been married six years and trying to conceive for two years. We had been through the temperature taking every morning, the legs in the air after intercourse, the sperm counts—all to no avail until an internist did two gas insufflations. I became pregnant shortly after the second one. I was delighted to be pregnant, couldn't wait to wear maternity clothes, and had no morning sickness.

It was an uneventful pregnancy and I looked forward to my delivery date of January 8, 1959. I planned to have natural childbirth. The popular book at that time was *Childbirth Without Fear* by Grantly Dick Read. There were no classes, but I had read the book and my older sister and several friends recommended it highly. I had been through an expectant mother class, but it only covered caring for the baby and a walk through the hospital's labor and delivery rooms.

The medical clinic I went to had no obstetrician when I first became pregnant, but there was a doctor finishing his residency who became my doctor when I was four months pregnant. He reminded me of a St. Bernard—large and friendly. He wasn't too interested in Read; I'm not sure he was familiar with his teachings.

I saw my doctor on December 30th and he said the baby would probably be late—to expect a January 15th delivery date. On the morning of January 2nd, I awoke when my water broke at six in the morning. The doctor advised me to wait until the contractions were steady before going to the hospital.

I arrived at the hospital at twelve-thirty in the afternoon. I was put in a labor room with an eighteen-year-old woman who was having her first baby. She asked me if I was as frightened as she was. Actually, I was euphoric—the grand adventure was about to begin!

My doctor arrived very quickly and I began to suspect that something was wrong. After examining me, he explained that the baby was breech, that the cord was wrapped around its foot, and I would have to have a C-section.

He wanted my feet elevated while arrangements were made for surgery, but the right bed couldn't be found, so he summoned my husband from the waiting room to help him lift the bed in order to put blocks under it. It was panic time. All I could think was that we had waited so long and now we might lose the baby.

At two o'clock I was taken to the operating room. The nurse told me, "Don't look so scared, you're having this baby the glamorous Hollywood way." It didn't seem very glamorous to me.

I was given a spinal and was awake through the whole procedure, but I was draped so that I couldn't see what was happening. Actually I don't think I would have wanted to see the surgery.

At 2:22, Susan Beth was taken from my womb and held up for me to see. My husband was not in the room with me. He saw her for the first time in the nursery. The spinal began to wear off before they finished closing me up, so I was given something to kill the pain. I woke up in the recovery room.

I spent the first twenty-four hours in a haze of pain, medication, and nausea. The baby was not allowed out of the nursery. The next two days she was brought in every four hours during the day for me to give her a bottle.

I had planned to breastfeed, but the nurses tried to talk me out of it. When they couldn't, they agreed to let me try. Then she was brought in every four hours around the clock, although the night nurses disapproved of having her feedings interrupt my rest.

The phrase I heard most often from the nurses was, "You've had a baby and major surgery." I grew to hate those words. I had some information on breastfeeding, but no mentor or guide who had actually done it. There was not much support.

A few days after the baby was born, the doctor told me, "I knew she was breech a few weeks ago, but I didn't tell you because I knew you'd just worry." I stayed in the hospital a week. When I went home, I couldn't drive for four weeks. I could only take sponge baths for another week.

I still remember how long it took just to get clean and dressed in the morning. I also remember how good the sponge baths felt. Just taking care of the baby exhausted me. My wonderful mother-in-law stayed two weeks and did all the housework.

I felt cheated. I had missed one of the great experiences. I hadn't been tested and I would never know how I would have stood up to this experience. In some ways it was like failing to pledge a sorority. I felt I didn't measure up as a woman.

It was also hard physically, and no one seemed to understand my feelings. A support group of women who had been through this would have helped immeasurably and would have given me some perspective.

During my first checkup I asked the doctor about future births and was told, "Once a C-section, always a C-section." I was depressed.

Somewhere I read the following quote by a woman who had

had a C-section: "They take our babies from our bodies and tell us we're mothers." Her bitterness echoed mine, but it was comforting to know someone understood.

Months later, I read an article that some doctors were rethinking this and that it might be possible to have a normal delivery after a C-section. When I became pregnant for the second time, I asked my doctor again, but his response was the same.

He said that, since I had waited so long for my babies, it wasn't worth taking the chance of my uterus rupturing during labor. You can imagine my feelings when, during the second C-section, the two doctors commented on how well I had healed and how strong the scar tissue had become.

As the time approached for my second and third C-sections, I would panic. That baby was in there and the only way out was through surgery and the awful pain that followed, the nausea—each time they tried different techniques to ease it—and the long recovery. There was also the fear that something would go wrong and I would die.

I did get to pick my children's birth dates, but that was small consolation. I also got to go into the hospital the afternoon before surgery and have a delicious dinner. My husband could visit from six to eight.

My doctor would drop in between seven and nine to chat. "You're not worried, are you?" was his usual comment. The anesthesiologist usually arrived about ten to brief me on the surgery and to tell me not to smoke any more cigarettes until after surgery. This was the only time during all my pregnancies that smoking was mentioned.

He was followed by a nurse bearing the dreaded enema packet. Once a nurse brought me dinner and cackled, "Enjoy that fancy dinner and the chocolate cake, honey, 'cause it's not going to be with you very long." Around eleven a nurse would come to shave me.

Once a rather bedraggled Episcopalian priest showed up at midnight. Although I was of that faith, I had requested on my hospital form that I not be visited. He came in and proceeded to tell me his woes and to quote, "I have miles to go before I sleep." He did nothing to calm my fears and finally left. So much for getting a good night's sleep before surgery.

Breastfeeding was more acceptable when I had my second baby in 1962. The hospital had added a rooming-in option, which I would have liked, but you had to assume full responsibility for the baby during the day. I couldn't do that.

When the spinal wore off during the birth of my third child in 1965, they gave me laughing gas instead of the usual shot. I had a terrible nightmare, so traumatic that I still remember not just the visual images but the terror it evoked.

Although I was thrilled to have my babies and I became adept at handling the recovery process, there was always a sense of incompleteness in having them delivered by C-section.

I am a very different person today than I was at twenty-nine. The children are grown and gone. I have grown and stayed. But, at fifty-six, there still remains a sadness within me, and I am glad to have had the opportunity to explore it after all this time.

Marilyn Bartick
Alexandria, Virginia

♡ *Marilyn Bartick was unprepared for childbirth and was shocked by much of what she experienced, but she never loses her very dry sense of humor in the telling.*

I was born October 1935, married June 1959, and was expecting my first child on July 26, 1962. From when I figured conception took place, I privately placed my due date sooner. I had a marvelous pregnancy, feeling better than I ever had in my life.

My then husband was not enthralled with becoming a father. He always referred to me as "she's pregnant," not "we are going to become parents." There was terrific pressure from his first-generation American-Jewish parents for us to have a boy.

They even came in for a week in July for the anticipated birth and ritual circumcision. They left mad at me for not delivering sooner and accused me of miscalculating the due date. During their week's stay, my husband took my side and told them we were expecting a girl.

Much can be said of my attitude toward the sex of the forthcoming baby. I always wanted four little boys and was totally unprepared for a girl. The culture I came from valued boys much more than girls. I always felt inadequate about this.

Also, I only had brothers and my two closest girlhood friends had only had boys. But I have had a lot of rotten luck all my life.

I figured I would have a girl. I anticipated a silly, giggly little creature rather than a tough, practical little boy I could relate to.

My husband voiced no preference, preferring not to talk about the pregnancy or anticipated baby. He just did not think or discuss it with me. He did, however, reluctantly accompany me to a Red Cross baby care course each week for a month. During this course, labor and delivery were not mentioned, only how to prepare for the baby and take care of it, once it was born.

I did take a tour of the hospital for expectant mothers. Labor and delivery methods were not discussed. The obstetricians in the group practice I went to never discussed it and I never brought it up. In truth, I never thought about the actual labor and delivery; I just remember someone way back telling me that it was a little like menstrual cramps, a problem I had had since age fourteen and have always lived through.

As my due date approached and passed, my ex-husband asked me if I would deliver close to payday, as we could pay for the baby out of current income. Both his parents and he thought of me as a human incubator.

As an aside, I always referred to the unborn child as "her" or "Melissa." In picking out the birth announcements before delivery to be printed, I gave them both names at the store and bought blue things for the baby.

I did have a book given to me by the obstetrician, called *Expectant Motherhood,* but I never read much about labor and only noted that it said contractions were painful, so that labor can be easily identified, and suggested that, between them, one could knit and visit with one's husband.

Also, the doctors had given me a sheet on the last trimester which included instructions on when to call in terms of the frequency of contractions. I had no fear of labor and delivery because I never gave it one thought.

My due date came and passed. On Friday, August 10, as I went to bed, I felt mild discomfort, much like menstrual cramps, and I did not sleep well. I got up several times during the night to go to the bathroom. In the morning I told my husband I hadn't slept well, and he said the same thing.

At ten o'clock, I had my weekly doctor's appointment. I had noticed blood-stained mucus from my vagina. I said, "Today is the day," and he said, "No, it will be another week."

I went home, and at one P.M., mild contractions started. We were new in Washington and had no family—just my downstairs neighbor, who loved babies and often spoke to me with great anticipation of the birth but never of the birth of her two.

Not wanting to alarm my husband, I went downstairs to the neighbor and we timed my contractions. When they got to be ten minutes apart, I went upstairs to my apartment and called the doctor, and he said to come to the hospital.

When I arrived, I went through admitting like any other patient, and I was brought up to be prepped. The nurses gave me an enema and sent me into the washroom. I was upset because there was no sink to wash my hands afterward. Meanwhile, my discomfort continued.

I was then taken to a labor room with two beds. I requested a private labor room but there was no such thing. The reason for the request was I thought my husband would keep me company during labor and chat between labor pains. He never came in. He had just dropped me off and gone home.

The OB of my choice was on duty and he came in to check me, didn't say anything, and left. Then the contractions became stronger; I was yelling with each one. I never felt such excruciating pain in my life.

At different times I yelled, "Please give me something. I promise I'll never have another child." No response. I heard screams from other rooms. I yelled for my husband, who wasn't even there.

I yelled, "If you don't give me something, I'll jump out the window." The response from an unknown source was, "Go ahead and jump. You'll still be pregnant."

The OB stopped in again and, instead of inquiring how I felt, just examined me without a word. He left again. The nurses

came in periodically to listen to the baby's heart. The doctor
came in again and explained he was very busy delivering other
babies and complained I just was not moving fast enough. He
then broke the bag of waters. Still no anesthetic or hope of any.

He came back in a couple of what seemed like hours and
gave me a shot. He said I could probably get up and eat. Food
was the last thing on my mind.[16]

About six hours must have passed and in walks my husband
in a white coat. He said I would just have to relax and left the
room. The doctor came in once or twice and upbraided me for
not progressing more quickly with my labor and gave me a shot
to speed it up.

In a little while, which seemed like an eternity, in comes
another doctor, an anesthesiologist. He and the nurse turned me
over and gave me a shot, and then put adhesive tape down back
and attached a vial to it. They quickly explained that this was
epidural and, if the pain came back again, I would get some
more. They didn't explain what *epidural* was; I only knew the
pains stopped.

So I lay quietly, feeling the contractions but no pain. Next
door was the doctors' lounge and I could hear *Death of a Sales-
man* on the TV. During the commercials the OB would check
me.

Then a nurse came in clutching her abdomen. I asked her if
she was pregnant and she said, "Yes." (I later learned she was
in labor and delivered at a nearby military hospital one and a
half hours before me.) The nurse would listen for the heartbeat
and told me to push.

I was pretty tired. It was at least one o'clock in the morning
and I was bushed, but I pushed with all my might, like eliminat-
ing a bowel movement. She told me she could see his head and
black hair. I corrected her to "her" head and kept pushing with
all my might.

Finally, she wheeled me into the delivery room with an anesthesiologist at my head, the doctor made a cut, and then he

pulled a screaming baby out with forceps, slapping her bottom and telling me, "You have a healthy baby girl."

"That's Melissa Claire Bartick," I said. Then I felt an uncontrollable urge to scratch my nose, but my hands were fastened in straps. The anesthesiologist did it for me.

I was so happy but I noticed the baby was all bloody. Due to my husband's squeamishness, I said that he could wait until the afternoon (it was 3:37 A.M., Sunday, August 12, when I delivered), when the baby was cleaned up. But the nurse said, as a favor to me, she could do it now. I thought my husband would be so disappointed with a girl.

After my episiotomy was sewn up, I was wheeled into a hallway with other women who had just delivered and where my husband was waiting.

I said, "Herb, we have a girl." He just sat there and kissed my hand while the baby, wrapped in a receiving blanket, just bawled. I said to pick her up from me; I was so tired. I held her for a minute and saw her charcoal blue eyes: that meant she was going to have my dark brown eyes—my God, she was beautiful. As my husband kept kissing my hand (the tenderest night in my twenty-four-year marriage), all I wanted to do was vomit and go to sleep.

Eventually I went up to my room and slept an hour or two. For two of the four days of my hospital stay, I couldn't sleep, I was on such a high.

Baby two—difficult pregnancy but quick birth. I needed no anesthetic, since it was like mild menstrual cramps, but I was given an epidural anyway. Anticipating an eight-hour labor, my husband went home to take care of the older child. When I called a nurse and asked what was on my leg, she said, "The baby's head." I was wheeled into delivery and it was another girl. The bag of waters broke at six-thirty at home and I delivered at nine.

When we called my in-laws to tell them of the second daughter, my mother-in-law said, "You better roll over and try again." Girls just didn't count for much.

Today Melissa is a student at Berkeley in a joint M.D.-M.S. program, and I have never discussed the pain of childbirth with her, but told her only the doctor checked me at commercials, which she found amusing. Her sister is studying international affairs at the University of Virginia.

When I asked the neighbor if she knew childbirth was so painful and why didn't she tell me, she said she knew but didn't want me to know. I've done that to all my friends and daughters.

Gomathy Venkateswar
Calcutta, India

♡ *Gomathy Venkateswar tells a lovely story of the 1966 birth of her unplanned but welcomed third child in Calcutta. In the "nursing home" where she gave birth, Gomathy was enveloped in a community of women, most of whom were strangers to her, who gently helped her along to a happy conclusion—the birth of a child who, she was sure, was destined for some kind of greatness.*

It's still a secret joke between my husband and myself about the pregnancy that resulted in Shyama's birth. She came about so unexpectedly and, as I vehemently claimed, at a time when my husband and I had no sexual contact under the advice of my doctor, who had said that any pregnancy would be detrimental to my health because I was under prolonged treatment for a chronic stomach ailment.

My husband and I had followed the doctor's advice so carefully that, when I missed my period in December 1965, and I started my morning sickness soon after, I just could not think straight. Finally, both of us started to say it must be an "immaculate conception."

My health throughout the nine months was excellent, never better, I would say, and, as I went about my household chores, no one guessed that I was expecting till I announced it to close

116

family members like my mother and my mother-in-law and to my two sisters.

My mother said, rather bluntly, "I thought you were smart and now you have gone and spoilt it all. You have a girl and a boy. What do you want a third one for?"

My two children, aged six and seven, knew nothing till my husband asked them casually, just a couple of weeks before the date of arrival, whether they would prefer a puppy for a pet or a little baby in the house? It was the pup that got the unanimous vote, at first, but, on second thoughts, the children told their father that a baby would be a better idea, but only on condition that it was fair and didn't cry.

Both conditions would be difficult to meet, for where can an Indian baby be fair of skin, and, again, where can one find a baby that did not cry? My husband and I decided not to worry too much on the tall order placed by the children, and I waited out the last days anxiously.

I explained to the children that I would be gone for a few days to the hospital and, before I could finish, my son said, "Take your own time over it at the hospital. Look out for the best baby there and bring it back quickly."

Then arose an argument between the brother and sister as to whether Mummy should bring home a baby girl or a baby boy. My son insisted it be a girl as he wanted to be the only son in the house, and his older sister yelled that she wanted Mummy to have only her as the girl in the house.

The doctor had calculated August 14 or 15, 1966, as the due date. On 18 August I was still at home, feeling quite fine, though a little slow in my movements and tiring easily. In the evening, when my husband returned from work, I said I would go to my obstetrician for another checkup.

I had to wait almost two hours before she got to see me and she was most surprised to see me there and said, laughing, "I can see you are still whole. You should have had your baby last week. Come let me check your blood pressure and hear your baby's heartbeat."

She took my blood pressure, found it rather high, and said, "You should check in to your nursing home tomorrow. I'll telephone the matron-in-charge to prepare for an induced labor."

Then, as an afterthought, she said, "As a South Indian you do put a lot of faith in auspicious birth stars and appropriate time, isn't it?" I nodded my head and she said, "Well, here is a good opportunity for you to choose the best within the next three days and tell me."

I went home and asked my mother-in-law to consult the Hindu Almanac, which has all the information regarding auspicious days, favorable birth stars, even the best time of the day or night. Going through all this detailed information, it seemed almost tailor-made that I choose the 21 August, because everything about the day was so right. It was the star that one always related to people with the highest in academics, or even to genius.

As per Chinese horoscope, 1966 was called the Year of the Horse and the double sixes in the year make it special by their almanac. In the Hindu astrological studies, the star sign under which Shyama was born is called Swati and is considered a lucky one for people bent on academics and research and fine arts. Great musicians, scholars, litterateurs, and orators in India have been born under this star.

In the Hindu Almanac there are twenty-seven different stars in a month, which again follows the lunar calendar. So, in an English month of thirty or thirty-one days, sometimes one can have the same star occurring twice—once at the beginning of the month and, again, twenty-seven days later.

It may sound complicated, but all children have their horoscopes compiled soon after they are born with the details of their planetary configuration at the time of birth being drawn up in a chart. An astrologer can more or less predict the outlines of a person's future, and a Hindu lays a great importance on this.

Even at the time of marriage, the horoscopes of the prospective bride and groom are compared to see if they are compatible,

and there have been several occasions when marriages have
not taken place on the basis of the incompatibility of the two
horoscopes, and the parties concerned have abided by it. One
may even say perhaps the reason for the lesser percentage of
divorce or broken homes in this part of the world comes from
the utter reliance one puts on one's stars and one's horoscope,
which we believe shape our destinies.

I was quite excited as I telephoned my doctor and told her
the family had decided on the 21 August. She just said, "What
day of the week is it?"

I replied, "Sunday."

"That's perfect. It suits me very well."

"What do I do?" I inquired.

The doctor said, "I'll phone the sister-in-charge at the nursing
home and ask her to prepare a room for you, and you just check
in by seven A.M. on Sunday and leave the rest to us."

I had a suitcase ready for weeks for the baby's arrival—a
complete outfit that was sent by my mother from Bangkok,
where my parents were for the last few years on a United Nations assignment. The baby dresses and nappies were so dainty
and exquisitely embroidered that I could hardly wait for the
baby anymore.

So that Sunday morning, twenty-four years ago, with nothing
to tell that I was going to have a baby soon, I stepped out of
the car and walked to the reception counter, gave in my name,
and said that the sister-in-charge was expecting me in the maternity ward. The pretty receptionist got up in a hurry and said
she would get me the wheelchair, but I just smiled and said I
was feeling very fit and would climb up the stairs.

The sister-in-charge came to meet me and said, "I've been
asked by the doctor to fix you some pain. Come, love, I will
start you on that soon! Just relax in the room for a while, and
try to go to sleep."

I changed to the long white shift that the nurse asked me to
wear, and picked up a magazine, but could hardly read. I was

so keyed up as to what I was to go through that I could think of nothing.

I tried to think of my two children, whom I had kissed good night the previous evening and dropped them at their grandparents' place without telling them about my going into the nursing home. I was a bit worried about my son as he made such a fuss about eating, and wondered how my mother-in-law was going to manage.

The sister-in-charge bustled in with a tray and said I was to drink up two ounces of castor oil and, after about an hour, she said, a bath in a tub of hot water would do the trick! So it was by eleven A.M. I was beginning to feel the twinges of pain and the dragging sensation in my legs.

I was told to keep walking, which I did, as I walked the long corridors of the maternity ward, up and down and back again. The other occupants in the ward looked at me and smiled, and I envied them the comfort of their unloading. I was hungry, no one had asked me whether I wanted anything to eat, and I just wanted to lie down and go to sleep.

It was now a little after one and the nurse had taken me to the labor theater, and there again she made me walk round and round the operating table. The pain was coming at long intervals and still bearable.

I inquired whether the doctor had arrived but the nurse said she would be there when the time comes. I just got up on the labor table and lay down exhausted, and then the nurse, who had washed up and put on the examining gloves, said, "Let me see how far you have dilated," and then broke off in surprise.

"Your waters have ruptured. Why didn't you tell us?"

I weakly replied, "I didn't even know. Please give me something to eat. I haven't had a morsel to eat all day."

The nurse was very apologetic and ordered me a hot chicken broth. She hurried away to call the doctor. The pain had increased in intensity and length of duration.

Lying there on the table under the glare of the lights, I remembered my previous two confinements, when my mother had been present throughout the labor and had held my hand tightly at the very moment of birth and congratulated me, saying I was very brave and had not even made a cry.

I had answered her by saying, "Really, Amma" (the Indian word for *Mother*), "it didn't hurt at all."

I wished my mother was with me now. She had begged that I should fly to Bangkok for this confinement, but that would have meant leaving the two children for so long, and, if I had taken them with me, they would have missed school. So I had decided to have the baby in Calcutta, and Mother promised she would come to see the baby as soon as she got the news.

The doctor seemed to have arrived even before I realized it, and she just said, "Come on now. Bear down hard. The baby is ready to arrive."

I felt I had no strength left. All of it had drained out in the miles of walking down the corridors I had done all day. All I wanted to do was sleep, but the pain was searing. I weakly pressed down but to no avail. Nothing was happening and the pain was so intense that tears just poured out of the sides of my eyes.

The doctor sharply rebuked me and said, "Come on now. You are not even trying. It's not your first baby. You know what you must do. Bear down hard and it will all be over."

I gave a tremendous effort and the red-hot blanket of pain that engulfed me made me cry out one long drawn-out, "Amma . . ." and it was all over.

She lay there between my legs with a mop of black hair and large eyes. She was fair and ever so pretty. It was 4:05 P.M. That's all I remember till I heard my name called gently, and I opened my eyes to see the faces of my loved ones.

We named her Shyama—a name full of meaning in the Indian connotation, and today, at twenty-four, she has graduated from Smith and is continuing her advanced doctoral program at Columbia University. We are inordinately proud of her and, with a twinkle in his eye, my husband calls her "The Best."

Nancy Harrison
Conroe, Texas

♡ *Nancy Harrison had four more children after the daughter whose 1967 birth she describes below. But she never stopped thinking about the little newborn girl with "lots of dark hair" who was given up for adoption. Nancy satisfied a lifelong need when she met her daughter again in 1989. She knows she can never replace the mother who adopted her child and raised her, but, she concludes, "I want to be a factor in her life. I think you can do that."*

From an interview with Nancy Harrison taped May 11, 1990:

Donna's father was someone I had just basically started dating. I was actually dating Larry, who became my first husband later on, more seriously at the time. Donna's father was just kind of an off-date. Larry was the son of some friends of my parents and, at the time, I wasn't real serious about him. But Donna's father was real popular and he was a senior that year and I guess I just was thrilled that he asked me out.

I remember the night that she was conceived. We went to some kind of club all the "in" crowd of the school went to, and we ended up going parking because the club got raided. But I wasn't real popular and I was wanting to get in the "in" crowd, so that's why. I probably was more popular than I thought I was.

We kept dating until he found out I was pregnant and then,

when I told him, he just kind of dropped me like a hot potato. He knew I was dating this other boy, too, so he just kind of said, "Well, it was the other boy's, forget about me."

Until now. He knows now. There's no denying it. She's got his nose. He has an Italian nose. She definitely has my chin; all my kids have my chin. But she's got, really, more of his looks than mine. . . .

I knew right away. I counted the days and I was very firm on days and I was always right on time. I counted the days back and I knew for sure it was him and I knew for sure when I got pregnant. I went to the doctor myself and confirmed it.

I was excited. I don't know why. I always was looking for somebody to love, and this was going to be somebody to love. I didn't know how to handle the situation and I had a real good English teacher that I talked to, and she told the principal and the principal called my mother [stepmother] and my mother told my father. (I think at the time they were required to tell, you know.)

When the school found out, they kicked me out. My parents got me into night school. There was a short period of time in between when I wasn't going to school and I have a very distinct memory from that time. My mother had a real good friend that we had known ever since we had been in Texas . . . that was her Avon lady. And she was due to come over, and my mother sent me to my room and told me not to make a sound while she was there.

We never talked about an abortion. At that time—1967—it was illegal. My father is very law-abiding. Later [after it was legal] I had three abortions, one of which my parents took me to.

My dad did take me to the boy's house, to his parents' house. The boy wasn't home. My dad got into a fight with the boy's father. I was so embarrassed. I don't know what my dad wanted to accomplish by going there—maybe just to vent his anger or something.

They wouldn't let me get married because Larry offered to

marry me at that time and stood beside me the whole time I was pregnant. But they wouldn't let me get married and they wouldn't let me keep the baby. My father still had so much control over me, I guess I was just too scared to lash out with my own feelings. I just abided by what he said.

I couldn't stay at home. My parents couldn't have that. People would see me. I went to the home for unwed mothers when I was starting to show. We lived in this old house; it was pretty dilapidated but it was a neat old house. I came in June, the first of June, as soon as school was out. I started summer school. They had the shacks in the back where we had summer school. It was a joke, really. They gave us the test before the test. . . . They said, "Here's the answers; we'll have the test tomorrow."

The first two weeks I was there, I cried my eyes out. I felt abandoned. I felt alone. I didn't want to do this. But, after I cried for about two weeks, I pretty much accepted it, just went on from there.

It was very frowned upon not to give up the baby after you went and stayed there. There were a couple of girls that changed their mind at birth, but there was a lot of no-noing about that. Every weekend my parents and Larry came up to see me. Larry was a good man. He still is a good man.

We did a lot of walking around here. It was the only thing we could do was walk. And one Saturday afternoon near my due date, I started getting little cramps, and we knew that, once you started getting pains, if you walked real fast, that would really bring them on. So we went trotting around the neighborhood, this roommate that I had and me. As a matter of fact, it was my roommate's due date. I wasn't due for a couple of weeks. But I knew I was past due really.

We walked for a good couple of hours, and by then, my labor pains were probably about half an hour apart. And we went up to the bedroom and I lay on the bed and we were timing them . . . and it took forever. I was in labor a long time with Donna.

About midnight, the pains got close enough together, like five minutes apart, for us to go to the hospital. And then, when we got to the hospital, of course, everybody called my parents and they met us up there and Larry came, too.

I would grab the back of the bed with my arms up and they'd say, "No, no, you can't do that. That pulls the baby up." It was very hard labor. I said a few choice words to everybody that was in the place. Everyone took turns coming out (I don't think they could stand the profanity too long at a time).

I remember asking Larry, "Why does it hurt so much?" And he said, "If it didn't hurt, you wouldn't appreciate it."

I'll never forget that. But they knocked me out when it came time to deliver. Because of the adoption situation, they didn't want you to see the baby born. So, after the actual birth, she was probably about three days old when I saw her. They kept us in the hospital five days and they gave us the option to see the babies or not.

I said, "If I can't do anything else, I want to do this." So I did see her, just once. It was kind of an uneasy feeling, knowing that I wasn't keeping her. I didn't know how to actually hold her, because I couldn't hold her close, because that would make me feel too close. I almost wished I hadn't seen her at the time that I was holding her. I wanted to hold her and look at her, but then I didn't want to, because I was having to let go.

So the only thing I remember is thinking that she looked like her father and that she had dark hair, lots of dark hair. She was the only baby I had that had hair when it was born.

If I thought there had been any way to change my parents' mind, I would have. But I knew my father and this was a set decision with no way to change it. There was Larry in the labor room with me and my parents there—if anything was going to be changed, I felt like that would have been the time to change it. And I don't remember anyone coming to see me from the time of delivery until it was time to pick me up, five days later.

I don't think they would have allowed Larry to come. I think they just allowed him in the labor room because I screamed so bad. They were pretty lenient in the labor room, but I think that was the end of it.

When I got home, I was leaking milk like crazy. My brother and sister were like eight and ten years old—maybe nine and ten, but they were young. They didn't know why I had left home or any of the circumstances at that time. And I was quite self-conscious; I was flooding everywhere, as far as my breasts and everything. Mom and Dad didn't tell them until four or five years later.

Donna was born in October. I had to go to the homebound schooling at the Home for the rest of the semester until I was allowed back in school. I remember it being about two weeks later when I signed the papers at the adoption agency to give her up.

At that time I talked about it a lot, but I didn't think about it. I've always dealt with situations by talking about them and getting them out of my system that way, rather than grieving.

But I went back across the street to the Home and I remember just sliding down to the ground along the fence, crying at that time. Then I told myself, "It's over and you just gotta keep going." And that's what I did.

Twenty-two years later, on May 15, 1989, Nancy learned that the daughter she had given up for adoption was trying to find her. After undergoing counseling and exchanging letters and photos—as required by the social worker who brought them together—Nancy and Donna finally met, on June 23, 1989.

We said "hi" and we hugged and then she gave me a gift, a picture frame that says "Treasured Moments," and it had the date we met on it. I have it sitting in my windowsill right now with one of the lousy pictures that we took that day.

We talked a few minutes and then her adoptive parents came in and I met them, and then we went to the big office where my husband and sons were and then everybody met everybody and we've been meeting everybody ever since.

Having a Baby

I was pretty much overwhelmed by the whole thing. Donna was *short!* My boys are big and it felt funny to be with someone shorter than I was. I didn't just like her right away; I *loved* her right away. It was like being her mother just right then, which has been really difficult to subdue—kind of hold back. I don't want to take away from what her mother has been to her, but I want to be a factor in her life. I think you can do that.

We see each other quite often, we've been lots of places together. She's been out to our house a lot, I've been to her house, her mother's cut my hair, permed my hair, we've been to lunch a lot of times. And they've come to Dallas to meet my parents and my brother and sister.

Donna and I both love spaghetti. That's all we ever eat when we're together is spaghetti and lasagna.

She's a good girl—very loving and caring and considerate. I would have preferred to have been able to have raised her myself and I feel jealous of what her adoptive mother has had, but I really do think that she had a better life and I'm glad for that. She's got a really terrific mother.

JoAnn is very secure in her relationship with Donna. Donna has always been very proud of being adopted. But a lot of it has to do with the way JoAnn raised her in such a loving atmosphere, and giving her the attitude toward me that it was a loving thing. A lot of adoptive parents, they're scared that the birth mother's going to come in and take their child away. I don't think JoAnn ever had that fear. She just took Donna and said, "This is my child," and raised her in that manner.

Once we had met, Donna had to go on and try to find her father, too. I was very excited about it, very curious as to his reaction, what it would be. Because after I had Donna, I saw him one more time. I went with some friends of mine to a football game and he was there. I went up to him and told him. I said, "You had a daughter." And he totally ignored me, and, you know, I knew it was his, she looked like him.

He just walked away. He was there with some other girl and he didn't want to hear about having a baby, not at a football game. I never saw him again after that, never. So I've always been curious since he's always denied it, and especially when all of this came up, as to what his reaction would be.

And I was frank with Donna and told her he denied it in the beginning. "I don't know. . . . If he gets one look at you," I said, "he can't deny it, but I don't know his reaction." So, when school started up again, she went to the high school and got the yearbooks and she said, "There's two boys with the same first name."

I didn't remember the last name, but, once she said the name to me, I knew it was the right one. She got the pictures and she looked up the name in the phone book. And there were only a few, so she called them.

Well, actually she had a friend call. The girl got hold of his mother first and left her name and said that she went to school with him, which was a lie, and for him to call her, and, when he called her, she told him why she was calling and he agreed to meet with Donna.

I think he must have known it was true. He called back and talked to Donna several times on his own before they actually met. He asked her all kinds of questions about me to make sure she really knew me, which was kind of weird after all this denial. I guess, once he met her, he knew. And Donna has a nine-year-old half-brother who looks just like her.

Now they're friends. He calls her about once a week and they meet—I don't think as often as we do, but they do meet. They both have the same nose, for sure. But I think she's got his eyes probably a lot, too. She's got the brown eyes and his nose.

Now I'm doing these panel presentations with Donna and JoAnn and interviews because, at the time that Donna contacted me, I did not know that this program was available, or I would have already done the search. I guess, because of that, I feel like, maybe by being so open, maybe there's somebody out there that was like me, that wants to do it and might find out that it's available.

JoAnn Daigle
Pasadena, Texas

♡ *Nancy Harrison put me in touch with her daughter Donna and JoAnn, Donna's adoptive mother. The three women have done several panel presentations together to inform others about the process of searching for birth parents or for a child given up for adoption—how it works, what can happen, and what you feel when you finally find the person you have been seeking.*

The greatest thing that ever happened to us was our kids. When our son was two and a half, we reapplied for another child, and four months later, we got Donna. It was love at first sight: she was so tiny with orange fuzz for hair. [The heavy black hair the baby had when she was born had fallen out by the time she was given to JoAnn Daigle.]

I have never been able to describe the feeling I had the first time I saw her. I don't think I would have been more thrilled if I had delivered her myself. In fact, I've always thought I appreciated my children more because they were adopted.

Our kids were raised knowing they were adopted. Donna thought it was special and would bring neighbor kids in for me to verify the fact. When she was about thirteen, she started to get curious about her birth parents, and we assured her that when she was old enough, we would help her in her search.

Through the years she would call the adoption agency and

talk to them, and they always took time to have long conversations and reassure her. When she was nineteen, I went with her to start her search.

Ten months later, our family and a few friends met Nancy and her family at the adoption agency. It was like a family reunion and, after two hours, we all had lunch together. Since then, we have spent a lot of time together and grown to love each other. (I had always loved Nancy, anyway, because she gave birth to Donna.)

Three months later, Donna met her birth father and also talks to him often. Last January, Donna got married and all the families were there. We were so proud that we could all be together for Donna.

Donna is expecting our second grandchild in December and I can't wait.

Donna Fehl
Pasadena, Texas

♡ *Donna seems to have opened up her heart to include her birth mother, Nancy, without diminishing in the least her very close relationship with JoAnn. Now twenty-four, she married on January 12, 1991, and, on December 10, 1991, she had her own little son, Daniel Tyler Fehl, known as Tyler to his many relatives.*

As a child I do not remember being told that I was adopted, but I did grow up knowing. I was proud of it. My adopted mother and father say that they told my brother and me from the day that they brought us home. They felt that telling us from day one was very important and, now grown and educated about adoption, I agree with their decision.

Mother and I recall moments when I would bring every kid in the neighborhood over and say, "Tell them, tell them, tell them I'm adopted." I indeed felt special.

As I started to get older (about the age of ten or so), I really got curious about my adoption. I would look for people that looked anything like me. I had a couple of girlfriends in middle school that favored me a lot and we decided that one of them was my half-sister and that her father had been part of the reason I was adopted.

Then, when I went on to high school, I had a class in sociology that made me feel that I wanted and needed to know more

about myself, my family history, and I wanted to know *why????*
My parents had always told me that, if I ever wanted to search
for my biological family, they would help in any way that they
could and would be behind me 100 percent.

So I talked to my mother about doing this search and we went
to the adoption agency to check into the procedures that they
required. The social worker strongly suggested that we attend
some of their search support groups. After attending only two
of these, I decided that I needed to wait. I was not ready for
all this (rejection, et cetera).

Later, after having some medical problems, I felt that I was
ready and that the search really needed to be done. So my
mother and I contacted the agency again and went on with their
procedures. I want to say that the search support groups that
they have are very, very, very important. They helped me, my
mother, and father prepare for anything. And that is how you
have to go into a search like this. . . . *BE READY FOR
ANYTHING!!!!*

After one year they finally contacted my birth mother. I could
not explain the excitement and nervousness that I felt when I
received that letter. Anyway, we met and, about four months
later, I also met my biological father.

As far as changing my relationship with my adopted parents,
there is absolutely *no way* that it could. I have parents, they
adopted me, they raised me; therefore, they are my parents.
When I searched for Nancy, it was not because I was unhappy
at home. It was because I wanted to know more about where I
came from, not to look for another mother or father figure.

When I met my biological father, we talked and he said to
me, "There is no way that I can replace, make up old times,
or be any kind of father figure for you, but I can use all the
friends that I can get," and that has really stuck with me, because that is the way that I want it. I want two new special
friends.

Growing up adopted has always made me curious what kind

of child could I make???? What would he/she look like?? I want a child of my own blood, but would consider adoption, also.

I think adoption is a wonderful thing. If it was a bad thing, then these girls would just have their babies and abandon them, not feed them, et cetera. But, instead, they choose to let their baby have a life . . . a chance at something they would not be able to provide for their baby. So I have a very positive attitude about adoption and do not see even one negative thing about it.

Sherley Hollos
Pennsylvania

♡ *Sherley Hollos has dedicated most of her life to offering women health care options. For twelve years she ran both a birthing center and an abortion clinic. She hopes someday to start a hospice. Her account of her own birth experiences in 1970 and 1974 reflects the same concern that women should receive the health care they want and need—and not some impersonal, standardized process over which they have no control.*

My first child was born May 12, 1970. Being thirty when I got pregnant, I had listened carefully to all my friends who went before me, read Elizabeth Bing's book.[17] So I shopped for my OB—called my old GP who gave me the name of an OB. I visited with one and asked if husbands were allowed in the delivery room. He said no—though he would like it, the hospital wouldn't.

So I thanked him, left, put my ear to the ground, and heard of a doctor who delivered at two hospitals in the area. I went to him and loved it. He's a risk taker as I am, respects women, and said I could do whatever I liked during my pregnancy, including downhill skiing. (I didn't ski because I ski more or less out of control keeping up with a more skilled group of friends.)

We owned a VW bug at the time. Rumor had it that if one delivered in a bug, VW would give you a $500 certificate/bond. I was all for it. You see I never thought I wouldn't be able to deliver by myself. I thought all this hype about pain and "medical event" was just that. But my husband is more conservative and wouldn't go along with that. (I was tempted to delay so that the inevitable would happen.)

We went to natural childbirth classes, which I loved. They were taught in the home of the Irish instructor—about eight couples—lots of "air time" for all of us.

Three days after my due date, I lost my "plug" about six-thirty A.M., called Doc around eight, puttered around the house marking contractions, and left for the hospital at plus or minus noon. Our doctor was famous for missing births—which, again, didn't faze me 'cause I didn't depend on him.

So, I was surprised to find him at the hospital (he had just had a delivery). He examined me, said I was breech, and said labor would be slower—the buttocks are not as good a battering ram as the head. He left for his office hours.

My husband and I settled in and around six P.M., to our delight, found I was fully dilated. Except for the usual transition, when I thought I'd throw in the rag, it was no big deal.

The doctor returned, said he'd do an extra-large episiotomy in case of problems with the breech and would have anesthesia in the room in case of an emergency C-section—but he told me that, if I could sustain my push at the end, it would probably be fine.

So I did, and she came with a few seconds of twisting and turning—no forceps. Not knowing what a vertex birth was like, it seemed fine to me—like playing three sets of tennis and winning. I felt sorry for my husband that he experienced it only vicariously as I think giving birth is the ultimate orgasm!

I champed at the bit to get out of the hospital and three and a half days later I was home.

My second birth was February 24, 1974. I got pregnant two weeks before I opened an abortion clinic and couldn't understand why I was so tired and sleepy! I worked at the clinic right to the end, a) because I felt fine (I used to say I should go into proxy pregnancies—this was pre-surrogate-mother days—

because I loved being pregnant and adored labor and delivery—what drama!), b) because I thought it was good for women seeking abortions to see that abortion is a chapter in some women's lives and that we weren't baby haters—we have a counselor now working in her ninth month, and c) my doctors were the ones who started the clinic with me, and if I went into labor, I'd just climb up on the table and deliver.

My second child was vertex and a piece of cake to deliver—it was fun to have the doctor I worked with at the delivery; there was lots of joking around. My second had ABO incompatibility.[18] I wasn't allowed to nurse until the baby's bilirubin count came down, and the nurses threw my expressed colostrum down the drain. They put her under lights twenty-four hours a day (bandaging her eyes, poor dear), which was/is the usual therapy. It wasn't that they thought the breast milk caused her jaundice, but that it prolonged it, because the baby was still exposed to the source of incompatibility.

Since I couldn't hold my child, I went home the second day and rested up to the point that I stopped bleeding. After badgering the doctors and hospital for four or five days, we got her on her first-week birthday. Today a bilirubin level of 13 isn't a big deal but then it still was.

My first OB was then doing home deliveries and, though I'd switched to be with the docs who started the abortion clinic with me, I stayed in touch with him and begged him to let me see a home birth. At two A.M. one wintry night he called and said my chance was close by.

I jumped into clothes and got to the house just as the birth was taking place. What a high—I was elated for weeks. Then I thought I'd have a home delivery service. After reading lots and asking lots, I decided home delivery in the U.S. wasn't efficient. I spent many hours brainstorming with the head of the National Association of Birth Centers, and looking at houses near our local hospital where my docs practice. I formed a nonprofit corporation in October 1978, found and financed a house in July 1979, and the birthing center had its first birth in February 1980.

I thought normal deliveries in the hospital were a misuse of resources—overkill. I also felt traditional birth belittled women (you're not capable of understanding, you're too emotional, et cetera). I like to be in control. In traditional delivery women are worked on (example: "Who delivered your baby?" The answer should be, unless it was a forceps or C-section delivery, "I did!").

Hospitals do things on their time for their convenience. When I gave orientations at the birthing center, one of my phrases was, "The midwife needs to know you well so she can work unobtrusively with you, so the baby will be born according to your unique rhythm, not according to the center's perceptions or assumptions of your need."

Patricia Bernstein
Houston, Texas

♡ *My own story tells how three much-loved daughters came into the world so differently that, in most ways, it never seemed like one birth prepared me for the next. It was those dramatic differences in birth experiences that inspired this book.*

My first daughter was born on June 1, 1970, in a small hospital in central Massachusetts. I was twenty-five and had been married for three and a half years. I was teaching English part-time at Smith College and my then husband was studying for his Ph.D. in English at the University of Massachusetts.

During my pregnancy I read Marjorie Karmel's *Thank You, Dr. Lamaze* (as mothers before me had read *Childbirth Without Fear*) and so came to the contemplation of natural childbirth. Of course, I said to myself, I wanted to be awake and alert and in control when I had my baby. Of course, I wanted to learn how to cope with the pain. Of course, I wanted to breastfeed my own child.

My husband and I took Lamaze classes from an inspiring and beautiful Swedish woman, who was herself the mother of three. But the big childbirth battle of the era was getting fathers into the delivery room. We were all determined about that. The largest local hospital continued to resist. I will never forget calling and discussing the matter with one of the nurses in labor and delivery:

"We can't allow fathers in the delivery room," she said. "My goodness, if we let the father in the delivery room, he might faint and then the nurse carrying the baby might trip over the father and drop the baby." Right. And then an eagle might fly in the window and carry the baby off to its nest.

So we chose to go to a smaller hospital in a smaller town some distance away, where fathers were permitted to enter the sacred precincts of the delivery room and actually watch their own children being born.

My pregnancy proceeded as spring came on—one of those rare and beautiful New England springs with warm weather and sunshine and early-blooming roses. I grew up in Texas and never reconciled myself to the long New England winters in the nine years I lived in the North. The coming of sunny days was like a new miracle to me every year. I spent so much time outside that one of our friends said the baby would be born with a sunburn.

Two days after my due date, my water broke at two A.M. My mother (who had come from Dallas to help out) and my husband had long been asleep, but I had stayed up late to read and wash and roll up my hair and had just climbed into bed when I felt this inner "thunk" and jumped up just in time to splash water all over the floor. I still remember the pervasive, earthy odor.

I administered my own enema-in-a-bottle to myself (no hospital enemas in hard labor for me, thank you very much) and that probably helped to bring on very strong contractions immediately. We arrived at the doctor's office a little before dawn. The doctor met us there and examined me and told us, although I was only slightly dilated, to go on to the hospital. My contractions were rapidly growing stronger.

We drove up north through the woods, hoping to stumble on the right road that cut sharply west and across the river and come out right in front of the hospital. We had always driven to this little country hospital from our home before, never from the doctor's office, and we really didn't know the way from this direction. But I looked up between contractions and managed to see the right sign, and we came out of the trees and arrived at the front door of the hospital just as the sun was coming up.

Although I was in a lot of pain, I remember that morning with great fondness and gratitude. Many women have awful tales to tell about nurses and doctors who were cruel or simply callous to them during their labors. And many women, who feel tremendous love and affection for their doctors and nurses in that great rush of emotion at the time of the birth, look back on the experience later and feel that they were not, after all, given very good care.

But time and two more births (and all that I have read and seen about childbirth since then) have never dimmed my warm feelings for those nurses and that doctor. I don't know if I was the only woman laboring that morning in that small maternity ward, but I felt as if I were. One nurse stayed with me almost the whole time and others helped when they were needed.

My doctor, a single woman in her late fifties, had devoted her entire life to her obstetrical patients. She followed us up to the hospital and was also there, in and out, throughout my labor. Everyone involved was warm, cheerful, supportive, and focused on helping me have my baby. I wish I could tell them right now what they meant to me.

The labor was hard back labor. The breathing I thought I had learned didn't help much. My husband pressed on my back, and when he pressed hard enough, that relieved some of the pain. I felt like I couldn't catch my breath between contractions. But at least things progressed quickly—especially for a first baby.

When I was about seven centimeters dilated, the doctor decided it would be safe to do something about the pain. Despite my plan to have the baby naturally, I didn't protest: at that point it sounded great to me.

They took me to the delivery room and administered a paracervical block with several shots in the cervix. All at once, the pain was gone but the contractions remained firm and the baby's heartbeat was strong.

After that, I enjoyed myself. My poor mother, distraught with memories of her sixty-eight-hour labor with me, couldn't stand it in the waiting room any longer. She had feared I would experience what she had—long hours of intense pain and no progress. She somehow talked her way past the "guards" and into my labor room and almost fell over when she saw me laughing and chatting with my husband and the nurses. She couldn't believe my labor was going forward without any suffering.

About ten A.M. they took me back to delivery and my husband suited up in gown and mask to go in with me. Yes, I was put in the dreaded lithotomy position, on my back with legs up in stirrups. But they wrapped my legs in something warm and fuzzy like sheepskin and they lifted and supported me while I pushed during contractions.

I felt, if I remember it honestly, that not feeling pain actually *helped* me to focus and push harder and more fearlessly than I could have done if I had been afraid of how much it would hurt. I also found out that pushing was one thing I *could do*. And that stood me in good stead with every birth I had. I was surprised to hear myself making strong, prolonged grunting noises with every push, but the nurses encouraged me: they said women usually grunted or groaned when they pushed effectively.

There was an episiotomy but it was small and I didn't feel it. There was my daughter's head—dark hair. And then, in a few more pushes, there she was, in a slippery whoosh at 10:27 A.M. She was quite purple and soon cried, and I looked at her and declared, "She's purple, but she's beautiful!" She was beautiful then and still is.

She cried enough to turn herself thoroughly pink and then quieted. Her daddy held her first before they even washed her off, and then, I held her close to me and looked into her enormous blue eyes while they stitched me up. She was tiny—only six pounds, two ounces, but healthy and very pretty and perfect. Her gaze was full of curiosity. I felt she was asking me questions and I answered her in my heart while I babbled nonsense to her out loud.

"Yes," I was saying to her in my head, "I'm your mommy

and I will take care of you, and I do love you, and you will always be my darling.''

When she was born, I was feeling a little light-headed from the pushing. Only later did the full realization and relief hit me. The maternity ward was not air-conditioned and I lay through that long, hot day and couldn't sleep or even really rest—I was so filled with excitement and relief and reliving the whole thing over and over in my mind.

My husband brought me roses and I left them in the sunny window and they wilted. But it didn't matter. I started nursing our little girl and that worked well. Her daddy marveled at her quiet alertness in the nursery. While the other babies howled, she looked around, as if to say, "Hmmm, so this is the human world." (There were never more than six babies in the nursery the whole time we were in the hospital. Part of the time there was only our Katherine and one other baby.) Katherine was so tiny but seemed so awake: we thought the other babies looked big and gross and clumsy and stupid next to her.

Of course, when we got her home, things were much different. She had colic for *seven* months. I was so exhausted, there finally came an afternoon when I went to bed with an agonizing headache over one whole side of my face, almost unable to speak coherently. I was so tired I couldn't think of the right words for things anymore.

I think the customs of the times, which I didn't have enough sense or knowledge to ignore, had a lot to do with it. I was only supposed to feed her every four, or at the most, every three and a half hours, and let her cry in between. Horrible stupidity but I did it, watching the clock, full of fears and anxiety, listening to her cry.

And the pediatrician started her on solid foods at *six weeks*— even worse stupidity—but I did that, too, though she clearly didn't really want the food and was constipated for days at a time.

But she emerged from all of that, somehow happy and sweet-natured in spite of my bumbling and bungling. I did nurse her until she was weaned to a cup at eight months and she was extraordinarily healthy throughout that time, except for the colic.

Then lots of things changed. In 1971 we moved to Houston. In 1973 Katherine's father and I got divorced and, for ten years, I worked and raised Katherine on my own—all that time wanting more children, especially more little girls like my dear Kaki.

In 1984 I remarried and on May 9, 1985, Katherine, almost fifteen years old, finally had a sister, Jessica Elizabeth. That was a different story. I embarked on chapter two of my childbearing experiences, thinking that I was determined to have a more natural experience than the first time and believing, in my innocence, that this would be more possible in 1985 than it had been in 1970. I was wrong.

The problem was that I believed the hype. I knew that fathers—and even, in some cases, other family members and friends—were now admitted to labor and delivery. I knew that some hospitals had added homelike birthing rooms to the maternity wing that were designed to suggest your own bedroom at home.

I was also vaguely aware that the C-section rate had skyrocketed since 1970, but didn't know what that meant in terms of how labor was conducted.

I soon found out. My OB/GYN was a charming woman who had helped me through a very early miscarriage a few weeks after our marriage, with a lot of nurturing and kindness. But, when it looked like this pregnancy was going to take and I began to ask some serious questions about birth procedures, I discovered that beneath the charming bedside manner was a woman who believed in massive intervention in the labor process, much of it quite standard by now—including subjecting the laboring woman to an IV throughout labor as a routine procedure.

An IV! I had already had a baby without an IV and I knew darn well it wasn't necessary. I also hate needles in my hands.

The doctor's argument was that we had to be prepared for emergencies and it was sometimes hard to get a needle in a vein in a crisis situation. I thought that was the most absurd thing I had ever heard. According to that reasoning, I thought, with our record of freeway accidents in Houston, everyone traveling on Loop 610 or Interstate 45 should always have an open vein, just in case of emergency.

When I was five months pregnant, I finally switched to another woman OB who was less nurturing but had a reputation for uncompromisingly aiding and abetting interventionless births.

I realized, at this point, that between 1970 and 1985, childbirth had become an even *more* politically charged event—rather than less so. If I had been willing to arrive at the hospital door and be conveyed, like a sack of flour, down the standard birthing assembly line, accepting all the usual interventions that increase the risk of a C-section, there would have been no conflict. But if I wanted birth to go *my* way, rather than according to standard procedure, I saw I would have to arrange for it strenuously and take every possible precaution in advance.

With all this in mind, my husband, Alan, and I also decided to hire our childbirth teacher as our monitrice—a kind of labor coach—during labor. We thought she would give us additional support and guidance and not interfere with the natural process.

However, despite all our precautions to avoid interventions (IVs, continuous electronic fetal monitoring, Pitocin, et cetera), we agreed—in fact, encouraged the doctor to take one step, that probably made everything else that followed inevitable. It was all a tradeoff, balancing relative risks. I knew my doctor was going out of town for a few days and I was afraid of getting a substitute who didn't know me or what I wanted. For this and other reasons, I agreed to have labor induced a few days after my due date had come and gone.

On the early morning of May 8, we went to the hospital and the doctor ruptured my amniotic sac. Then I was told to walk and walk and walk, to try and get labor started. But nothing much happened until fairly late in the afternoon or early evening when labor did at last begin but then proceeded very slowly.

Come about midnight, when I was only four or five centimeters dilated—although I had been in strong, but not really intense labor for some time—my doctor was afraid of bumping up against hospital policy that declared that, if the amniotic sac has been ruptured for twenty-four hours and the baby has not been delivered, a C-section must be performed to avoid the danger of infection. (I have learned since that, if a few basic precautions are taken, the risks of infection following rupture are really very minimal and there is no sudden increase of risk at twenty-five or twenty-six hours after rupture. This is one of those arbitrary protocols that results in unnecessary cesareans.)

I had become more and more discouraged as the night went on. I was in a lot of pain and felt like I was in a dark tunnel with no light ahead, no end in sight. I was also very tired from all the walking throughout the day. But I was willing to go on that way. I had found that the steady, deep abdominal breathing I learned from my Bradley instructor helped me far more than the complicated Lamaze breathing I had tried to learn fifteen years before. I could remember the deep, steady breathing and do it automatically.[19]

But when the doctor announced that she was putting me on Pitocin and we had to leave the cozy birthing suite and go to a standard labor room, I felt I had come to the very end of my rope. Our monitrice, who had been very ingenious and helpful in getting my labor off the ground and keeping me going, couldn't do anything to change the decision. We were all in the grip of merciless hospital protocols.

The Pitocin caused very intense, hard-peak contractions that hung at the top level of intensity for some time before they came back down and, it seemed, started over again almost immediately. I had had it. I asked for an epidural.

My sweet husband, who had put his heart and soul into helping me breathe with every contraction, had stood in the shower with me to try and get contractions started, had committed himself as firmly as I had to the best possible birth for our little girl, was quite distraught when he saw our birth plan going down the drain. I think *his* heart almost stopped when I received the epidural and began to shake and tremble uncontrollably for a few minutes. Then the baby's heart rate dropped way off and stayed down for a few awful seconds—a common consequence of the epidural.

I went to sleep almost at once when the pain stopped and was only vaguely, dozily aware of what was happening. But, if the baby's heart rate had not come back up rapidly, I would have been an emergency C-section candidate. Fortunately, her heart rate bounced back, she was fine, and, after an hour or so of sleep, I was fully dilated and ready to push.

From there, things went smoothly. I woke up, concentrated my efforts, and pushed her out handily—and there she was, another wee girl (six pounds, six ounces) but this time with paler eyes and a kind of reddish-gold tuft of hair like a stripe down the center of her head.

More delight and joy. More inability to sleep, riding on the birth high. I see in my mind to this day, my fifteen-year-old lying on her side on the hospital bed, gazing at her tiny sister, who was lying on the bed next to her, and hear her saying to me, "I don't think I've ever loved anyone as much as I love this little thing."

This time we did the postbirth business right. Jessica cried some but was basically an easy baby. I fed her whenever she was hungry. We slept when she slept. She had no solid food until she was five months old—and then she was so ready to eat that I thought she was going to climb into the bowl to guzzle up the last of her rice cereal!

It was amazing how easily we adapted to her and she to us. She walked at nine months and talked in complex sentences at eighteen months. She was still tiny: the smallest walking, talking person you ever saw.

Today, at seven, she is in advanced classes at school, and, no longer tiny, is also one of the fastest runners in her class. She has honey-colored hair, enormous blue-gray-green "Bette Davis" eyes, and a wonderfully rascally sense of humor.

And then there was Rebecca Floren. When we told my parents I was pregnant again, at forty-two, they were quiet for a long time and then said, without enthusiasm, "Oh, that's nice." Alan's parents were blunter. They simply said, "Why?"

Before the pregnancy was over, I had asked myself that question many times, too—although I knew the answer. We very much wanted another child and, with my biological clock about to retire and give it up, there was no time to waste.

I decided against using the previous OB. I still had some resentments about the way the last labor had been conducted, including a vivid memory of her telling me something along the lines of "Oh, shut up" at one point when I was moaning during one particularly bad contraction.

We visited with another (male) doctor who seemed far more relaxed and pleasant and still willing to let mothers birth as they wished. He admitted that he had once been a hippie and played in a rock band and his instincts were still somewhat countercultural. I also observed that his basic approach to medicine was professional but very laid-back in nonessential matters—the polar opposite of the customary *"I'm in charge here!"* medical personality.

After more interviews, including some long talks with a very earth-mother-style midwife who lived in our neighborhood, I rather casually (and without thinking it through) decided to have my baby at home with the midwife, whom I liked immensely, and forgo the whole hospital straitjacket entirely.

And so the months passed. I was working hard, too hard, trying to keep a business going and also complete some major writing projects. I saw the midwife monthly and welcomed her warm care and positive attitude.

But I see now that, deep inside, I was ignoring what was really happening with me. I was getting panicky about caring for another baby and keeping everything else in my life going at the same time and panicky about completing several major projects before the baby was born. My reaction was to kind of head-in-the-sand it. I had no time to think about the baby or the birth, so I didn't.

My midwife told me later that she never felt, in all those months, that she was really making contact with me emotionally. I know what she means. She would ask me questions about the pregnancy and my plans for the birth and I would evade her questions, responding with my worries about my business and writing and other obligations.

Finally, the matter of the impending birth was brought to my attention forcibly. My mind and body played a strange and awful trick on me.

When I was eight months pregnant, I woke up one night about three A.M.—startled out of a deep sleep. Suddenly, I was terribly afraid. Why?

I sat up on the edge of the bed. The fear grew and drove me up and out of the bedroom. I paced the living room, the den, the kitchen, finally put on my coat and went outside. It was cold and dark—late February, overcast, no moon, no stars, a chilly wind blowing. Even the neighbor's dogs, who usually barked most of the night, were quiet. I felt like the only person awake in the whole world.

I must be afraid of labor, I decided finally—afraid of the pain, afraid of that long cave I had been in with no light ahead in my last labor. Perhaps I had been too nonchalant when I made up my mind to have a baby at home. I hadn't thought it through.

It's simple, I thought. I would just tell the nice male OB I had seen several times (for backup, in case problems developed) that I had changed my mind, that I wanted to have the baby in the hospital. I went back inside to bed and was soon asleep.

I thought the problem was solved, but that night was just the beginning of what would become the worst experience of my life—worse than getting a divorce, losing a job, or having back surgery. I had been through all these experiences, but I had been through them as my own recognizable self. Now I was about to lose my self entirely.

The next day I told my husband, the doctor, and the midwife

what I had decided. They were all surprised and baffled. I had fought so hard the last time to have my second child without anesthesia. Why was I now suddenly so afraid of labor pain?

"This doesn't seem like you," the midwife said.

"I'm sorry," I said. "I guess I just didn't think it through before. Maybe I just don't have enough pioneer spirit, after all, to have a baby at home. Maybe I was trying to fulfill some kind of philosophical ideal, and the truth is I'm too conventional at heart."

"Are you worried about the baby?"

"No, not really. I think she is fine and will be fine," I answered truthfully. I felt instinctively that my third daughter (we knew she was a girl, too) was doing well and would be born successfully in any setting. I was afraid for *me*.

"So," she said, at last (she always asks the hard questions), "do you feel better now that you've decided to have the baby in the hospital? Do you feel safer?"

The truth was that I didn't feel better. Over the next few days I seemed to feel worse and worse. Day by day, I grew more panicky. My sleeplessness increased. I would go to bed very late, exhausted, and awaken an hour or two later, stiff with terror, panting, my mind racing with outsized images of interminable, pain-soaked labors—or being wheeled in, flat on my back, unable to breathe, for cesarean surgery.

Night after night, while my husband and my children slept, I was alone in the dark, struggling to keep my tears and screams inside.

After an hour or two, I would sleep, wake again, finally capture a couple of hours of truly sound sleep in the early morning. I dreamed over and over that the baby had been born and everything was fine, but, when I awoke, I was still pregnant and still afraid.

I simply couldn't explain what was happening to my midwife and childbirth educator friends—all of whom I consulted. They saw me still walking around, functioning, doing what I had to do to keep everything going, and they just couldn't understand that natural childbirth wasn't an issue with me anymore. I was too sick inside to care. I just wanted the birth to be over.

At last, when I reached full term, I went into the hospital on March 31, 1988, for an induced labor.

It was a labor and delivery almost entirely without pain, if such a thing exists. I got the epidural before I got the Pitocin drip. I also got completely paralyzed and unable to move anything from the waist down during the last two hours of labor. I couldn't complain much about that; I had asked to be shielded from pain, after all. They had done what I had requested.

Nevertheless, I did still push the baby out myself, despite everyone's skepticism that I could do it with such "profound" temporary paralysis. (I could almost see, behind the doctor's frown, a neon sign blinking in his mind, "Forceps! Forceps!") Only the midwife, who agreed to keep us company in the hospital and see us through this mess, kept encouraging me and believed I could do it. She said later she could feel the baby move and turn every time I pushed.

One little thing that happened . . . it was very insignificant in comparison to all the big things that happened before and after Rebecca's birth, but it was emblematic of the difference in atmosphere between my first birth and my last two births . . .

I was pushing and I began to make the same kinds of loud grunts I made when I pushed out my other two babies, and one of the nurses said, very impatiently and not looking at me, as if she was embarrassed, "Don't do that. You'll push better if you don't make any noise."

I was startled and thought to myself, well, okay, I think I can do it without noise, if she insists. But, when I thought about it later, I was very annoyed and am still very annoyed. Who was she to tell me what kind of noises I could make, for heaven's sake, when I was having *my* baby?

And so Rebecca was born—she was bigger than my other babies, by a good two pounds (which may have had something to do with my breathing problems and carrying problems, in general—I also wonder if her weight somehow related to a biochemical imbalance that caused the anxiety, as well?). Yet I had no incision and no tearing.

We were so relieved and happy. Little Rebecca had dark hair and light eyes and it seemed to me later (though it wasn't possible) that she met the world with a smile from the first day. She seldom cried and, from an early age, simply beamed her bright smile at everyone she met.

For two or three days I felt normal again. I convinced myself everything was okay. Then the fear—now little snakes, tendrils of an unnamed, unfocused anxiety—began to return. It was as if we had, through days of elaborate ritual, exorcised the attic of our house, thanked the priests, and sent them home, and then discovered that the demons had simply relocated to the basement.

Once more, I couldn't sleep. Anxiety and agitation attended me almost constantly. I nursed and bathed the baby and did the laundry by rote, but I could not care for my toddler or concentrate on the conversation of my teenager. I couldn't nap or even put my feet up and rest.

My husband and my sister, who was visiting from the East Coast, took over everything as I went spinning down, down, into a whirlpool of uncontrolled emotions—all the while regarding my own condition with shocked disbelief.

Here I was, a woman who had managed her own business for five years, had raised children with great love and joy, had America's most supportive husband, had never had the faintest shadow of a psychiatric problem before—become a weepy creature of fears and alarms, unable to read or talk to her three-year-old or even settle down in one place for more than five minutes.

I tried everything. I took long walks around the neighborhood in the early spring weather that blew warm and soft one day, cold and wild the next. I discovered neighbors who had a magnificent rose garden and visited often. I was trying to fix in my mind images of giant mauve and peach blooms to rock me to sleep at night.

I taped my own relaxation monologues and hid away in a back bedroom, cross-legged, with eyes shut, listening to them over and over. I even went to a "cognitive therapist" and tried to train my thoughts to face, dissect, and banish the horrific images that plagued me.

I was fighting to avoid drugs—tranquilizers, antidepressants—because a grim female psychiatrist had told me I could not possibly take antidepressants or antianxiety drugs while I was nursing the baby. She thought I should simply end the breastfeeding and stuff myself with medication.

She didn't understand. I *had* to keep nursing the baby. It was one of the few links to reality I had left, all that made getting up and living through one more awful day possible.

"Your fixation on breastfeeding is merely another symptom of your illness," she said. "When you feel better, you'll realize it's not that important."

Maybe not for her. She had children of her own, she said, but she didn't look as though she had ever hugged them, much less nursed them. For me, I thought, if I'm not nursing my baby, I'm not a mother and then what am I? Why am I hanging around here on this earth at all?

Gray days turned brown. I saw "bad things"—something amorphous and evil—out of the corner of my eyes. Food tasted bad. I had to force myself to eat. I brushed my teeth a dozen times a day, trying to abolish a constant sour taste. The house seemed dark. I was afraid of cloudy days and dusk. I was afraid to close windows because I feared I would feel suffocated. It was all crazy, I knew, but I couldn't help it.

I even came to be afraid to take a shower in the morning. I literally couldn't stand to be alone that long. Every day I stood in the shower and sobbed.

My husband was bewildered and weary. He had planned a long leave from work so we could enjoy this baby together, as we had the last. Now he found himself afraid that his wife and his family were headed toward some kind of final crack-up. Nevertheless, he took on all the household chores, played all day with our three-year-old, patiently drove me from one doctor to another, held me at night.

I hated myself for what I was doing to him and my oldest and middle daughters. My teenager was frightened. I feared that the three-year-old would soon know something was wrong, too. At night I clenched my teeth and forced myself to read her a bedtime story, struggling to keep the tears away.

Finally, three or four weeks after baby was born, when I was facing my husband's imminent return to work, my sister's return to her home two thousand miles away, the demands of my own business and my older girls—not to mention this new, little life that seemed so threatened by my illness—I managed to get the right referral, at last, to a psychiatrist who was also a psychopharmacologist, an expert in mind-affecting medications. This doctor, a gentle, compassionate man in his sixties, whose face seemed to me to contain all the wisdom he had acquired in thirty-five years of listening to human outpourings, heard my story and said at once, "I think I can help you. I think it is possible to do what you want to do." This was the best hope I had had since the first night I awoke in fear. I believed him, and he was right.

He prescribed a very minimal dose of an antidepressant that had been in use for many years and had even been taken by women during pregnancy. I, in turn, agreed to let the baby have two bottles a day and to nurse her the rest of the time—to reduce her exposure to the medication and give me time to sleep.

After only four or five days on the drug he gave me, I returned almost completely to my old self. My depression and anxiety began to recede. I found I could function and run my life once more and slowly I grew independent and optimistic again. There were bouts of anxiety for some time to come, but I could manage them and they grew less and less troublesome.

One early summer evening, I sat in a swing in our backyard, holding my infant girl in my arms and humming "Hush Little Baby" to her while tears of relief rolled down my face. I was so grateful to be able to love and care for my baby and embrace my life again.

In my predepression innocence, I had no idea what a terrible thing "postpartum depression" was. I had always thought it was a deep discouragement that women suffered who had fussy babies, little sleep, and no support from husband, family, or friends. I thought it was a logical reaction to bad circumstances.

Postpartum depression can be, I learned, a biochemically induced horror that can strike without warning at women who are happy with their marriages, want their babies, and are surrounded by support and love. It can happen to women who, like me, have never experienced any form of mental illness and probably never will again.

I also learned once more that health problems that are exclusively women's have received little attention or study in our society. Postpartum depression has been known for, literally, thousands of years—yet, in one of the most medically advanced cities in the country, there was almost no information available on what drugs can be used by nursing mothers.

Times are changing, of course—and I suppose these things will be studied in time. But it's so easy, even now, for a doctor to simply take an infant off the breast and not have to worry about complex unknowns like how drugs affect breast milk. Thank God, I finally found a doctor who was willing to look at the situation from my perspective and try to help.

There is something else to be faced in all of this, apart from the whole issue of postpartum depression. I don't think I was really honest with myself through two pregnancies about what I actually wanted with the births of Jessica and Becca. What I now believe I really wanted was to re-create my first, almost idyllic, birth experience.

I was willing to accept some pain with birth but I don't think I ever really wanted the extreme pain I associated in my mind with the last stages of undrugged delivery and birth.

This is not to say that I don't believe in natural childbirth. I still think it is the ideal way to go—and almost undoubtedly the best thing for the baby. All the common hospital interventions in birth—anesthesia, Pitocin, C-sections—can have powerful negative effects on both mother and baby. These are risks doctors don't discuss while they eagerly elaborate on the risks involved in home birth or the risks of not having an IV or a continuous electronic fetal monitor throughout labor.

I still, therefore, have great respect for women who do have their babies without artificial aids. I still believe every woman could benefit from the kind of knowledge conveyed in classes like those given by the Bradley instructors—and could benefit from the wholehearted *effort* to do without drugs. But my instructors would say a halfhearted commitment won't see you through; they would say you have to be sure and be resolved.

The truth is, I guess, I am weak when it comes to pain. I am a pampered city child of the twentieth century. I realize now that I actually liked being in the hospital and being taken care of for a few days. I liked not having to have full responsibility for the baby's care at the very beginning—although I wanted to be able to have her with me whenever *I* wanted to have her.

I guess, best of all, I liked the paracervical block, which released me from pain but left the contractions and the power to control my birth intact. Most doctors, of course, don't do paracervicals anymore: paracervicals are said to have caused an unacceptable rate of fetal bradycardia (abnormally slow heartbeat). And for some women the paracervical provided no pain relief at all. But I found it much less intrusive than the epidural.

This past May I went back to Smith College for my twenty-fifth reunion and I took my oldest daughter, Katherine, with me. Part of our plan was to visit the places her father and I lived when we were newlyweds and the year after she was born—and, of course, I wanted her to see the country hospital where she actually came into the world.

I had dreamed of visiting the hospital, going upstairs, and seeing the babies in the nursery and telling Katherine how we watched her, looking around quietly while the other babies hollered. I even thought vaguely that we might find one of the nurses who was there twenty years ago when Katherine was born.

We found the place all right and the building looked the same as it had—but it was no longer a hospital. Just one of the many hospitals that had fallen victim to the current difficult health care climate, it had been converted into a nursing home. There was no more maternity wing and there were no more babies; in fact, it looked as if the second floor wasn't being used at all anymore.

I couldn't even take a picture of Katherine in front of the building. We had run out of film.

I'm afraid the kind of birth experience I had there is pretty much gone, too. I was lucky. I had my first baby just at the end of the "knock 'em out, pull 'em out" era and just before technology grabbed hold of childbirth.

But maybe I'm being too gloomy. Certainly, there are still birthing center births and home births and even some hospital births that are similar to my first one in terms of care and nurturing and simplicity and focus on the birthing mother and her needs. But, of course, as a deliberate choice on the part of the mothers—to avoid the interventions and reduce the risk of a cesarean—most of these births take place without pain relief.

I'd like to see women who choose to have babies in hospitals and choose at some point to have pain relief also given control over their own births and individualized care that allows for the wide variance in the way women naturally labor and have babies.

I'd like to see all the hardware and the rules and the many unnecessary C-sections shoved out of the way, so that more new mothers can feel once more the delight I felt when my oldest child first lay on my arm and looked at me with such grave curiosity in her dark blue eyes.

Lydia Griffin
Columbia, South Carolina

♡ *Lydia Griffin is the tenth child of Florine Bond, who describes the births of her thirteen children earlier in this book. I was struck by Lydia's buoyancy, verve, and strong sense of the dramatic in describing her one and only childbirth experience, in 1972.*

Although her life was full of hardship at the time of her son's birth, Lydia tells her story with excitement and anticipation. She acknowledges that she has made mistakes and has learned from them, but her overall attitude is positive. She leads us to believe that she knows her child will bring something good into her world.

At the time my son was born in August 1972, I was twenty-five years old, unmarried, and still living at home with my mother and two younger sisters, Essie and Valerie. My two older sisters and one younger sister were married and gone, as were all six brothers.

I helped Mom around the house cooking and cleaning, doing laundry, and getting groceries. Essie, three years younger than me, already had a two-year-old son. She had gone back to college and her boyfriend gave her money, which she shared with Mom. I worked part-time and kept my money, since Mom and I had the agreement because I "helped out."

Life was tough with three "girls" in one house. It was really four women, if you counted my mother. There were tensions between the three of us with Mom in the middle—money was a big issue. Mom would tell me, "Just keep the peace."

I had finished high school but hadn't done much else. I had no drive to do anything. I was perfectly content to deal with things as they were—that is, until my son was born. I knew my job had no future and I had no place to go. Looking back, I don't know how I ever lived like that!

Valerie and I were expecting at the same time, delivering ten days apart! I never got Mother to say how she really felt, but I believe she was embarrassed. She didn't *say* anything.

My brothers were furious. They didn't expect any of us to do anything like this. We were too good, not like other girls. We were supposed to have been perfect ladies and waited for weddings. They slept around, but we were supposed to stay up on the "pedestals we were placed on by them." I couldn't believe what I was hearing!

My pregnancy was easy until my fifth month, when a series of urinary tract infections began. There was a lot of pressure on my right kidney, which caused it to malfunction and nearly shut down. The problem went on for the entire pregnancy and beyond. It was a painful and scary time, since UTI can cause miscarriage and/or damage to the fetus.

I prayed everything would be okay. At the beginning I knew to stop smoking, so I did. I also started walking and eating healthier. I was in school until my seventh month, walking the mile to and from the bus stop, unless I had late classes or it rained.

I never had morning sickness because I had prayed I wouldn't. I hated to throw up. Swelling ankles was the only other health problem I had. My mom had a pair of black orthopedic shoes that solved the problem, even though I looked like a grandmother wearing them.

Clinic visits were at the county hospital where OB patients were herded from one long, narrow corridor to be seen by the specialty doctor our conditions required. If we saw someone we knew on one side, chances were we'd run into them again on the other side before the long day ended.

Only women with female problems or us pregnant ones were seen on either of the two days each week. It was always amazing to see how the bellies differed and to notice the unusual ways of walking that developed because of the unaccustomed roundness.

The seats at the clinic were those hard and uncomfortable but colorfully molded "modern" monsters that only a kid could be happy with. Many times the doctors stood in the crowded hallway telling their patients the latest, due to a shortage of private places to talk.

Smoking was allowed back then so we had to put up with the annoying smoke unless we found an empty seat elsewhere. Many of the ladies had other children. Some appeared to be good mothers while others made me wonder why they were doing this a second time. They didn't seem very excited about having a child, which was quite sad. It was apparent that they'd rather be doing something else far away from the hospital.

The doctor told me when I was due to deliver but I disagreed. He insisted it would be September, but I knew it would be August since I counted back and recalled that "special" night. I finally had to tell the good doctor that I didn't remember him "being there." So he stopped, turning red.

After the exam he informed me that my pelvic area was large enough to hold a ten-pound baby! I calmly said, "And when he comes, you can have him!" He laughed. I decided he would come on August 13th, weighing a lot less than that.

During my seventh month the windows needed to be washed. It had always been my job. Pregnancy didn't change anything. My brothers were too busy, as usual, so I climbed aboard the milk crate as I always did.

This time things were not usual. I could feel myself falling. I just knew that my belly was going to hit the protruding bricks, no doubt killing my baby and me, since the impact would have pushed him into my heart and lungs! Instead, I landed on my bottom, legs folded under me, Indian-style. Neither of us was hurt! I had a huge black-and-blue bruise the size of a saucer on my leg. I knew that God's hand had been on us. This was my way of knowing that He had forgiven me for my transgression. He had spared both our lives! That meant a lot to me.

I would have made it to August 13, had it not been for the exciting preparations for Valerie's baby shower. It was scheduled for Sunday afternoon, August 13, while I was in labor (as it turned out). Guess I didn't realize that those trips to the basement had been just the catalyst my baby needed to begin his entry into the world.

When I showered that night, my belly felt "funny." It was unusually hard and had dropped lower. I didn't sleep well at all. I really missed sleeping on my stomach. I tossed from side to side, feeling the initial pangs of labor beginning.

At two A.M. it got serious. I put up with the pain for hours, but finally had to wake my mother. She was calm. I had already started getting dressed. I tried to relax while she got ready.

We called for the ambulance. My friend Loretta's husband was part of the crew. He cheerfully announced that he had delivered "a couple babies," adding with a laugh, as he noticed my shocked face, that he "would love to deliver mine!"

The thought had never crossed my mind! There was no way he was going to deliver mine; I would be too embarrassed, I thought to myself. I managed a "No thanks, Dave. We'll wait for the doctor."

I didn't stay long at the hospital. My contractions were two to three minutes apart but too brief to warrant admitting me. I returned home and went back to bed. It seemed that, as soon as I fell asleep, the pains started again. This time they were much worse! Within a two-and-a-half- to three-hour time span, we were headed back to the E.R. That was about 8 A.M.

My girlfriend Luddie had given me instructions on how to breathe when the "pains got bad." When the nurse found me panting, she said, "That's a good idea! Who told you to do that?"

The only answer I could manage between contractions was a sob. "My girlfriend," I said, then went back to panting. I'm not sure it really worked, but it sure kept me busy until the pains subsided. The nurse patted my shoulder, smiled, and walked out.

All I could think was, This is silly, all this pain for a few hours of fun! I decided right then that I would never go through this again! I remembered my decision as a teenager to have "at least five kids." There was no way, if this was how it was going to be! *Once* was plenty!

My water broke. I had no idea what was happening. I rang for the nurse at the onset of it, thinking it was an ordinary pee. When the nurse arrived, my entire low back and bottom were wet. I apologized, saying that I was sorry: "I tried to hold it." The nurse told me what had happened; no one had explained about that happening.

The baby still wasn't ready. The nurse came in to "prep" me. She cleaned the pelvic area with a solution that must have been stored in the refrigerator. Wow! It was cold!

She also shaved off all my pubic hair. Once she was finished and gone, I dozed off. It was good to escape the pain and the chilled air of the room. The pain was beginning to make me sick to my stomach.

I felt a pain beginning way down deep inside of me. I knew it was time. There was intense pressure against my pelvic bone. I signaled for the nurse. After looking at my bulging belly, she determined that "it was not time yet."

I let her leave the room and awaited the next pain. I could feel something moving down there. I lowered my hand and felt hair. I knew it couldn't be mine. It was the baby's head! I thought to myself. I wondered what time it was, hated not knowing.

Earlier someone had informed me that my mother was in the waiting room. I wondered how long she had been there—not all day! I knew the baby's father wouldn't come . . . he didn't believe the baby was his.

Since I had found hair that didn't belong to me, I rang for the nurse to tell her. She came but immediately rushed back out, after looking for herself and seeing the head pushing its way into the world. She stopped long enough to remind me that "The area is sterile; your hand should not be down there." I only shrugged. It was too late now.

The doctor arrived, muttering to himself. He asked me to sit up, which wasn't easy in my condition. But I managed. The pains were coming faster and getting worse. I had a contraction while he was touching my low back with something cold and wet.

I glanced back to see what he was about to do and spied this monster needle in his hand! When I asked what he planned to do with that thing, he answered, "I'm going to help you have your baby," sounding annoyed. I wondered if needles that size were only for overweight patients . . . it was as long as my hand!

As I felt the prick of the needle, I had a bad contraction. I heard him curse and mutter to himself as he pulled away. He'd said, "Oops!" to which I said, "Excuse me, Doctor, but you don't say, 'oops!' with a needle that big in my back!"

No doubt he agreed. He called for a nurse and, when one answered, he ordered blank cc's of something, and some kind of needle. She arrived carrying a vial and a normal-size needle. He gave me a shot in the hip and helped me to lie down.

No sooner had I stretched out than they were putting my feet up in the stirrups. It didn't take more than a few seconds before the baby began cramping my stomach like I'd never felt before! As things began to blur, I could hear the nurse saying, "Don't push." All day they'd said, "Push." Now, when I felt the greatest urge to push, I was told not to!

My mother, no doubt with hands neatly folded in her lap as she slept, later informed me that she only heard me scream once. During the entire ordeal I had moaned a lot with silent tears running into my hair and ears, down my neck, onto the pillow. It was quite wet.

I wanted to push so badly. I wanted to get this over with. I was cold and tired. The next thing I heard was this woman screaming. I wondered where she was. It sounded so close. I didn't know it was me until I felt my mouth stretching open. I have never felt that much pain! That scream must have come from the bottom of my feet and run through my entire body to reach my mouth with such an eruption of sound!

I could feel the baby as he exited my body. At 3:55 P.M., my seven-pound, four-ounce, nineteen-inch-long bouncing baby boy was born! I could hear a little "pop" or should I say "plopping" sound? I had previously asked God for a boy, knowing that this would be my only chance.

The nurse leaned over to tell me, "Mrs. Bond, you have a boy." I was thrilled! I had my boy. "Thank God," I said, then passed out.

The hospital must have been short of nurses. The best of them were in the nursery. I don't know where they found the not-too-bright one who came to the room the second time we got to see our babies. She started with those new mothers closest to the door, leaving two babies while delivering four. She picked up my son and started toward the white girl across from me. We had shared the same delivery/labor room.

"Hey," I called to her, "this nurse is switching babies on us!" The poor nurse froze, then quickly turned to look at me. I replied to her stare, "I've seen him twice, I know what my baby looks like: his father. Please bring me my baby and give that woman hers."

The nurse had stood unmoving as I spoke, unsure of what to do, until I said that she could try looking at the names on their bracelets.

She was trying to figure out how my baby could be whiter than a white woman's. The expression on her face was enough to make me laugh, but I didn't. She already knew how foolishly she'd acted. Someone else brought the babies next time. By the way, my son's father may be lighter in color than I am, but he is black, also.

I chose the name Benjabi N'gandi for my son. I put together the two names which "fit" my last name (and that I could pronounce) from several lists my sister had of African tribal and regional names together. These names also made the statement I wanted to make. I wanted strength and symmetry. The name fits him perfectly! He is strong, bright, and symmetrical! He also has a wonderful sense of humor and a beautiful smile!

My son and I discovered that there are worse things than being unmarried and pregnant, just as there are worse things than not having a father who lived with you. As our lives progressed, we found that there were people who actually envied us!

My son and I love each other. If I had to do things all over again, I wouldn't change a thing! As long as I could have "my Ben," who made it all worthwhile!

On May 4, 1991, Lydia Bond married John Chapman Griffin, a coworker at the hotel where she is a switchboard operator. The wedding took place in Lydia's living room. Ben was the official witness at the ceremony.

Barbara Crotty
Houston, Texas

♡ *Unlike women of an earlier generation who had a couple of unpleasant childbirth experiences and* then *sought a different approach, Barbara Crotty knew from the beginning that she wanted to do things her own way. Of course, by 1981, when Barbara's first child was born, feminism and the persistent natural childbirth movement had prepared the way for her to strike out on her own.*

I think I began a retreat from conventional submission to medical doctors the first time I visited a gynecologist. I was left, undressed under a paper sheet in a chilly room, lying on a table with my feet up in stirrups. As I waited and waited for the doctor, I had to keep staring at the ceiling, to which was taped a cartoon clipped from, of all things, *Playboy* magazine. The cartoon depicted a woman in exactly my position with a doctor sitting on a stool between her legs, audaciously tickling the bottom of her foot and saying, "Cootchy-cootchy-coo!" This did not give me a sense of comfort.

As an active feminist in college, I was especially interested in gaining and sharing information about women's health. I wanted to demystify my body so that I could know when I really needed a doctor and when I could take a simple measure to help myself. I wanted to be able to discuss my condition with the doctor intelligently, rather than being patronized and confused.

I learned how to give myself a vaginal exam, using a speculum, flashlight, and mirror, and to recognize normality in my own body, as well as common vaginal disorders. It felt good to begin to take charge of my own health.

Hence, when I became pregnant during my last semester of graduate school, my approach was to seek out as much information as I could about various approaches to birthing. I quickly realized what a controversial issue it is!

What I was reading and learning in my childbirth preparation classes, which were taught by a lay midwife, was quite at odds with what I experienced in the doctor's office at the City Public Health Clinic. As a financially destitute student, I took advantage of the free prenatal care offered by the city, which was actually more comprehensive than the care most obstetricians' practices offer—including nutritional counseling and education sessions about birth, baby care, and birth control.

However, the checkups and deliveries were done by young doctors on obstetrical rotation, who were very rigid in their adherence to traditional hospital routines for birth. I imagine I was the only patient who ever came into that clinic with a birth plan, citing my personal requirements for my birth experience: no routine IV, no shave or enema, only intermittent fetal monitoring, freedom to move around during labor, freedom to eat or drink as I wanted during labor, and so on. I couldn't get one of the dozen or more doctors who checked me to agree to any of my wishes.

Then I heard about a hospital about sixty miles away, in Cleveland. There was a two- or three-year-old in-hospital birth center there, staffed by certified nurse-midwives. I went to visit and saw their four birth suites, each including a family room with a hide-a-bed sofa, TV, telephone, toy box, and comfortable furniture; a bedroom with a double bed and homelike furnishings; and a private bathroom with a shower.

There were cabinets in the bedrooms where all the birth supplies and emergency equipment were unobtrusively stored until needed. There was also a shared kitchen for the use of the patients' families and the midwives. Unlike the hospital delivery room, it did not look like a place for sick people.

There were no routine procedures. Everything that went on was subject to the wishes of the birthing family. To my husband and me it looked like the perfect combination of our wish for a homelike, family-centered birth with the safety of the hospital. The maternity ward was only an elevator ride away, if we should need the emergency facilities available there.

When we discovered that the relatively short postpartum stay at the birth center made the total cost about the same as the city hospital, we decided to have baby there, despite the sixty-mile drive.

My prenatal checkups with the midwives were always a joy. On arrival I would weigh myself and check my urine for protein and glucose with a paper dipstick. This freed them up for difficult tasks. They trusted women to be intelligent enough to tend to these simple chores.

After always being denied access to my own medical charts and never being told the results of blood pressure checks unless I pressed the office nurse about it, I was very happy to be accepted as a member of my own medical team. The midwives took plenty of time to tell me what they were checking for and why, and to answer any questions or concerns I might have. It was common to spend an hour at a checkup. Dads and siblings were a common and welcomed sight at the birth center.

During that pregnancy I was twenty-seven and finishing my master's degree in geology. I stayed active, going to classes and doing the field work for my thesis, which involved tromping through streams and brush. I also took long hikes at local parks.

About five weeks before my due date, my Braxton-Hicks contractions became so frequent and strong that the midwives advised me to rest in bed when I could and take a glass of wine each day so as to avoid premature labor. That was boring, but I did hold out until only ten days before my due date.

Oddly, a friend who was flying in from Connecticut to be at the birth had had an intuition that she should come sooner than planned. . . . We had to send someone to the airport for her because I was in labor when she arrived.

I had awakened in the predawn hours of June 9, 1981, with contractions. I timed them from five A.M. until seven A.M. and realized that they were fairly regular. Not twenty minutes apart, as we had been taught to expect at the onset of labor, but more like four minutes apart.

At seven A.M., my husband, Kevin, got up and we started writing down the times of the contractions. They continued through the morning, varying between three-minute and seven-minute intervals. I remember that time as exciting. I was anxious to go to the birth center to experience what I had been anticipating and preparing for for so long.

After a couple of phone calls to the midwives on duty, they told us to come on up at about two P.M. The drive up was uncomfortable for me, so I was relieved that I was dilated sufficiently to be admitted when we arrived. At that point I was at three centimeters.

We were left pretty much alone all afternoon, with infrequent visits by a midwife to see how I was doing. My friend arrived from the airport. I was into active labor by late afternoon. I was encouraged to drink fruit juice and eat lightly, if I wished.

The dinner that was sent from the cafeteria for my husband and me was stuffed cabbage rolls with tomato sauce—not the sort of food I was interested in! Consequently, I really didn't have much to eat, and it turned out that my baby was posterior (facing my front instead of my spine, which occurs in about 25 percent of all births), so the labor was very long.

As the hour grew later and I grew more and more tired, I began to feel discouraged. I wondered what would happen if I just passed out. I kept moving around, changing positions, from hands and knees to standing to the rocking chair and whatever else anyone could think of. Beyond that time, my memory is foggy because I was so exhausted.

I got in bed to rest awhile and the midwife did a vaginal exam. She said my bag of waters was really bulging and suggested breaking it. We said okay. When it broke, I guess I went into transition because I vomited up all the apple juice I had been drinking.

I recall a sensation of being afloat in a warm sea. Somehow the bed was tidied up around me and I was put on an IV for fluid replacement. I can't remember when I started pushing, or how long it took, but I remember that I did not do it in a controlled manner.

I knew that, when I pushed as hard as I could, the burning sensation at my perineum would go away, so I did that, oblivious to the commands of my birth team to hold back. When the baby's head came out, the rest of his body shot out right away, "like out of a cannon," everyone said. I had considerable tearing, but nothing that caused me long-term problems.

It was a boy and we named him Sean Michael and he was put to my breast right away. His umbilical cord was too short to reach, so it was clamped earlier than we had wanted.

The postpartum time was the most fun! It was five A.M. when he was finally born, just about twenty-four hours from the time I began early labor. For most of the morning, Kevin and Sean and I slept together in the double bed where I had given birth.

At regular intervals a nurse would come in quietly to check the baby's and my vital signs. There was no need for him to go to a nursery! He was staying nice and warm, skin to skin with his mom and dad.

Later in the day a nurse brought in a baby bathtub on a cart and showed us how to bathe him. I confess I was preoccupied with my bottom and my contracting uterus, so the bathing lesson was mostly received by Kevin.

We stayed in our suite that night and made a leisurely departure around noon the next day. I was a little sad to leave! Difficult labor notwithstanding, it had been a wonderful stay and I was very proud to have given birth by my own efforts, with no drugs to jeopardize my baby.

It was mentioned that if I had been at a traditional hospital—

because of my long labor and slow progress—Sean probably would have been born by cesarean section.

We decided to make a little brother or sister for Sean when he was about two. We were living in Houston then and I had been going to a certified nurse-midwife for my gynecological care for a few months. I knew that she was doing home births, but I wasn't sure if we wanted to give up the security of the hospital.

On the other hand, I knew we would be unhappy in a traditional hospital setting, so I set about taking hospital tours before I was even "showing," to see if Houston offered any alternatives within hospitals. I was discouraged by what I found.

A key question for me was, "Will you let me keep my baby with me constantly?" The answer was always that there was a mandatory minimum nursery stay of four hours. Remembering how I felt about Sean at his birth, I couldn't imagine letting my baby be taken away.

If we could have, we would have liked to fly back to Ohio to birth at the birthing center again. That being out of the question, we decided to study up on home birthing. We felt more comfortable knowing that our caregiver was a certified nurse-midwife (CNM) as opposed to a lay midwife. I knew that many lay midwives are highly qualified, but I felt I had no standard by which to assess them.

I knew that a CNM was a registered nurse with further education in normal birthing, was licensed by the American College of Nurse-Midwives, and was supported by one or more physicians who would serve as backup care in an emergency. The cost was surprisingly low, especially considering how much time our midwife and her partner spent with us.

We were screened at our first visit with respect to such factors as obstetrical and general health history, current health status, whether or not we were smokers, and our degree of motivation to take responsibility for the birth in terms of nutrition, exercise, and preparation of an emergency backup plan.

We attended a series of six classes at the midwives' office

where we discussed the questions and concerns of the clients. I felt those classes lacked preparation for labor itself. Only one session was spent discussing relaxation and other techniques for coping with labor. We used the book *Special Delivery*, by Rahima Baldwin, as a manual. It was very informative.

We arranged for a couple with whom we were close friends to come to the birth as Sean's caretakers. He knew and trusted them, and we felt he would be comfortable with them. We prepared him to attend the birth by taking him to a film at the midwives' office and by talking with him often about what it would be like. We planned to let him watch or not, depending on how he handled it. Our friends, Joan and Tom, could take him out if he wanted.

My contractions started coming at fairly regular intervals around six A.M. on March 26, 1984, four days prior to my due date. We called Joan and Tom to warn them that this might be the day, and to ask them to call in periodically from work and school.

Late in the morning my husband remembered that we had invited a little boy and his mother to come over for lunch and to play with Sean. It was another client of our midwife who was expecting a few weeks later. We decided to go ahead with the visit!

They came over and we had a fun time. I was still in early labor and it was exciting to share it with them. As they were leaving, around three P.M., Joan and Tom arrived, laden with all the supplies we had asked them to bring—all their pillows, their tape recorder, and some other items.

Joan and I went for a little walk. I decided to go by the local ice cream shop. No sooner did I start eating my ice cream cone than the effect of the walking kicked in. I started having contractions that caused me to stop and hold on to something, and I really had to concentrate on breathing and relaxing. I didn't want to face the walk of about two blocks back to my apartment, but we took it slowly and it was okay. I count my labor as really starting then, at about four P.M.

Tom heated up a casserole I had made ahead of time and we all had some dinner. The midwife arrived with her six-week-old baby and had dinner with us. I folded Sean's diapers, chatted, and generally enjoyed myself.

I think it was only the last two or three hours that were really intense. I was not aware of it, but Sean was bathed and put to bed as I focused on Kevin's eyes and we chanted together, "Open, open, open." I tried to visualize my cervix opening and the baby coming through, as I breathed through the contractions.

I usually hung around Kevin's neck, and he applied pressure to my lower back with his hands. For us, eye contact was very helpful.

Eventually, while I was sitting on the toilet and he was squatting in front of me, I began to cry. I said, "I don't know if I can do this anymore"—the classic statement of a woman in transition.

I decided to lie down and rest a bit. By now it was something like nine-thirty P.M. I rolled over to get comfortable and splash! My water broke. The midwife checked my dilation: nine centimeters! Wow! I had raced through the last four centimeters. No wonder it seemed so intense and I was feeling so uncertain.

I remember fearing the onset of those last contractions, calling to Kevin, "It's coming!" so he would be there with me. He was so steady, so wonderful. I remember thinking over and over, I love you, I love you.

When it was time to push, I must not have had an overpowering urge, because I asked if I should. I had pillows propping up my back, one foot resting on the leg of one of the midwives on my left, and the other foot . . . I don't know where. Second stage is hazy in my memory.

The phone rang, everyone told Joan to answer it, and then the contraction came that brought the baby's head out, as Joan was telling the midwife's husband that she would have to call him back. My breathing was very fast and panicky, which I know now was not good. I let out a loud yell.

The next contraction followed very quickly and the shoulders were born. The cord was around the baby's neck two times, but it was swiftly and calmly clamped and cut by the midwives and there was no problem.

A little girl! She gave a lusty cry and I took her in my arms right away. It was 10:03 P.M. Sean was asleep. It was peaceful. We admired her and talked in hushed tones as we waited for the placenta.

In a few minutes Joan appeared with a plate of fruit and cheese and crackers. I ate most of it by myself! I felt really good. This time I had only a very slight tear, not even first degree, and no stitches were necessary. My friend Joan, who is a nurse, was laughing when I got up and started taking pictures of everyone else. Having only witnessed hospital births in nursing school, she did not expect a newly delivered mother to be up and about. In the photos I look worn out, but happy.

Around two A.M., when Colleen was four hours old, Sean woke up for some reason and came in to meet his sister. Unexpectedly, Joan had spent more time caring for the midwife's baby than for Sean, since his bedtime had occurred earlier in the evening.

I was so happy to have birthed at home. I have warm, fond memories of that night.

Sandi Gutierrez Heimsath
Austin, Texas

♡ *Inspired by her mother-in-law, who had five natural births, Sandi Heimsath treats birth, in the story that follows, as a joyous challenge. She and her husband greet the whole experience with enthusiasm. The only minor glitches in the process occur when an officious doctor, uneasy with the role of supporting actor as the birth unfolds, causes Sandi's self-confidence to fail her momentarily.*

My mother never told me anything about her birth experiences and it seemed to me as though her lips were firmly cemented shut during my first pregnancy. I never asked her anything and she never offered anything.

I do remember one time when I was little, she did say, "When you were born, I almost died," and she looked at me with accusing eyes. She refused to elaborate other than to say that she had had to have a C-section. I mentally shrugged, knowing that I probably didn't have much control over the circumstances of my birth, even though I *was* an active participant.

I grew up, therefore, assuming that, because my mother had had a difficult birth, that I would, no doubt, as well. I never bothered to question the inevitability of a C-section.

Where my Filipino family was silent about emotions and opinions, I had married into a family antithetical to my own. When I first met my husband and his family I was struck by the con-

174

stant din. There were endless stories told around the dinner table, and they found me an alert audience.

Ben's mother, Maryann, fascinated me most of all. Almost singlehandedly, she had raised five children while her husband grappled with the complexities of running his own architecture firm in an unstable economy.

Though she performed all the proper motherly duties of caring for her noisy brood, she still found time to start a darkroom in the basement and shoot and develop her own film and design and build her own stained-glass windows. She learned to design and build furniture, including the two little wooden beds that my two older children now sleep in each night.

I had heard from her eldest daughter that Maryann always had had natural childbirths and had nursed each child. Birth was perceived as a natural process, not something to be suffered through. I wondered at that attitude and how different it was from my own mother's. Perhaps everything was not genetically predetermined.

My mother-in-law's secondhand experiences were to become critical during my own pregnancy, birth, and the ensuing months. In hindsight I realize how heavily I relied, not on information that was consciously studied or my own mother, but on the experiences that were already implanted in my deep unconscious.

Pregnancy with our first child was blissfully uneventful. I walked around Back Bay and enjoyed private walks along the Charles River throughout the spring and, more slowly, in the summer. As my stomach grew and grew, my moods fluctuated wildly, just as the books said. "Hormones," said the books. "Hormones," sighed my husband.

One day in early September of 1984, hugely pregnant, I was quite ready to be on with the miraculous event. An afternoon set aside for elegant window shopping ended in a suspicious wet flow into my underwear, which I verified in the ladies' room of the Copley Hotel. Membrane break? Entirely possible, particularly since I was so close to my due date.

I called Ben from a pay phone. "I think we should go to the

hospital now. I'll meet you at home," I said, and promptly hung up. At last. It was going to begin. I walked home as briskly as I was capable, smiling the whole way.

Ben, who, at the time of the call, had been at his drafting desk, later told me of his disbelief: *"You're walking home???"* he said to the disconnected telephone.

The route to and from the hospital had been minutely scrutinized in advance and various routes planned. Everything hinged entirely upon whether or not a baseball game was being played at Fenway Park. In a sports-crazy town like Boston, no one in their right mind ever drove near Fenway before, during, or after a game, particularly if they were in a hurry. Thank goodness, Ben said to himself. no game. He would use the most direct route to the hospital, which would pass the front gate of Fenway Park.

By the time I strolled into the apartment, Ben was there, ready for anything—if not a bit miffed at what he thought was my flip manner. He waited for me to change my wet underwear but refused to wait for me to take off my nail polish. "Enough is enough." He wore a tight smile.

It was seven minutes from our door to the hospital emergency door. In the examination room off went the underwear, on went the hospital gown. On the second try the nurse succeeded in getting a sample that contained amniotic fluid.

"Yes, there is amniotic fluid and you'll be staying to safeguard against infection," she said. "You'll be moving to a recovery room until your contractions are stronger. During active labor you will be in a labor and delivery room. Chances are that you will be feeling some action late tonight or certainly tomorrow."

The room, with two beds, was empty, so we made ourselves at home. At the end of visiting hours Ben reluctantly left for home at a nurse's urging. "You'll need as much rest as possible," she said. It was the only time we had been apart since we had been married.

By early morning I began to feel "uncomfortable," much like

menstrual discomfort, in regions below. "Those are contractions. Your labor is beginning," said one of the nurses. "Oh," I said. No problem. If this was all it was, it wasn't going to be very bad at all.

Ben came at seven-thirty P.M., bearing the *Boston Globe,* the *Wall Street Journal,* and various magazines. "The apartment was so empty," he said.

Meanwhile, I was ready to begin my "special hospital book." My hospital book had been most carefully chosen, and, since labor with a first child usually took many hours, so the literature said, I fully expected to read a majority of Waugh's *Brideshead Revisited.*

Thus we remained that morning with the light pouring in from the plate-glass window, reading, until just before noon. I was having to look up more frequently from *Brideshead Revisited* to breathe through the contractions. *In and out and in and out and in and out* at the first level of breathing.

"Let's move you down to L and D," said the nurse. And so on to the wheelchair to the new wing of Labor and Delivery. I remember clearly one beautiful watercolor of an orchid whose soft colors bled all the way to the edge of the page—hanging on the newly painted walls in L and D. By the time the contractions were firmly established, we had walked along those walls around and around and around, stopping only occasionally to concentrate on a particularly intense contraction. Ben would time the contraction from my mark and I would concentrate on the building wave.

"These are muscles," I would say to myself through each contraction. "The muscles are working to move the baby down and the closer and stronger they get, the sooner the baby will be here." It was my mantra. It gave structure to the process. Ironically, later, a nurse would say exactly the same words to me.

Sometimes we would come back to that room with the break-away bed with its metal this and that. I remember very clearly the clock and its stiff jerking second hand, and the rocking chair that looked big enough to hold an elephant, and, since I was an elephant, I sat in that rocking chair, feet flat on the floor, and rocked.

By late afternoon, miles later, a nurse came in and checked me with a gloved hand. "If you like, you may try taking a shower," she said. At the time I was concentrating on a contraction. Speaking to Ben, she said, "She will not be able to use the whirlpool, since her membranes are broken, but, as long as you stay with her, you may use the shower. It will help her relax."

The shower was wonderful. Ben held a shower spray over my back and neck and shoulders and the water flowed all over me and his running shoes. I stood forever, aware only of the pinpoints of water. The nurse was right. It really was relaxing.

And then suddenly I began to feel dizzy. "I feel dizzy," I said. "Get me back to the room, please." Gown on, towel on hair. Head pounding and uneven movements, leaning heavily on Ben's arm.

The shower had indeed served the purpose of hastening dilation. When the nurse checked again, I had progressed from 5 centimeters to almost 8.5 centimeters.

"We're almost there," we said to each other and smiled between breathing, counting, and contractions.

We were working as a unit, Ben and I. We were locked together. During the last hour, we were lying on that breakaway bed with the belt of the fetal monitor adjusted precariously around my middle that was tightening and relaxing of its own accord. Ben was focused on me, helping me breathe by breathing himself loudly, very close on my face so I could see him as I had taken off my contact lenses. We were working together even as the tempo increased.

"Just a little rim left before you can push," said the nurse. "Keep going. You're doing great."

At some point during that last fuzzy hour, my doctor, with a bald head and a fringe of white hair, had entered the room and was sitting quietly in the back, just watching. Finally he stood up and said, "This is your last chance for an epidural. Do you want one?"

I was stunned. Epidural. Wasn't that if you couldn't handle the pain anymore? Wasn't everything going just the way it was supposed to? I looked first at Ben, then at the nurse, and then back at Ben again. For the first time I felt unsure.

Ben and the nurse were on either side of me, looking at me as I lay inclined on the bed. The doctor could not see either of their faces. The nurse was looking at me very intently and very, very slightly shaking her head.

The next contraction came and went and I forgot to breathe. The nurse rose quickly and escorted the doctor outside, speaking to him in a low voice. She returned at once. "I told him to give us fifteen minutes. Let's get this baby born."

And then, there it was. An animal urge. The books called it "the need to push," but they never discussed the intensity with which it came.

"Don't push yet!" said the nurse.

"Quick, Sandi," said Ben. "Blow it away." He blew, puffing up his cheeks like the old images of the North Wind in Greek mythology.

"Blow into your cheeks," he said. "Don't push."

Don't push? I thought, HA! *How, how* could you not push? I inadvertently pushed again during the next contraction and, for that moment, I felt that I wasn't on top of the situation.

But then, almost as suddenly, the nurse said, "You're ready now. *Push. Now.*"

Push? ALL RIGHT!

At the nurse's suggestion, we tried squatting during the contractions to make use of gravity to bring the baby out. At the next contraction, Ben and the nurse would quickly pull me to my feet in a squatting position. The vigorous activity was just what I needed and I remember being pleased that I could move as quickly as I did each time. I thought of the young wife of the Chinese farmer in *The Good Earth* and how she would deliver her babies alone, squatting over a bucket.

Pushing was an unspeakable relief. I took all the energy that was spent for the past few hours in not taking part in my body's activities and pushed with all my will.

And then he was there again. The doctor whose name even now I cannot remember.

"The baby will be born now if you have an episiotomy," he said, standing in the middle of the floor, blinking behind thick glasses. It was as though he wanted to be involved in the birth and now there was almost no time left.

"He is right," said the nurse. "You are beginning to tear. It'll be a simple cut and you will heal cleanly." She was speaking almost apologetically.

Tearing? Oh, that was the burning sensation during the end of the last contraction.

"All right."

And then the doctor was giving the orders, almost whistling at the task. Instruments, the cloths, the table, the stool. When the cut came, I had the impression of slicing steak and I didn't like it at all. But there was no time to think because everything happened all at once.

During the actual moment of birth, everything seemed to pour out. There was a sliding, sliding, and then an incredibly heavy weight moved down and through and out in the space of one breath. And it was done.

"My baby. My baby." Our hearts were so full. We couldn't say anything more.

And then the baby, wrapped in a towel, was placed on my chest. Life. She was moving against me for the first time, warm and wet. Ben and I, heads close together, were grinning like idiots, smiling and smiling, cooing and cooing.

"She'll think we're a two-headed hydra," said Ben.

And, when the business of administering the Apgar test was finished, the nurses came without number to chortle and delight at the new child. ("Look how tiny her wrists and ankles are!!") I smiled at that exclamation. Of course, she would have a slender form. Wasn't she half Asian?

I was struck by the dichotomy between what was happening with the sewing of the incision below and the ensuing euphoria above. A clear division of heaven and hell. I can still remember the tugging of the needle and the sutures, and the top of the doctor's bald head, bent to the task of repairing the point of exit.

Later, I would feel as though the area was crudely repaired with the coarsest of knitting worsted, as sitting to nurse was quite painful. The episiotomy took longer to recover from than any other element of the birth itself, and I recall being irritated that the books never spoke about its aftermath.

Beyond the excitement of the beautiful new child in our arms, I remember being *incredibly* hungry. I had eaten no solids since the night before, only Jell-O and clear sodas. Even Ben, perpetually hungry, had simply forgotten to eat.

One of the nurses went to see whether she could cajole two trays of food from the cafeteria, which was ready to close down. We ate dry institutional food with great gusto.

In those months after Kristin's birth, I had many chances to think about my mother's attitude toward her own birth experiences. Resentful and afraid, even in retrospect, she was a product of the fifties in America where birth was supposed to be a misty blur. When she saw her granddaughter for the first time, her awe that the birth had been without complication, without drugs or forceps, without fear, was transparent.

The most delightful revelation for me was my father's behavior and attitude. He was completely unafraid of holding the newborn, of walking her to and fro, of making faces at her, but, most surprising of all, he was completely unembarrassed about my nursing.

It seemed incongruous, coming from a family that had always been obsessively modest. But, then again, it made perfect sense. He was the eldest son of twelve children, whose mother was endlessly pregnant, from a loud and jolly family that included cousins, nieces, nephews, aunts, and uncles, that seemed to be always growing—of course, he would look upon birth as the most natural function of all. And, no doubt, he had seen his own mother nursing sibling after sibling. For him, not so far removed from the Old World traditions, "natural childbirth" and nursing the baby was the obvious way to do things. In the end, it was my father who quietly gave us the positive support that we needed as new parents.

And the final gift that the nurse gave us—the woman who, for at least an hour or two, had joined us in the center of the universe—were her parting words: "You both are a fantastic team."

Robbie Davis-Floyd
Austin, Texas

♡ *Robbie Davis-Floyd has a Ph.D. in anthropology and folklore and has published a number of professional papers, many of them on the subject of childbirth. One of her papers is entitled "Birth as an American Rite of Passage." Certainly, for Robbie, her second birth became a very dramatic "rite of passage."*

I have given birth twice: the first time to a daughter by cesarean section in the hospital, the second time to a son by vaginal birth in my home. The two experiences are as different as dark and light, day and night, but the lesson that I learned from each experience was the same: to trust myself and what I *know*.

The first time I didn't; the second time I did, but even then there were moments when I lost that trust, and I can see now that each of those moments, although painful to live through, was a gift, a mirror there to show me that what the midwives say is true: there is an inner knowing in us; it's there and all we have to do is be silent and listen.

In 1979, when I was pregnant with my first child, I *knew* the baby would be a girl. I *knew* that without a flicker of doubt. I bought only little girl clothes and furnishings at the baby store, and I planned to name her Peyton Elizabeth—my mother's maiden name plus my middle name. People laughed at me when I told them, no, I had not had an amniocentesis—I just "knew" that she was a girl. So I learned not to say much about it, and it didn't occur to me to trust myself to know more.

When I became pregnant again, four years later, I *knew* the baby was a boy. I bought only little boy clothes and agreed with my husband, Robert, that he would be the one to choose the name. Robert had his own kind of "knowing"—when I gave birth, he was sitting on the bed behind me; the midwives put the baby in my arms; Robert put his arms around me and the baby, looked down at him, and called him Jason.

I was amazed. It was not a name we had ever discussed. Robert said it just "came up to him from the baby," and he *knew* it was right.

There were other things that I *knew* this second time, and that, unlike the first time, I trusted—that the baby boy would weigh exactly 10 pounds (he did), that my labor would be three days long (it was), and that I would need a totally supportive environment that included warm water to get through it (I did).

The contractions for my second birth began around ten A.M., just like the first time, only this was four and a half years later (January 18, 1984). I straightened up the house, like the first time, and then I went to the store to lay in supplies for the people we expected: two midwives, who were wanted for their expertise; Rima, a rebirther and very dear friend, who would be in charge of "directing the energies"—a critical function, as it turned out; Peter, a photographer who was studying midwifery and loved to photograph births; and Phillip, a close friend who had asked to be present for this birth. It would be his job to keep the hot tub filled and the water warm.

I returned home to the rhythmic ringing of hammers on wood—my husband Robert and several of his friends were climbing around on top of the temporary room they had constructed around the hot tub, which we had placed just outside our front door.

I couldn't believe my eyes. In the time I had been gone, they had practically finished the room. Double sheets of plastic had been nailed across the wooden supports to serve as walls, which had been further insulated with almost every blanket and quilt in the house.

Truly, my husband had constructed a "womb room" for me— his labor had prepared a special space for mine. Although it was the dead of winter—19 degrees outside—with all those blankets on the walls and the space heater going, that room stayed as warm as a real womb for three days!

Around ten P.M., the midwives came and checked me and unpacked their bags and went to bed. They said, "Don't get in a hurry! This is going to take a long time—you're not even in real labor yet. You're only four centimeters!" And that scared me because it was just like the first time when I was "stuck" at four centimeters in the hospital for hours.

So, around midnight, looking for some comfort and reassurance, I got into the bathtub (the hot tub wasn't ready) and stayed there in the warm water, with Rima rubbing my back, for a long time.

The midwives got up periodically to take turns sitting with me while I stayed in the bathtub. And they told me, over and over, not to get my expectations up because I still wasn't in real labor.

One midwife said, "Honey, I know it hurts, I know it feels to you like real labor, but these contractions are just very early ones. They are going to have to get a lot longer, a lot stronger, and a lot closer together before you're going to be in real labor."

And I didn't really believe her, because the contractions were just like the ones I had had the first time, and the nurses hadn't said anything about them being "early labor." It wasn't until day three that I finally understood the difference.

By three A.M., everyone in the house was asleep but me. I had dried off and climbed into bed to snuggle with Robert. He dozed off blissfully, but I lay awake and breathed through contractions all night. Around seven A.M., Phillip came and told me that the hot tub was ready.

It had taken hours to fill, because we hadn't installed a water circulation system of any kind (we had been able to find a used hot tub for only $300, but the machinery to hook it up was too expensive). Phillip and Robert were having to fill it with a hose connected to the hot water heater, which could only produce enough hot water to run for a few minutes at a time.

So Phillip had been heroically augmenting this by heating huge kettles full of water on the stove and then carrying them to the womb room and dumping them in. He presided over that kettle-laden stove for three days; his labor, too, was an essential ingredient in mine.

I was thrilled that the tub I had wanted to labor in so much was finally ready. I have always felt most blissful floating in water or soaking in a hot shower, and most peaceful looking at water, whether in oceans, lakes, rivers, or swimming pools. I swam throughout my pregnancies—the pool was the only place where I felt weightless, totally supported by my environment.

I slipped eagerly out of bed without waking Robert and, in the middle of a contraction, sank into my hot tub's celestial blue, welcoming warmth, feeling just like Eve in Eden. The water inside and the water outside of me seemed one.

The midwives got me out of the tub to check me after they woke up. I was still four centimeters, so they told me to call them when the contractions got stronger, and went home to take care of their children! I got back in the tub and stayed there most of the morning.

I spent hours that day having contractions in the tub's warmth—I even ate lunch in there. Peter had made me a big sandwich with sprouts and other nutritious ingredients and a smoothie-milkshake made of fruits, protein powder, and juices.

After noon my contractions began to space out more and more until finally around two P.M. (about the time I was waiting for the OB to come back from church to do the C-section before), the contractions stopped altogether. I was out of the tub and dressed by now and I was shaking with fear because I didn't know what was going to happen or how to deal with it.

I told Rima that I wanted her to do something to make me feel better. I trusted her so completely—I felt that it was within her power to release me from this paralyzing fear that I wouldn't make it and would end up in the hospital with another C-section. So Rima, her husband, and a massage therapist who was also present staged a ritual for me.

Rima put a tall candle on the floor and we all made a circle around it, and, at Rima's direction, we started stating our fears, one by one, and then throwing them into the fire to symbolically release them. Everyone present participated, and the fact that Rima and her husband were so unself-conscious and natural about the whole thing made it easier for me not to feel silly about throwing things I couldn't see into a tiny candle flame.

The ritual was very cathartic, especially for me, because one of the fears I had was that I couldn't communicate with Robert, that he would think I was being ridiculous during labor and wouldn't support me. But when he started doing the ritual like everyone else and stating his own fears, I felt a sudden rush of openness between us, and after the ritual was over, I went to him crying and he really opened up to me and held me for a long time, just standing there in the living room in our magic circle.

After that, I suddenly realized that the hour when the cesarean had happened, four years ago, was long past, and that I had finally entered completely uncharted territory. I was free! The past pattern no longer had the power to map itself onto my present experience! My relief was overwhelming.

I got into bed to rest, and the massage therapist gave me a wonderful and relaxing all-over body massage, during which the contractions began again, coming about every ten minutes. They stayed at that rate all that night, so I was even able to sleep quite well for about four or five hours.

A contraction awoke me at dawn. I felt tremendously refreshed and extremely grateful for such a wonderful sleep. The contractions were still coming every ten minutes, so I ate a good breakfast and got back into the tub, which Phillip had managed to keep warm for me overnight.

Soon the contractions picked up in intensity. By noon they

were coming three minutes apart, and I was in serious distress. The midwives came back, unpacked, and checked me and announced with great glee that I was now five centimeters! They said, "Now, you're *really* in labor!"

By midafternoon I was arching my back in the tub during contractions, pulling on Robert's arms, and pushing against the side of the tub with my feet. It was the only way I could stand the pain without going nuts. The contractions felt like one person was stabbing me in the stomach with a knife and twisting it, while another person was stabbing me in the back with a long sword and pushing on it.

The pain was so overwhelming that I vowed I would never again harshly judge a woman for asking for anesthesia to avoid feeling such pain. I "got it" that you have to be *completely* committed to taking the experience as it comes.

I found myself repeatedly envisioning a window in the sky. I kept thinking, If I could just step through that window, I'd be in Tahiti. Later Jane English (who wrote a book, *Different Doorway: Adventure of a Cesarean Born,* about her experiences with remembering her cesarean birth) told me that the "window in the sky" was my programming from my own cesarean birth, in which I had indeed been "rescued" through such a window!

In the midst of such pain as I would never have believed I could survive, I had a problem with my midwives. When I hit active labor, Phillip had gone to pick up my daughter, Peyton (age four and a half), from her gymnastics class. She didn't want to take any chances on missing the birth.

After she arrived, she spent a lot of time sitting on a stool at the edge of the hot tub, eating potato chips and watching me labor. Often she would help me chant during contractions. Robert and I had been chanting for hours, and I was truly impressed by how much of the pain could be channeled through me and out by a powerful sound like "Raaaaaaaaam."

But, during one particularly sharp, twisting, and lengthy contraction, I decided to try an experimental scream to see if that worked any better to release the pain. When I screamed, Peyton clapped her hands over her ears and ran out of the womb room crying. Then one of the midwives came in and bawled me out for screaming and scaring my daughter. I couldn't believe it.

Peyton and I had spent lots of time talking about all the strange things I might do in labor, the weird sounds I might make. I knew that she would be okay about the scream and, anyway, it hadn't worked as well as chanting so I had no intention of doing it again. But here was my midwife, ruining the few short minutes of rest I had between these incredibly long, back-to-back contractions.

I started to cry and I told her that I was tired of her negativity (this was the fourth negative thing she had laid on me since my labor began) and that I just wanted her to be positive for the rest of the birth. She left the room in a huff, and then the other midwife came in and started to lecture me about being mean to the first one.

I was stunned. I felt like somebody had put a lid on the hot tub. Here were the two women I needed the most to support me, and they were both mad at me and telling me so. I was so upset that the labor stopped. I couldn't afford to lose them so I begged the second one to forgive me. She got off on a tangent about who could she ask to come in to replace the first one who had told me not to scare my daughter. Once again, I couldn't believe this was happening.

I had to tell her, no, I don't want to replace anyone, I just wanted them both to be positive and supportive and not yell at me. I felt like a three-year-old apologizing to Mommy. Midwives are often very powerful women. I knew that later I would find this incident hard to forgive, but, for right now, we had to get on with the birth.

In desperation I looked at Rima, and I said, "Rima! You're in charge of the energies here! Do something to get us past this!" And she did. She began chanting in a very soothing and beautiful tone. Robert and the second midwife and Peyton (who had indeed recovered quickly) picked up the chant, and then the first midwife came back in and picked it up, and so did Phillip and Peter.

They encircled the hot tub, holding hands and chanting. My contractions resumed in synchrony, stronger than ever, and I chanted my pain and my joy at the restoration of our precious harmony, and the womb room sounded and resounded like a Catholic cathedral.

After an hour or so more, I had to get out of the tub to go to the bathroom. When I finished, I noticed that the bed had been freshly made up with my favorite sheets and quilt to receive my newborn and me. It looked so inviting! I dived onto it in the middle of a contraction and suddenly everything changed.

Without any preplan, I simply gave up and surrendered to the overwhelming force of the contractions. Until that moment, I had been struggling to maintain myself as separate from the pain, but suddenly I just let that effort go, and I said to the pain, "Take me, I'm yours."

Then a miracle happened. I felt that I, body and soul, *became* the pain, and, once there was no more separation between me and the pain, there was no more pain! I lay there on the bed, utterly relaxed, breathing softly, in total peace. I could hear the midwives whispering, "Good, that's really good."

I could only maintain that altered state as long as no one divided my attention, so I lost it when people started to speak to me. (If I ever labor again, I will seek that state for the whole labor, now that I know it truly exists. But, for me, given my past history of trying to control, it's a real miracle that I achieved it at all this time!)

Unaware that I was in transition, feeling only that with each contraction I would surely fly through the roof or leap through the window, I was truly amazed that the house did not simply explode as a result of this tremendous force inside of me.

I crouched on the bed in terror and panic and panted to Robert that I could not do it, that I thought I would die. His strong hands grasped my shoulders, and his calm voice said firmly, "Focus on me." I peered at him through a fog of agony and fear and his liquid golden brown eyes poured strength, peace, and love into me.

Suddenly I heard Rima, who had been rubbing my back, exclaim, "Oh my!" and I felt her stand up. My waters, intact until that moment, had broken and anointed both Rima and my best quilt. Truly, there was water everywhere with this birth!

Soon (around six-thirty P.M.) the midwives asked to check me again. I couldn't believe my ears. They said, "Robbie! You're ten centimeters! You're ready to push! Where do you want to have your baby?"

I blinked at them in confusion. "Baby? Oh! In the tub. In the hot tub!" I don't remember getting there. The next thing I knew, Robert, swimsuit-clad, was sitting on the molded seat inside the hot tub, while I, naked, crouched on his knees and tried to find a good position for pushing.

Now I have to tell you something that is very personal, but I am going to include it here because it was wonderful and, if you know that I did it, maybe that will give you the license you need to break a few social rules and have this pleasure, too. In spite of the fact that our hot tub was surrounded with people, and that one of the midwives in her bathing suit was right in there with us, I turned facing Robert and I whispered in his ear, "Please rub my clitoris!"

The energy that I was feeling was intense, and, accompanying the intense pain of the contraction, was an equally intense sexual desire. In the hospital he wouldn't even get in the shower with me, but here in his own home he overcame his embarrassment and complied with my request. Very quickly, I had an incredible orgasm! It was an island of ecstasy in the midst of an ocean of pain.

You can bet that, if I ever give birth again, I will be wanting to do a lot more of that sort of thing, and I will make sure that Robert and I have the privacy for labor that will enhance the passionate nature of the birth experience.

About twenty minutes into the pushing, the midwife (who had just finished reading *Williams Obstetrics*) got very nervous because the heart tones were dropping, and I heard her mutter under her breath something about going to the hospital if they got any lower.

I looked at her through the haze of pain and energy required for pushing, and my entire body suddenly flooded with the absolute certainty that my baby was fine. I *knew* there was no danger. I leaned forward and opened my mouth to communicate the wonder and the certainty of this *knowing* to my midwife, but another contraction seized me in its bony grip and I was unable to speak.

So the midwife, still nervous, asked me to get out of the tub and push on the toilet. She felt that the baby was stuck on the ischial spines and was worried that his oxygen supply might be compromised.

I complied. Later I asked the midwife if it would have made any difference to her perceptions of the danger if I had been able to tell her what I *knew*. She said, "Oh, yes, absolutely! I have learned to trust birthing women to have that connection with the baby and with their bodies. If you had told me, I would have relaxed and trusted you."

But I do not regret the experience of getting out of the tub, even though I had planned to give birth in the water, because the second most important lesson of the birth happened to me as I ran down the hall to the bathroom. The walls of the hall, and all the other people running down it with me, suddenly fell away, and I was completely alone in a universe of my own making.

And I *got it* that this time there would be no rescue. There was no white knight in shining armor to rescue me from the dragon of pain. No one and no thing could do this for me. It was totally and completely up to me. And I had set it all up so that it would come to this existential moment of realization that *I had to do this thing*. The only way out of it was through it, and *I* had to do it.

I put my heart and soul and every muscle in my body into pushing the baby past the ischial spines—the "stuck place" the midwives called it. The pain was unbelievable! But it was tempered by my newfound determination. *I* was going to do this thing, no matter how much it hurt. There was tremendous relief in that commitment.

There was also relief in my subsequent discovery, at long last, of how to push. I had been straining the wrong muscles and I finally figured out that, if I bore down from my diaphragm, I could actually gauge the proper angle to push from and into. After that, my pushes became much more effective.

After twenty minutes of pushing on the toilet, the midwives announced that the baby was past the "stuck place," and his heart rate was back up. I accepted being on the toilet as useful at the time, but I was not at all happy about it. So I was very relieved to get out of that ignominious position.

It's strange—even though my official plan had been to give birth in the water, I *knew* from the beginning that I was not actually going to do that. I knew that I needed the water for labor, but my bed has always been my "safe place." So, when I got up from the toilet, I instinctively headed for the bed.

Robert piled on first, with his back to the wall, and I got between his legs, semi-upright, leaning against him. It took me then about fifty minutes to push out my baby. Here is what that was like:

For a long time there is only pain and pushing into the pain. Then a sudden sharp burn intrudes on the deeper pain that I have almost gotten used to, and, taken completely by surprise, I cry out. Peyton, gazing raptly from her bird's-eye view on a high stool at the foot of the bed, throws her hands over her ears for an instant, then takes them off again, relieved to see that I am back to my guttural grunts and moans.

And then the midwife's voice says, "Reach down. Reach your hand down." And I reach down—what am I reaching for? And my hand encounters a head—warm, wet, enormous. I will never forget that sensation—it is imprinted on my hand's palm and my heart's memories. And I rest between contractions, cradling my baby's head in my hand.

I am in joy and at peace, but the midwives are concerned. Something about shoulder dystocia. When are they going to get off it, I wonder. I *know* that all is well. But I can sense their anxiety and I understand, so I willingly forsake my peace and push for them, not waiting for the next contraction.

If I don't get the baby out fast, they will turn me over on my hands and knees and I can feel my body rebel against the thought of any change in position. So I galvanize again—a deep breath, an internal focus on that muscle in my diaphragm, a precise gauging of the angle of pressure, and . . .

I have tried but I cannot describe the overwhelming relief and release I experienced when the baby suddenly flew out—on film all we have of that instant is his body's blur. I sank back into Robert's arms, carrying with me the impression of my newborn lying on the bed, asleep! no less, after all that—so peaceful. I *knew* him. I knew he was okay—just taking his own time to come to terms with this sudden change in dimensions.

But the midwives didn't know, so they woke him up and fussed him, trying to suction the meconium out. I didn't want to pick Jason up right away. I just wanted to stare at him, to take two or three minutes to get used to the overwhelming relief of no more pain, to come to an integration of the suddenness of this transition that had thrust both of us into a different dimension of life.

But the midwives wouldn't have it. They thrust him crying into my arms and started a long cycle of telling me what to do— try breastfeeding in this position, no, that one, try patting him, try turning him over. Too much noise!

I did what they said but felt increasing frustration, which was hard to integrate with the overwhelming gratitude I was feeling toward them for their very evident and much-needed skills. I couldn't get a sense of what Jason needed with all that going on.

After about half an hour of their fussing, Jason was still crying and the midwives finally left us to be alone. Then I held Jason up in front of me and I silently asked what he needed. Instantly I *sensed* that he needed to be in the water. I asked Peter, our photographer, to fill up the baby bathtub with warm tap water and put it on the bed.

As soon as Robert and I lowered Jason into the tub, he stretched out his little body to its fullest extension, opened his eyes, and looked at all of us, pulled my finger into his mouth and sucked it vigorously, and then suddenly went limp in the water in total relaxation, all his tension gone. He has been an extremely mellow child ever since, even-tempered and easy to soothe.

For me to give birth at home required a complete shift in beliefs, from reliance on the knowledge of others to reliance on my own *knowing,* from separation and detachment from my body to full integration with it, from assigning to others responsibility for my life to accepting that responsibility fully myself.

This shift is a process that was not completed before the birth and is not complete now, for these things that I have been learning are the goals of many thousands that embark on paths of spiritual learning and growth. For me, both of my births were steps along that path.

Henri Childers
Houston, Texas

♡ *Henri Childers thought she was completely committed to natural childbirth before her first child was born in 1985. Afterward, she changed her mind.*

We had thought we were the most prepared couple to ever have a baby. We had read books—all of the books. For months, I had haunted bookstores and libraries to find anything about conceiving, pregnancy, and childbirth. The back of my car looked like a bookmobile and I was sure I was getting suspicious glances from some of the librarians who had seen me pacing the same shelves for weeks on end. We had attended classes, especially the natural childbirth classes, and were convinced that that was the best way to have a child.

In our quest for the perfect childbirth experience, we had discovered *Husband-Coached Childbirth* by Robert A. Bradley, M.D., and had become so excited about his down-to-earth approach that I had written to California to find a local coach-teacher. For several months we had sat around on the teacher's living room floor with six other large-bellied couples (in most cases, just the women) and had listened to horror stories of what the medical profession was trying to force on unsuspecting and uneducated parents-to-be.

We were not going to be a pushover for the system and diligently practiced relaxing and breathing while we continued reading. We were ready—or so we thought.

The due date was January 13th, but that was my birthday and I had said I hoped it would be later. I really didn't want to share my birthday. I got my wish. At exactly 12:05 A.M. on the 14th, the first contraction woke me.

This was no Braxton-Hicks; this was a real contraction. The difference was immediately recognizable. By six A.M., we decided to make that long-anticipated call to the OB. As soon as we had called and waked him, the contractions stopped. I had heard about babies with a sense of humor, but I didn't think the doctor would be quite so amused, so by eight A.M. I called his office to cancel our arrival and lay down to resume my nap.

Already the baby did not want me to sleep. As soon as I quieted down, he started pushing again. By two P.M. we decided we had been at home long enough and were ready for some expert opinions. We called the hospital to let them know we were on our way.

We had preregistered so we went promptly to our floor of the hospital and settled in our "labor room." Thinking back on that ten- by fifteen-foot space, "closet" would have been a more accurate description. Henry stayed just long enough to get me undressed (how very like a man) before he was off to the office.

Remembering our training, I climbed down from the bed and took to the hallways, feeling very foolish indeed. Every ten minutes or so, I would have to stop, lean heavily against a wall or chair during a contraction, and wait for the room to stop churning. The worst part was having so many solicitous strangers stop to offer assistance. However, we were many, many hours from transition.

Henry returned around five P.M. to find that very little progress had been made. There had been some dilation but it was so slow. By seven P.M. we had made it to five-plus centimeters. After a long discussion (no, we didn't want drugs; no, we didn't want the water broken), the decision was made that we would be better off at home where I might be able to relax and get some sleep. The doctor sent four Seconals (sleeping pills) and instructed Henry to get some food in me, then give me two, then two more later if the first two didn't work.

On the way home, again Henry stopped by his office. I still have the most vivid memory of lying in the back seat, moaning and cursing his strong work ethic. I was miserable and now seriously believe I was just beginning to hallucinate. By the time we got home (a good forty-minute drive, even at that time of night), I was totally unable to get out of the back seat and do not remember getting to bed at all.

I do remember Henry bringing me some chicken noodle soup and standing over me like a sergeant, demanding that I eat. I had the strongest urge to throw the whole tray at him, but felt too bad.

I started crying for the hospital and kept telling Henry that something was wrong, I shouldn't hurt this much and "Please call the doctor." At first, he didn't want to, but wanted to give the sleeping pills a chance. Finally, I gave him no options as I headed for the phone, so he reluctantly made the call and we were back in the car on our way to the hospital.

They had not even changed the sheets in our labor room; it felt like home. After a quick examination they announced that I had been going through transition, had advanced from six to nine-plus centimeters and that a baby should be here shortly. This was about ten or ten-thirty. They put Henry in his "greens" and we waited. Once again, nothing happened.

Though we had long insisted that letting nature take her course was the best way, we had to admit that I couldn't go on much longer. Henry and I had had several serious battles about drugs. I had been the strong proponent of "natural," but now I was insisting on anything they could do. I remember a nurse coming in with a shot (Demerol?) and having Henry argue to wait a little longer and me telling the nurse to ignore him. I was having this baby and I wanted something *now*.

The doctor came in to break the water, hoping that would help the baby pass into the canal. Every contraction was forcing the baby's heart rate seriously below the desired rate, so they kept switching me from side to side in an attempt to keep the baby from distress.

Shortly after the water was broken (I can still see the long instrument that looked so much like a knitting needle), everything stopped. They decided that I was so tense and tired that I was resisting the baby's attempts to come down the canal. Maybe an epidural would let me relax enough for the baby to come on down. I remember Henry's stony face in opposition as he left the room when the anesthesiologist came in to begin the epidural.

I don't remember pain as the anesthesiologist began probing for the right spot to begin the epidural. What I vividly remember was the tension that mounted in the labor room as everyone watched the monitor and saw the baby's heartbeat drop to a dangerous 54 beats per minute. The activity in the room quickened immediately as a normal heartbeat should be from 150 to 200. We were about to lose this baby after so many hours, weeks, and months of trying.

Without stopping to consult or discuss, the OB took one end of the table I was lying on and the anesthesiologist took the other end and they began to run down the hall toward the delivery room. They didn't have to explain to me what was happening. I knew the grave situation we were in and was crying for them to hurry. Along the way someone threw out to Henry that they were going for an emergency C-section.

In the delivery room many hands were moving at once as one quickly slopped orange antiseptic on my stomach while another strapped my arm to the immobilizing board to insert the IV catheter. My last conscious memory was, Oh, please hurry.

My next memory is the groggy certainty that I was dying. The effects of the anesthetic were sending my head sloshing into some outer region where I knew I had no control and felt I was losing a conscious part of me.

I remember a recovery room nurse trying to quiet me with the usual assurances that I was going to be all right, but that only made my demands for a priest more adamant. I was absolutely certain I was dying and somehow a priest was the last human being I wanted contact with. For a person who is not particularly religious (a believer, yes; religious, no), just hearing myself asking for a priest scared me more. Thankfully, I then receded back into deep unconsciousness.

The next time I woke up, I realized that I had regained a little self-control and immediately began calling the nurses to get me to a room. Along the way, they stopped by the nursery and brought this little white bundle to me and held up Kelly, our new son. Still groggy from all the drugs, I held out my hand for at least one touch and vaguely wondered why it looked like he was smiling at me.

Later, they explained that he had been born with an incomplete cleft lip. It was minor, no more than a wrinkle. The palate was fully intact and they couldn't find any other problems, so they assured me everything would work out fine. After coming so close to losing him, a little bummed-up lip didn't bother me at all. Besides, my nephew had been born twenty years before with a cleft *palate* and I remembered the many operations and many difficulties.

I thought, Well, if you have to have a birth defect, this is the one to have. One simple operation should be all we were faced with. I slept without worry.

At the time, Henry and I were so shaken by how close we had come to losing Kelly that we were just grateful everything had worked out in the end. Kelly was not breathing when he was first born and even his five-minute Apgar tests were not good. Now, he seems to be functioning normally without any residual effects from the long, difficult delivery.

Later, I would question many times how our OB let us get into such a tight spot. Taking some of the responsibility, I knew we had stressed to him how adamant we were about natural childbirth and had questioned him on every detail of delivery methods. He said that he had just tried to fulfill our wishes.

Yet, forty-nine hours from the onset of labor, particularly with an elderly primigravida and one so small, there should have been many red flags before we got to the emergency stage. After telling our story to other medical professionals and having time to really consider the whole case, I feel the doctor erred in not performing the C-section a lot sooner.

Though it is rare for a woman today not to be able to deliver vaginally, it does happen. Apparently, my birth canal region tapers off drastically toward the end and the baby's head simply could not go any further. When the epidural was administered, the region began to relax, which allowed the umbilical cord to slip between the baby's head and the pelvic bone, which immediately cut off the oxygen supply. The record officially reads "Prolapsed cord," without extraneous details as to why.

Even though the birth experience did not turn out the way we had wanted and planned for, somewhere near the end, I remember abandoning all the desires for *my* experience and began concentrating on the larger goal. We were there to have a baby, not just a satisfying experience for the parents. That realization changed my whole outlook about C-sections and drugs. Whatever was necessary was all right with me.

Here we are, three years later, faced with another round of delivery room jitters. When asked whether I am considering a vaginal delivery, I quickly give an emphatic "Not a chance."

Postscript: Henri's second son, Alex, was born without complications by scheduled cesarean in February 1988.

Peggy Eggers
Evergreen, Colorado

♡ *After three cesarean births, in 1976, 1977, and 1980, Peggy Eggers, herself a childbirth educator for many years, was absolutely determined that the birth of her fourth child in 1985 would be different. She was supported by family and friends and her own carefully nurtured and cultivated belief in herself, but also by the fortunate fact that, by the mid-eighties, the old dictum "Once a cesarean, always a cesarean" was finally being superseded by a more flexible approach to births after cesareans.*

A few years back, I took stock of my life. As an active wife, mother, and childbirth educator, I was certainly busy enough. The phone rang frequently; the calendar was full. Yet, deep within, I felt a nagging sense of the incomplete. Even after three children and a certification in childbirth education, I still didn't feel whole in my understanding of birth. You see, my children had all been born by cesarean.

Each time I taught about birth, I couldn't help but wonder if I was speaking truly. While I assumed an air of confident authority, my thoughts were full of insecurity. I knew my classes were providing people with valuable information, but my inner turmoil hung like a shadow over any feelings of success. Something was missing. Should I have another child to find out what it was?

As a first-time expectant mother, eight years before, I consider myself quite typical. Assimilating the pervading social opinion, I believed that if I ate my yogurt, exercised regularly, and practiced my breathing, I would assure myself of a truly rewarding birth experience.

My doctor had informed us that our child was presenting breech, but I didn't ask what that meant. I trusted that he was competent, my husband Peter was involved, and my body was healthy. Somehow I would "be delivered" to the tune of happy laughter and meaningful interchanges. Like so many other first-time mothers, I hadn't prepared for the unexpected.

I was in labor with Megan for many hours. Peter was sensitive to my needs and encouraged me through each contraction. When I was close to full dilatation, the doctor announced that the X-rays showed our child sitting Indian-style over my pelvic bones. The safest route of delivery would be by cesarean section. The father's attendance wasn't even considered at the time and Peter was whisked away as I was prepared for my surgical initiation into motherhood.

Plugged into an IV, catheter, and emotional turmoil, my body was laid out on the operating table. My face was brave, but my psyche shuddered. During surgery, I watched the doctors' heads and shoulders moving and bobbing and felt very detached.

I wanted to concentrate on the positive, but my clearest image was that they were carving a holiday turkey. I was present, yet unacknowledged.

There was certainly joy in Megan's birth (on January 31, 1976)—joy, relief, and a sense of awe. The image of our purple daughter being lifted from me into life is etched on my brain. But, no matter how strong and cheerful I tried to be afterward, it hurt. It hurt to move; it hurt to have to ask for help. Most of all, it hurt to say I'd had a cesarean birth.

I stuffed myself into my jeans and my doubts into oblivion. I refused help from friends, said everything was fine. Inside, I questioned myself, felt distant from my husband, incompetent as a mother.

A year later, the unexpected once more occurred—I was pregnant again. I was told that I had "cephalopelvic disproportion" (CPD), which meant that, should I carry this baby to term, his head wouldn't fit through my pelvis, and that I should prepare for another cesarean birth.

Fear motivated us to become acquainted with the options available and make our choices within those options. Two issues were important. First of all, I wanted to go into labor. The benefits were well documented[20] and, with all the other intervention, it seemed significant for the baby to at least determine his own birthday.

Second, we felt strongly that our birth should be shared. Policy at the hospital where our doctor worked forbade fathers in the delivery room for a cesarean birth. We gave him the option of changing his hospital's policy, going to another, or not having us as clients. He agreed to go to another hospital where Peter could be present.

Gabe's birth, on November 2, 1977, was satisfying. My scar had been reopened, but my dignity remained intact. This time I felt included in the party—a welcomed and integral part. I reacted spontaneously to the emotions of birth and was able to express my joy openly with Peter. Our gladness flooded the postpartum months and my recovery was rapid.

To understand what we had experienced, we learned more. Peter and I began teaching about cesarean birth to the local childbirth classes. I told them what I had learned: that a cesarean birth doesn't make you a failure; it just makes you a mother.

With our third pregnancy, we again assessed our choices. Vaginal birth after cesarean (VBAC) was just being accepted as an alternative to a repeat cesarean, but we could find no local support for a VBAC when a mother had already had more than one cesarean. By this time, we felt comfortable enough with cesarean delivery, and committed enough to the benefits of hospital care that recognized the needs of the whole family, that we filmed Moria's family-centered cesarean birth, on September 26, 1980.

The whole issue of childbirth and choices fascinated me. I

began teaching full childbirth education classes and became certified as a childbirth educator through the International Childbirth Education Association. Still, I was in turmoil and the question became more urgent: Would we or would we not have a fourth child?

While I wanted very much to have a VBAC, was I willing to have yet another child to be responsible for? Or . . . I really wanted another baby, but was I willing to meet the challenge of a VBAC? Toward the end of the year, we had reached resolution. Getting pregnant was the easy part.

Now there would be a birth and it would represent the best of my abilities, but I had inevitable doubts. VBAC was much more widely accepted, but could I locate a physician who would support me in a vaginal birth after three previous cesareans?

If so, would I be able to assert myself in voicing my desires? What if I had another cesarean? Could I ever face a class again? Could I face myself? If I did deliver vaginally, did I have the strength to meet the challenge? Would I be proud of myself—could I approve of myself—as a birthing woman? Despite my training in the ambivalence of early pregnancy, I felt quite vulnerable as the time came to choose a birth attendant.

After interviewing several doctors, I had heard the words "risk," "complicating factors," "precautions," et cetera, so many times, I was discouraged. Under the "right" circumstances, they were willing to support me in a "trial of labor." But I didn't want to be put on "trial."

I had had my fill of being stripped and identified—processed, patted, prodded, and placated. All I wanted was the chance to give birth without intervention, unless it became necessary for a healthy outcome. There was potential for great psychological healing to be done, and Peter and I both wanted an environment conducive to accomplishing as much of that as we could.

Our fourth interview proved fruitful. The doctor answered our flood of questions fairly and thoroughly. Nothing we asked was too trivial, and he was convinced that a VBAC was safer for both me and our child. He said that my chances were over 75 percent of delivering vaginally.[21]

Despite the fact that I was thirty-seven, he saw no reason for me to be treated differently because of my age or previous obstetrical history. We explained the value we placed on being greatly responsible for our birth, and he respected our choices without judgment. We hired him on the spot.

Now I could get on with the business of being pregnant. I ate well, read voraciously, visualized my vaginal delivery, and started swimming—half a mile three or four times a week. Gliding and pulling myself through the water buoyed, soothed, and cleansed me. I would breathe myself strong to do another lap, leaving in my wake the worries, the doubts, and the frustrations. Swimming gave me muscle tone, built up my strength and stamina, cleared my mind, and heightened my sense of self-confidence.

Peter and I wrote our birth plan. We found the act of writing our desires in black and white for all to see further clarified our thoughts. We decided to invite our children (ages nine, seven, and four) to the birth, and my mother and my friend Susan to be with them. Susan's husband, Willy, was asked to take photographs.

As a cesarean father, Peter had had the responsibility of driving me to the hospital, informing the nurses when I needed pain medication, and making sure I had help at home postpartum. It may not have been ideal but at least it was familiar. The unknown length and outcome of a VBAC made him question his ability to function as my sole partner. Since both of us wanted to keep our birth intimate and autonomous, we chose our friend Catherine to be Peter's support.

The last days lagged on. It seemed that every other face at the supermarket was a former student asking, "Are you going to do it 'right,' 'naturally,' 'normally' this time?" I groped for appropriate responses, each time confronting my own self-doubt. Every other day, I immersed my bulbous belly into the lap lane and renewed my sense of confidence and power.

Finally, contractions began. Peter and I were determined not to go to the hospital until active labor because we wanted to avoid any intervention out of staff boredom. After nine hours at home, my water broke, so we headed down to the hospital. We arrived just after midnight on Labor Day 1985.

Our friends and family gathered, each quietly finding a comfortable spot. I visited with them, walked the halls, took several Jacuzzi baths, moaned softly, and did a large, undulating belly dance to keep my pelvis loose. My body felt like a comfortable old friend embarking on a powerful new journey.

The staff came in and out performing professional duties but respecting our request for privacy and autonomy. The doctor was in the hospital for my entire labor and checked in every few hours. He never left without some reassuring words, showing his confidence in my abilities.

While Mom attended the children, Peter, Catherine, Willy, and Susan—in the best of partner fashion—met my needs without disregarding their own. They stayed calm and reacted in love, giving me all the room I needed to ride the contractions with the poise of surrender. Though my labor moved at a stately pace, I never felt anxious eyes or anyone trying to predict either my progress or my behavior.

Somewhere below any conscious surface, I knew that fear was holding me back—fear of the unknown. I had taught the process of birth to hundreds of couples, but this was new—this physical drama that went way beyond what anyone could describe or explain.

And there was the additional worry that maybe my first doctors had been right—maybe I was too small. What if I got this far and someone stepped in and took over? I don't remember much frustration in that long, long time—more of a feeling of dreaminess, punctuated by the visceral grip of contractions.

Eventually, I felt the need to get on with it. With some regret and some resolve, I left my dreamy state and dragged my hugeness to a sitting position, so gravity could contribute to the baby's descent.

With a contraction I hung myself like a pregnant pendant

around Peter's neck. I rocked delicately on my toes, tilted my pelvis, closed my eyes, and bore down into the pain. Between contractions, I sat on the edge of the bed, received, relaxed, and went blank.

Gradually, steadily, I felt the urge to push. I felt forces within me that needed no guidance. I discovered that birth is a place where power lives—a power that can only be tapped by surrendering completely.

I looked at Peter. With hours of hard work behind him, he was gearing up for the final sprint. I had seen that look in his eyes before: it was him at his best. He was fine. I was "deliverable." Mom and our children were ushered in, and the atmosphere changed to one of excited readiness. I maneuvered into the birthing bed, adjusting myself like an athlete checking her equipment prior to a performance.

Peter put on his gloves and two-stepped himself down to the action. An explosion in my body and the head burst forth . . . a moment to absorb the occurrence . . . another long, low urge . . . and my largest baby slipped into his father's waiting hands. No knives, no medications—just one body sliding from mother to father.[22]

Megan, our firstborn, severed the umbilical cord and we all let go. I felt alternately humble and triumphant, relieved and profoundly glad. And then we cried. We cried for the release of our fears, for our joy in Alex and in each other, for the twenty hours of hard work in birthing, and for the intense satisfaction of seeing a big goal met.

The children each had a special moment with Alex and then joined our tearful hugs. I don't really know what effect watching their brother's birth had on our children. They haven't talked about it much. But I do know that they witnessed their parents give birth with honest effort and great love.

They were very tender in their regard for both Alex and me afterward, keeping their sibling struggles quiet and encouraging each other to act responsibly. As he grows, they easily participate in his care. The unexpected challenge has been to help them remain positive about their births, in the midst of well-wishers extolling the virtues of the "natural" way.

As far as the natural way, there are some advantages. As a cesarean mother, I had viewed myself as a receptacle that needed to be surgically opened. Though breastfeeding promoted closeness, somehow I never lost the feeling that my baby had to violate me in order to be born. There was a distance that guilt kept inspiring me to cover up.

From the beginning, I have been most content to meet Alex's needs, to feel him close, and to sacrifice my desires for his care. It is difficult to know whether my attitude is a result of my easier recovery, personal maturity, or a vaginal birth, but the difference is marked and has reflected on my relationship with our other children as well.

While having had Alex without intervention doesn't make me an expert on birth, it does add a new perspective—that of participatory birth. With Megan, birth was unknown. I let the doctors birth me. With Gabe, I was the good patient. I asked for concessions but didn't question authority. With Moria's birth, I tried to teach other expectant parents graceful acceptance of the current status quo: "Once a cesarean, always a cesarean."

The joy of having my first three children was certainly genuine, but I found myself coming up with excuses and defenses about the way they were born. I felt a sense of loss over an experience in self-reliance that—under other circumstances—might have been, and a feeling of gratitude to the doctors for getting them here. Though I feel exquisitely grateful for my support and care during labor, I have no one to thank for Alex.

His birth was the result of forethought, determination, and a bit of luck. Through it, I learned that there is great responsibility in the creative process. I had to evaluate my choices, express my desires, accept support from my loved ones, and both build and rely upon my own inner resources. The challenge was great and so was the triumph.

All of my children were born in love. Alex's birth has helped me to love myself.

Rhonda Silverman
Merrick, New York

♡ *Rhonda Silverman, who calls herself a "home engineer" these days, reports that her firstborn, Elyse, is still "strong-willed and cannot wait, but a whip." Rhonda's second birth was in the hospital and required a longer, more typical period of labor. She preferred the first birth experience.*

Back in 1986 I had what I felt was an unusual birth story, which may be of interest to you. My firstborn, Elyse, was born September 19, 1986. She was born at home in the toilet by the hands of her mom, me.

I was in labor, not badly enough to run to the doctor. I did my walking and breathing. When my husband walked in from work, I was erratic with contractions. Well, within one half hour of my pacing, he suggested I call the doctor. I was still five to seven minutes apart, but not for one full hour as suggested by books and doctors.

Anyway, we called in, the pain was there, and the doctor decided to meet me at the office. As my husband proceeded down the block for our car (at the time we were in an apartment), I thought I had to make a bowel movement.

Needless to say, my Lamaze breathing didn't go too far in this case. My first big breath led to a push and out came Elyse's head, and the next push was into the toilet with the body. To this day, Elyse loves the water, almost the Leboyer method was practiced![23]

Well, I called my neighbor upstairs to come down. Elyse was still attached; I had wrapped her in a towel at this point and with my finger had taken some mucus out of her mouth.

After that, I opened my apartment door for my neighbor and husband, respectively, holding my new baby daughter, of course.

May I say that, to this day, she still does not have time to wait for anyone or anything.

I enjoyed giving birth at home better than at the hospital, as I did with our second daughter, Jaclyn, born two and a half years later. Internal exams and bedrest during labor are not for me.

P.S. I did get my delivery money back (refunded to me) and flowers from the doctor's office.

Suzanne Bancel
Seljord, Norway

♡ *American Suzanne Bancel reports on the births of her two sons in Norway in 1986 and 1989, vividly contrasting American and Norwegian attitudes toward childbearing and breast-feeding. She is extremely modest, however, about her own descriptive abilities and the remarkable nature of her experiences. "The [events of my life]," she says, "are more or less what everyone experiences—I just happen to see more snow while I am experiencing it."*

I came to Norway the summer after graduation on a program called Scandinavian Seminar. I went to a "folk high school" for a year—a noncompetitive alternative, yet very traditional school. I wanted to stay one more year to learn more Norwegian, and because I had this feeling something was "going to happen." January that year (1984), I met my husband, Dick—yes, he is Norwegian; no, his name is not.

We moved in together in May. He was living in a rural community of 500 (Espa), absolutely beautiful. Big pine forest on a hill overlooking Lake Mjosa. Dick was a sawmill worker at the time. I was unemployed for a year—a wonderful year with long walks in the forest, knitting, chopping wood.

The year after, I started at the Norwegian School of Library and Information Science. I took the train to Oslo each day (one and a half hours in, one and a half hours out). Among other things, I found the school to be *incredibly boring!* So my thoughts started wandering—hmmm, what can I do to make life more interesting—I know, have a baby!

Dick wasn't sold on the idea, but I nagged and nagged and got pregnant. I continued to commute each day until two weeks before Daniel was born. It was exhausting. I was nauseated the whole time—lost about ten pounds before I put it back on—gained really only six to seven pounds, and Daniel weighed five pounds! I experienced my pregnancy as physically and emotionally tough. I was quite lonely most of the time and often wondered if I'd made the biggest mistake in my life.

My husband found a job in Oslo and we bought an apartment right next to the school. We moved in one month after Daniel was born, so that I could continue school, with Daniel on my lap, which I did.

In many ways the Norwegian society is a lot more geared to children and pregnancy than I think it is in the U.S.A. I do not think the prevalence of teenage and/or unwed mothers is greater here, but their visibility and acceptance are. When you become pregnant, you can choose between your regular doctor or going to the local clinic for prenatal care. Every pregnant woman is entitled to free prenatal care, hospital treatment, and one postnatal checkup.

A woman who has given birth is required by law to stay home the first six weeks. After that, either she or her husband/lover or significant other (i.e., a mother or father) have twenty-six weeks' paid maternity leave.[24]

Just about everyone goes to a pregnancy class run by a nurse-midwife. All births are monitored by nurse-midwives, unless something requires the attention of an obstetrician. Norwegians are quite adamant about natural childbirth and as little drug and doctor intervention as possible.

The last few days before Daniel's birth were quite nice. I was at our home in Espa, baking Christmas cookies, writing papers, and packing for our move. Daniel was kicking away and kicking away. It was November and quite icy and cold.

I remember one night trying to get to our outhouse—it was a ways from the house, up a slight hill, and the hill was a sheet of ice. Imagine trying to get there with a *big* stomach and walking against the wind!

The day I went into labor I'd put my hair up in rag curls to pass the time. I took them out at ten P.M. I looked like an electrocuted poodle. I went to sleep and woke up at two A.M. with contractions that came about every twenty minutes. I called the hospital and they said I should come in no later than six A.M. since we lived half an hour away.

Then I looked in the mirror—Ah! Electrocuted poodle! I tried to brush it out—no luck—feverish hunting for a big scarf—found one! I tied it around my hair and it helped a bit.

Earlier that day I'd baked cinnamon rolls. I had planned to have a "last supper" with my husband—warm cinnamon rolls, candlelight, just the two of us. So I went to the kitchen, got everything ready, went upstairs, and whispered, "Dick! Dick!"

He grunted. I tried again. He rolled over and opened his eyes: "Er du bare sulten, eller . . . ?" "Whatsa matter, you hungry or something?" So much for romance!

We drove to the hospital and were there at six. I was checked in, my opening was measured (only two or three centimeters), and my contractions were checked—pretty irregular and not very strong. The nurse-midwife said we could go home if we wanted but implied it was best to stay when we were so far out in the country.

They suggested that I walk to keep my contractions going. So I walked and walked and walked. Dick and I walked around the neighborhood, watched people come and go to church, and walked some more. We were pretty tired by that afternoon—but still walking.

My mother was due to arrive that day. She'd been trekking in Nepal. Some friends picked her up in Oslo and drove her up to the hospital. My memory (I'm sure it's wrong) is of me sitting in the hospital room in a gown, having a contraction, and my mother bursting in the room saying, ". . . and all of a sudden this rhino came tearing through the underbrush at us."

My mother, our friends, and Dick stayed until about eight P.M. By now I was really tired. I'd only had a sandwich that day (and my cinnamon rolls!). I had blisters on my heels from walking and still no big opening. Mom went to a hotel nearby. Dick and I tried to sleep.

Around ten P.M. a nurse asked if I wanted a sleeping pill. They fixed a beanbag chair for me on top of a bed. (I've never figured that one out.) I took the sleeping pill and couldn't wait to sleep. I was sick of the whole thing.

That's when labor really began. I'll never forget trying to get off the beanbag chair and off the bed! How unwieldy! Oh! It hurt! All my labor pains were in my back and I was so tired. I screamed and moaned for about three hours. Dick was really good the whole time but nothing helped.

When I started to bleed, the midwife got me up on the bed (I wanted to stand—the idea of moving at that point was horrible). The nurse or midwife suggested relaxing with some "gas" (I forget the term in English), but I was too tense to breathe.

She left the room for a minute and that is when I opened—I think I must have opened about seven centimeters in one contraction. It was horrible—I really thought I was going to die. Dick looked pretty pale, too. I remember about four women ran in—two midwives, a nurse, and a "barnepleier" (a health worker with one year's training who takes care of newborns—weighing, feeding, bathing, cuddling).

They put my feet in the stirrups and said, "Push!" I couldn't; it hurt too much. I remember thinking then of all the birth literature I'd read where it was supposed to be so good to push. I was so tired and scared by that time. (Trying to decide whether to swear in Norwegian or English is an odd experience!)

Well, I had to push, so I screamed and pushed, and three of the team of four pushed from the outside, and *boom,* out came Daniel. "It's a boy!" My first thought was, Darn! I didn't realize until then how much I wanted a girl.

Dick looked pale, scared, amazed, relieved, tired, all at once. They took Daniel away immediately because he was so small— bathed him and brought him back dressed and warm. He was a funny, wrinkly thing!

I stayed in the birthing room with Daniel for two hours. I could hardly move. Daniel was in a crib next to my bed with his hand wrapped around my finger. It was nice. I was so drained, I couldn't feel more than that. Dick drove home to tell his mother and brothers the news.

On my long walks up and down the exciting hallway earlier that day, I'd discovered Vibeke, a woman from Espa who'd gone to the same pregnancy class with me. I asked to be put in Vibeke's room when they wheeled me out of the birthing room. My best memories of Daniel's birth come from sharing a room with Vibeke.

It was wonderful to wake up the next day and have someone to groan with and someone to share my experience with. Vibeke needed a vacuum [vacuum extractor?], so she didn't have any rosy memories, either. My eyes were bright red from burst capillaries and my voice was almost gone from screaming.

At six A.M. a sour nurse whisked into our room, turned on the lights, washed the floor, and whisked out. At six-thirty we waddled out into the hall for warm oatmeal soup—sounds horrible but it's part of every Norwegian woman's good memories of birthing.

Nursing is a *must* in Norway. I think 98 percent of all mothers nurse at least three months. Any good Norwegian grandmother will tell you, "Oats bring on your milk and give you your figure back!" Midwives and nurses scurried in and out and everyone talked about milk, milk, milk.

The nurses also ran around and took our temperatures and asked, "Have you farted lately?"—to make sure all the prunes were doing their job.

I spent seven days in the hospital because of some odd infection I had (fever, cramps)—probably just exhausted. I wrote two papers there, knitted, slept. All the time everyone was talking about breastfeeding. My milk came in quickly and in buckets. I had severe contractions every time I nursed the first week, which didn't do much for making me think of nursing as a positive experience.

I liked being on the maternity ward. My mother-in-law, a nurse's aide, worked on the next ward and could drop in often. One of the barnepleiers was from Espa and took "extra good care" of Vibeke and me and our babies. My mother was allowed to come and go as often as she liked.

What I experienced most strongly was a renewed awareness of my foreignness. There are so many cultural ties to pregnancy and childbearing that one is not aware of until placed in another culture. There were small things—some nice, like hot oatmeal, and scary things, like not knowing the midwife who delivered my baby, all the new vocabulary—*diaper, placenta, contraction*.

All the cultural differences I thought I'd come to understand seemed so superficial compared to the real *pressure* to nurse, *pressure* to have natural childbirth, *pressure* to oogle and google with pride.

The circumstances around my second son's birth were entirely different. I was working, had two minutes to walk to work, could look forward to maternity leave, and Dick was looking forward to number two, too. The delivery only took four hours and I had an epidural (wonderful). Being freed from the pain, I could concentrate on what was happening.

I thought Bjorn-David was wonderful from the start—except, *darn!* he should have been a girl! So I guess we'll have to try one more time! I think we will, and I'm getting used to being surrounded by boys, so a third boy wouldn't hurt.

I'd imagine that one's culture has as much to do with pain and blood tolerance as our individual personalities. I feel like a "traitor" when I say that neither pregnancy nor birthing was a great experience, if I am with Norwegians, but, among Americans, it seems a lot more acceptable.

On the other hand, I love being able to nurse *anywhere* in Norway—a café, a post office, at school—and that is a freedom

I haven't experienced in the States. I also love knowing I can stay at the hospital for seven days, if I need to, without worrying about expenses.

And *midwives are great*. I went through four midwives before Daniel was born: they all checked in the next day to see "what came out." The midwife who is there when the baby is born drops in before you leave the hospital to go through every phase of the birth, especially to discuss any "traumatic" experiences. I've probably been treated by eight midwives on shift for my two labors, and they were all warm, gentle, and professional.

Pauline Jonas
Westville Grove, New Jersey

♡ *Pauline Jonas describes below the sudden arrival of her fourth child with no one in attendance but her three other children, ages seven, five, and three.*

I was divorced. Sachi's father is a man with whom I had a very brief liaison (made so by my pregnancy). I was alone—my family lives in New York, and I didn't want to impose on friends. I decided giving birth at home was the best way.

After all, I was experienced, and the choice was further reinforced by my memory of being in hard labor in the winter, bouncing through the potholes on Philadelphia's expressway. I also had this fixed idea that I would labor six hours—I don't know why.

On the night of February 21, 1987, I began labor. I didn't get alarmed by those first wake-up contractions. It was around one A.M.

I couldn't sleep. I drew a bath—my baby dropped—I knew it wouldn't be long. I called a friend twenty minutes away and the midwife, who was one hour away.

My kids were all awake by this time. My sounds made no secret of my baby's urgent need. Ariella was seven, Jonathan five, Kristen three. Ariella suggested I call the hospital. So, frantically, I dialed 911.

You see, two of my children were born with shoulder dystocia (the shoulder presents itself square) and I needed assistance to turn the baby so they could slide out. I was petrified this baby would get stuck if I didn't have help.

But this baby was ready and waiting for no one. And I knew it. I tried with all my might to contract the birth muscles but it didn't work. So I quickly squatted on the floor at the foot of my bed and, a contraction or two later, put my hand under my baby's head and caught her, lifted her up to my breast, and, dazed, checked her breathing.

I had a basket all prepared for the midwife, and in it was a suction bulb. So I suctioned her nose. She was so peaceful—no cries, just eyes closed, breathing peacefully.

At this point the ambulance people arrived. Well, I was so out of it, they looked like apparitions. All was well and there was nothing for them to do.

They radioed the hospital about cutting the cord. By that time my friend arrived (the wife of my chiropractor—she had three at home). So she watched the cord until it stopped beating and the paramedic cut it about one foot from Sachi—to be sure the midwife had enough to take blood samples. (I'm Rh negative.)

The midwife arrived (I was still seated on the floor) and, of course, noticed immediately the placenta had not come out. So she helped deliver that. The crowd dispersed and it was then I was told I had a little girl. This was about twenty to twenty-five minutes after she was born.

From that point on, we all settled in to cleaning Sachi, stitching me (the midwife thought I had previously had an episiotomy—I had not—I tore in a nice, straight line), and bonding with Sachi.

For many days and nights we all talked about the birth. My kids talked about how they were frightened and how happy they were Sachi was okay. Would I do it again? Absolutely!

When I filled in the forms for her birth certificate, the people at our local municipal building thought I made a mistake. They figured somebody had to have been there. When we went down there to straighten it all out, Sachi was a celebrity at two weeks old!

Her name, by the way, means "bliss" in Japanese (I liked what it meant). Her middle name, Moira, means "teacher." She is quite outgoing, very affectionate, and really opens people's hearts—a real bundle of energy, not easily intimidated. She's everyone's darling.

Although I am not opposed to abortion, it just didn't fit for me with Sachi. I entertained the thought, but it just didn't take hold. That's why I spent so long researching adoption.

But there was a Spanish woman I knew, Maria, who would say, "Every child is born with a loaf of bread under its arms." So true. Sachi, and all of my children, have been a great bounty.

Myra Worrell
Winston-Salem, North Carolina

♡ *Myra Worrell embraces every aspect of pregnancy and child-birth with an uninterrupted flow of optimism and delight. She treats gestational diabetes during the course of her pregnancy—to the point that she had to take insulin—as a minor problem. She experiences her labor as essentially painless. Myra is an honest woman who describes all of her feelings, but she also knows how to throw open her arms and welcome the common miracles of life.*

I would like to share my pregnancy and birthing experience with you. It was the most wonderful experience of my life.

My husband, Shelton, and I were married March 2, 1986. He works as a hair designer and owns his own business. I have a master's degree in library science and work for the Forsyth County Public Library in Winston-Salem. We are African-Americans.

In November 1986, we decided that I should stop taking birth control pills so that "we" could become pregnant. And in January 1987, we hit the jackpot! I was thirty-one years old. For about two weeks after the doctor confirmed my pregnancy, I walked on eggshells—afraid to disturb the baby. Then, for another week or so, I thought there'd been a mistake and that I wasn't really pregnant. I didn't feel anything. Sure, I was nause-

222

ated, but I never once threw up, and I kept feeling as if my period was about to begin.

My breasts ached like crazy, but they'd always become sore whenever it was time for my period. However, by the end of the third month, I *knew* that I was pregnant. It was thrilling to observe the many changes taking place in my body.

My pregnancy went very smoothly. Around three and a half months the nausea left and, on May 4, 1987, I felt the baby move for the first time. What a *thrill!* I think that was what I enjoyed most of all—the flutters that turned into thumps, and kicks that turned into lazy stretches. *So sweet!*

During the fifth month, I was diagnosed as having gestational diabetes. I wasn't surprised because my mother is diabetic, as was her father. At first I was worried, but then I decided to trust God, follow my doctor's advice, and look forward to my healthy baby.

The doctor placed me on a diet and I took six units of insulin daily during the last six weeks of the pregnancy. I felt wonderful the whole time. If the doctor hadn't diagnosed me, I'd never have known the difference. I was told that the diet and the insulin would control my weight gain and the baby's, as well.

Babies born to women with diabetes usually weigh ten pounds or more. My doctor wanted to keep the baby's weight around eight pounds and my weight gain around thirty pounds. I gained thirty-three. Pretty good, huh?

I worked every single day during my entire pregnancy and felt terrific. My due date was October 8. On Monday, September 27, I had my weekly checkup. The doctor wanted me to stop work on Friday, October 2. He advised me to get lots of rest the next week.

On Friday, October 2, I worked all day and went home to prepare dinner. My husband got home around seven-thirty. We ate, relaxed, talked, and went to bed around ten. Around eleven I felt the baby moving in a different sort of way—as if it were rotating. I was also feeling very mild cramps.

At eleven-thirty I felt a trickle of water and thought I had urinated on myself. I also felt as if I needed to have a bowel movement. I went to the bathroom and, when I wiped, there was a pink tinge on the tissue.

I called my doctor, who was out of town. (I wasn't due for another week.) The on-call doctor said maybe I was beginning labor. He told me to get some sleep and come in the next morning for an examination. He thought by then I'd really be in labor.

I lay down but again felt the urge to have a BM. I went to the bathroom and sat down. But this time something let me know this wasn't a BM. My husband was sleeping like a log through most of this.

We got up and made the three-minute drive to the hospital. By the time I got to the labor room, the nurse examined me and said I was already seven centimeters dilated. That was about one A.M., and at 2:47 A.M., October 3, 1987, Joshua Immanuel Worrell was born. My husband named him. Joshua means "God of salvation" and Immanuel means "God with us." He weighed seven pounds, eight ounces, and was twenty inches long.

The most unique thing about my labor is that it didn't hurt. I'd heard many stories about the pain, but I didn't experience pain. The pressure I felt, however, was *tremendous!* I felt as if I could have pulled whole trees up by the roots! But I didn't need anesthesia. The nurses couldn't believe I was dilated at seven centimeters but couldn't tell whether or not I was having contractions. We hadn't even timed them because I didn't know I was having them.

I was aware of everything that was happening. My entire being was focused on having the baby. I knew my husband and the nurses were there, but it was as if they were on the edges of my consciousness. My husband was a champ. We didn't attend Lamaze classes, but he was there every step of the way!

When the baby emerged, the doctor and nurses and my husband were jumping up and down, clapping and saying, *"It's a boy!"* And he was perfect. I had an episiotomy and, as the doctor stitched me up, my husband was strolling around the delivery room, holding and talking to Joshua.

As they rolled me out of delivery to recovery, one of the nurses said, *"This woman knows how to have a baby!"* I felt so proud of myself—still do (smile)!

To sum it all up . . . the best thing, the most exhilarating things, were the pregnancy, the labor, and, most of all, a healthy baby. (I breastfed him.) What an awesome experience for a woman!

The downers were that my rear end felt as if a transfer truck had driven through! I had no idea that I'd be that sore. Also, breastfeeding hurt! The gestational diabetes was also a downer. It was more of a mind thing—accepting it, first of all, and then dealing with monitoring blood-sugar levels and giving myself injections of insulin. Incidentally, the diabetes goes away after delivery. I've been checked since and I am not diabetic. The baby was perfectly healthy.

The last downer was the "baby blues." They began about five days after delivery and lasted about a week. I cried for a solid week! I am generally cheery and was very up about the pregnancy and the baby. I had read and heard about the blues but thought it wouldn't happen to me—but it did.

My husband was great. He was loving and understanding. He started taking the baby and me on trips to malls! I've never been to the mall so much in my life! But it got me out of the house and that cured my blues.

Joshua is now three and he is the light of our lives. He is bright, happy, and rambunctious. Next week he begins pre-school at the Montessori Children's Center.

We are talking about having another child, although I am thirty-five years old now. Even so, I long to feel a life stirring within me again. I thank God for the honor and privilege of participating in the creating of life!

On February 27, 1992, Myra gave birth to her second child, a little girl named Amanda Diane Worrell.

Anonymous

♡ *In the following story a woman describes her own childbirth experience and the childbirth experience of her live-in lover or "partner," who is also a woman. The two women decided not only to each have a baby through artificial insemination and to raise their children together as one family, but also to use the same anonymous donor, "thereby relating the children, not just spiritually, but biologically as well."*

Today this is an unusual arrangement; it may well become more common in the future. But, for the present, the two women have asked to remain anonymous.

Families are created, not related. That much I had already discovered. For five years, my partner had been a woman who had children from a previous marriage. Even though they were already teenagers by the time that we got together, there was no doubt that we were a family. In fact, they spent the first year that we were together literally hanging on to my neck.

I loved them as if they had been my own children. In fact, I wanted the things for them that I would want for any child of mine: a sense of self-respect and well-being, being in charge of his or her life, a thorough knowledge of being loved and wanted, a well-reasoned intellect.

But the more time that I spent with these children, the more I realized that they did not have these things, and, with my coming into their lives so late, the more I realized that I would be unable to help them develop these qualities. As this became clearer and clearer to me, it also became clearer and clearer to me that I wanted to have children of my own.

When that relationship ended, my new partner and I, also a woman, began to talk almost immediately of having kids. It turned out, as we compared notes, that we both had always wanted to have families of our own. So, the decision to have kids on our own was very easy, and, since I am considerably older, it was also easy to decide who would have the first baby.

What took some thinking and planning was the *how* we were going to have the babies. From the start, we were clear on one thing. There would be more than one, and we wanted the father to be the same, thereby relating the children, not just spiritually, but biologically as well.

As we began to feel our way along in the process, we asked a male friend of ours if he would be a donor for us. He answered thoughtfully that he could not see fathering children with whom his relationship would be unclear. And that was for us a very valid point.

We had thought originally that it would be good for the kids to know their dad. But, as we thought more and more about it, we realized that, of our options, that one might not be the best. If the father was someone we knew, what would we expect of him as the father? What would the children expect of him as the father?

Would he send Christmas cards? Would he visit once a year? Would they be hurt if he forgot their birthdays? Would he want to make comments about how they were being raised?

In the end, it seemed to us that it would be easier on all of us if none of us knew the father. In the meantime, we discovered that someone we knew was a doctor who had a practice in infertility, and she had been helping women couples bear children. We made an appointment with her and decided after our first visit that this was the correct route for us.

After five months of being artificially inseminated, we discovered that I was pregnant. Once an early ultrasound showed that the fetus was successfully implanted, we were discharged from the clinic.

Because of my age at the time, thirty-eight, we decided that we needed to look carefully into our options for our OB/GYN care. We made an appointment with an obstetrician who was attached to a local teaching hospital. As far as we knew, except for my age, this was a normal pregnancy.

During our first visit to the doctor, we were absolutely scared witless because we were given literature that told us all the ways that this doctor could help us if we had a problem with the baby. They could treat hydrocephaly. They could handle spina bifida. If there was fetal distress, they had all the monitors and beepers available.

I remember leaving there feeling quite shaken, not realizing that there had even been all those things that could go wrong. And I just could not see going through what appeared to be a perfectly normal pregnancy dwelling on everything that might go wrong.

So I called a friend who worked for a major birthing center in New York, and asked her to recommend someplace close to us where we could have the baby. She recommended the only freestanding birth center in our area. It was right across the street from a community hospital, but it was an independent organization. We went to an orientation session there and felt at home right away.

When we came to our first appointment, we knew that we were at the right place. We were told that my chart would always be available for us whenever we wanted to read it. I would test my own urine and weigh myself when I first arrived. I said that, because of my age, I did want to have an amniocentesis done. The midwife said that they did not see the need for one, but, if it would make me feel better, to go right ahead and get one done.

Except for some high blood pressure in the final weeks, the remaining time of my pregnancy was quite uneventful. The midwives continued to prepare us by encouraging us to take a birth class and by helping us to fill out a birth plan with things that we wanted to have done the night of the delivery.

We decided that we wanted a low light level, soft music, and plenty of good food (we were to supply our own). I also decided, after seeing various pictures, that I would like to deliver sitting up on the bed. It seemed the most comfortable position.

The birthing suites there were just like bedrooms. The only things that were different than an average motel room were the sink and the countertop running along one side. Otherwise, we could have been in the guest room of a local inn. There were no monitors. No equipment. No *drugs!*

During birth class, the nurse had stressed that first babies are usually late and usually a long time coming. We should not get discouraged if the labor lasted several days. As well informed and well rested as possible, we awaited the big night.

Knowing that we had plenty of time, we did not rush to finish the babies' room. The holidays were busy, as usual, and we wanted to savor our last few months of time without babies.

Therefore, when we went to bed on the second night of my thirty-seventh week, and my water broke, we experienced some heavy denial before we finally accepted the truth. I was in labor!

We tried to remain calm, even though our immediate reaction was to laugh hysterically when we realized that we were not ready to have this baby. We hadn't finished his room. We didn't have any diapers. We hadn't packed a suitcase. We hadn't made any food.

We called the midwife and she suggested that we try to get some sleep. It was not unusual for contractions to begin quite a while after the membranes ruptured. We slept fitfully until early the next morning, at which point we *tried* to think of how we were going to organize ourselves to have this baby.

I was to go in to be tested in the afternoon, to make sure that the amniotic fluid was still clear. The midwife on duty that afternoon told us that everything was fine. Sometimes, she said, it took several days for contractions to begin, but, most often, they started within twenty-four hours.

I spent the rest of the day resting comfortably, while my partner rushed around the supermarket buying whatever seemed "essential" to having a baby and wishing that there was some way to explain to people in line that she was about to have a baby, so she really needed to go ahead of them.

That night at dinner, as I finished eating, wrapped in a towel to keep the amniotic fluid from flooding our dining room, I began to feel small cramps. Within several hours, the cramps had become contractions, and, by bedtime, the contractions were regular and coming about every five minutes.

We called the midwife, just to let her know, and she said to call her back when I had to concentrate on the contractions. To everyone's surprise, that was about twenty minutes later. By eleven-thirty P.M., I knew this baby was serious about being born.

We called back and said, "Here we come," and we got in the car. By this time, I was doing my breathing and wondering if the baby was going to be born in the car. My partner, meanwhile, was so relieved that I was finally in labor, that she actually started to relax. In fact, at one point, I wondered aloud if this was the slowest drive that we had ever taken to the birthing center.

When we arrived, it was snowing like crazy, and my contractions were every two minutes. In between, I hustled into the building and got into my nightgown. The midwife said that she had some paperwork to do and that she would be back in a few minutes to check me. We were alone in the building. The nurse was on her way.

The midwife returned shortly to examine me and said that my uterus was quite jumpy, that she would give it time to settle down while she continued to work in the next room. As she got up to leave, another contraction started. It was so strong that the force of it flipped me over in the bed from my left side to my right, and it ended with me pushing. It seemed that I had gone through transition in one contraction.

Then things started to get interesting. I remember seeing the midwife running around the bed. And I remember her telling me not to bounce the baby off the wall. Apparently, right about then, she had picked up her scissors, thinking that she should probably do an episiotomy, when I, in her words, "unzipped."

Out came the baby. It had taken only three contractions and here he was. In seconds, he was in my arms, all blue and bloody and cheesy and beautiful. While we oohed and aahed over him, he turned pink right before our eyes, and we began to rub in the vernix.

My partner and the nurse took the baby over to the countertop and began to care for him. Meanwhile, the midwife and I tried to coax the placenta to arrive with the same rapidity as the baby. We failed.

For the next two hours, the midwife tried everything she could think of to make that placenta appear. I walked to the bathroom. I tried nipple stimulation. I tried having the baby nurse. Nothing.

Finally, after she threatened to transfer me to the hospital, I delivered the placenta. Apparently, I did not want to go out into the snowstorm that was now raging outside. As soon as the placenta arrived, she was ready to sew me up. I swung my legs over the edge of the bed and propped them up on two chairs while she stitched. By the time that I was back together again, I was starving. So my partner went into the kitchen and made everyone breakfast.

She remembers that meal of bacon and eggs as one of the most complicated and drawn-out experiences of her cooking career, and she is a skilled chef. Two sleepless nights and an adrenaline overdose had finally taken their toll.

After breakfast, it was about six A.M., so we decided that we would take a nap. We put the baby into a small cradle and we all went to sleep for about two hours. When I woke up, I felt great. We chatted with the nurse for a while and filled in the birth certificate. The building was very quiet, as all appointments had been canceled due to the storm.

I said that I was ready to go home, and we began to get ready. But, as I started to get dressed, I realized that I was, in fact, not ready. So I lay down and went back to sleep for a couple of hours. But by the next time I woke up, I was definitely ready.

The nurse went up and hung a banner out the front window of the house that read, "It's a Boy!" and we all headed home. The baby was twelve hours old and looked like a loaf of bread bundled into the car seat. What a wonderful, funny, joyous time we had all had.

As a friend of mine replied when I told her that it had definitely been one of the top three moments in my life: "And I bet you can't remember the other two."

By the time our son was nine months old, we were ready to try again, and this time everything was to be totally different, and yet the same. This time, my partner was to be pregnant.

We both came from families where we had not only been the youngest, but the youngest by six years. Wouldn't it be wonderful, we reasoned, if the children could be close together?

After all, biology was not in our way. We didn't have to wait for my body to recover. We could start all over again with a whole new body. We thought that having them in diapers at the same time would be a great way to get diapers done with at the same time.

We called the doctor back and told her that we were ready to start again. But there were two major obstacles that we hadn't stopped to consider. When our son was born, he'd gotten very badly jaundiced, and it was during that time that we discovered that, through his father, he was a carrier for a galactose intolerance called galactosemia.[25]

When we returned to the clinic, we were informed that our donor was no longer being used because of this experience. We were stunned. We had been planning for this moment for three years. Having the same father for the children was the one fact on which we had been clearly focused since we started down this path. We went home in shock.

In the end that obstacle was much more easily surmounted than the next. We signed a release form stating that we understood the risk and took the responsibility for using this donor, regardless of the outcome. But, as for what happened next, we were completely unprepared.

We had been told the first time around that the average woman took two or three cycles to become pregnant. We were leaving town in six months, so we figured that we had plenty of time. But those six months came and went quickly.

Between starting work in a city two hundred miles away, finishing graduate school, selling the house, preparing to move, *and* chasing after a baby who hadn't slowed down since he almost bounced off the wall the night that he was born, we were exhausted. Not the most conducive atmosphere for conceiving a baby. Now we were in a real dilemma. We lived a four-hour drive from the clinic.

Two more years went by and we still weren't pregnant. In the meantime, we had tried fertility drugs, exploratory surgery, and prayer. And we always lived with the specter that the donor would leave town.

But, just as we were giving up hope and were discussing alternatives—my taking a turn at number two, for example—my partner's textbook twenty-eight-day period failed to arrive and we realized that she was finally pregnant.

With our dreams so far intact, we began to search for a new birth experience. Our first one had been so positive that we felt saddened by having to look for a new place. Nothing could ever be like that again—and it wasn't.

But, once again, we got lucky. We called an acquaintance who had just graduated from a local midwifery school and asked her to give us some suggestions. Stay away from the place where she had graduated, if we wanted to avoid "high tech," she said. But she had heard of one enlightened OB/GYN in our area who practiced with midwives. She hadn't met him person-ally, but had heard great things about him.

It turned out that, not only had his first child been born in the birth center where we had been, but that he had lived two blocks from a restaurant where we had worked, and we had waited on him. We had come home again.

The pregnancy proceeded almost without incident. Although my partner got annoyed at herself for morning sickness, food aversions, and extreme fatigue, we made it to the big moment without any major disruptions. In fact, all three of us were excited.

The baby was due in early January. We were hoping to make it past the holidays, but, based on our first experience, we weren't counting on it. Being self-employed and working out-doors, my partner had had to stay active. So, up until the Friday before Christmas on Sunday, she had been climbing over stone walls, jumping frozen creeks, and learning how to pee pregnant in the woods.

She had been delighted during the holiday shopping season to discover that she got almost instant service, no matter how long the lines, but it was a little difficult maneuvering through the crowds. Watering the Christmas tree was out of the question.

At last, Christmas Day arrived and we breathed a sigh of relief. Family gathered, scores of baby presents were opened, and we went to bed thinking that the final two weeks would be time enough to "get organized."

At dinner on the 26th, with our five out-of-town guests, as my partner got up to get second helpings, her membranes rup-tured. She excused herself and went upstairs to check the amni-otic fluid, and, finding everything normal, spent several minutes experiencing heavy denial all over again.

She confided to me later that she had carefully ignored the signals her body had been giving her all day—the signals that birth class and the books say are *so* obvious. She was as sur-prised to be in labor as our houseguests were to hear that the.

baby was on the way. I put down my wineglass and suggested that we call the midwife.

Contractions began almost immediately but they were spaced quite far apart. A sense of excitement and relief came over us, and we sat back to enjoy the anticipation of the arrival of the new baby. My partner wasn't in the middle of the woods in freezing weather, or stuck in one of the never-ending traffic jams that clog the roads around here, or one hundred miles from home—all of which had been her worst fears.

She was safe and warm in her own home, surrounded by friends and family, all of whom were willing to help do anything and everything. We didn't have to worry about child care or the house or the pets or the dishes. We were free to time the contractions.

In fact, we were considerably more relaxed than our house-guests. We went into the living room and continued to entertain neighbors who were dropping in to wish us a happy holiday. Our guests kept saying that they really thought it was high time we left now, they didn't want to be delivering a baby, thank you, and we continued to blah blah blah.

We put our son to bed and explained as best we could that the baby was on the way and that we might not be there in the morning when he awoke. He was a little excited, but was a lot more interested in knowing if he could sleep in his new tent that Santa had brought him than about the particulars of babies.

Near midnight the contractions were coming fast and hard enough that my partner was having to concentrate on them, and they were about five minutes apart. We headed to the hospital, since the midwife and the doctor were already there with a C-section.

We settled in and got as comfortable as one can get when one is about to have a baby. Since things had moved right along up to this point, we were expecting this baby to pop out just like the first one.

But it became clear, quite quickly, that this was to be a whole different experience. My partner's contractions slowed down as soon as we arrived, and we were back to chatting and reading the newspaper in no time. The midwife came and went, suggesting ways to get the contractions started again. We took walks up and down the hall. And the midwife tried jiggling my partner's uterus to wake the baby, who apparently had gone to sleep.

I marveled all along at the almost complete calm with which my partner was getting through each contraction. For me, each contraction had felt like an earthquake. In fact, I remember announcing each and every one by saying, "Here comes another one," and then watching everyone run around the room. Finally, about four A.M., she went into transition, and by this time, she was in back labor.

The midwife suggested that she try taking a shower, so we moved the whole show into the bathroom at the end of the room. I sat on the toilet in the lookout position while my partner stood under the hot water. I was quite sure that they would probably find us in there the next morning when they came to clean—two shriveled prunes and a uterus. But, eventually, we emerged and discovered that transition was almost over. It was now almost six A.M. and the midwife gave the word to start pushing.

My partner looked at the midwife and said, "Now, how do I do that?" The midwife and I looked at each other, and I said to her, "Oh boy, if she doesn't know the answer to that question, we're in trouble." And we were.

Apparently, the midwife later told us, her uterus was lazy, and it took nearly four hours of pushing to get that baby to move those last five centimeters. And, when the baby did move, it was from the strength of abdominal muscles, not from the contractions. We tried pushing from every single position that has ever been tried. She sat. She stood. She squatted.

Squatting seemed to work the best, so that's what we stuck to for a long time. There was a bar on the end of the bed, and when the contraction started, my partner would haul herself up onto the bar and push. The midwife had a little stool and she would perch underneath from where she would give directions.

At one point, I was sitting on the chair beside the bed with my head resting in my hands when I heard snoring. I looked up to see that my partner had fallen fast asleep. I looked at the midwife and again we laughed.

I said, "I bet you don't have many women falling asleep during pushing."

To which she replied, "It's not too common."

About this point, the baby decided to fall asleep again, too. The midwife looked at the fetal monitor and said, "Apparently, this baby likes pushing."

But, at last, around ten A.M., the big moment arrived. The top of our baby's head, which we had been staring at for the last two hours, seemed almost ready to erupt. The midwife got her scissors. She said that she felt that it had been long enough and she made a neat little snip. Two contractions later, out came the baby. It was at this moment that I ran out of film in the camera. After waiting for this all night, as the baby arrived, I was on the other side of the room loading the camera!

The doctor, who had arrived for the big moment, told me to get over there and meet my baby—forget the film. So I dashed back across the room to see the baby placed in my partner's arms. We all hugged and laughed and cried and then I loaded the camera.

After I had gotten the nurse to take pictures of the three of us, she and I took the baby over to the portable incubator where we started to clean her up.

Meanwhile, my partner was delivering the placenta and started to hemorrhage. Suddenly, the atmosphere, which had been very chatty, turned absolutely quiet, while the doctor punched my partner in the uterus quite sharply. It worked. The hemorrhaging stopped. Finally, we could start to enjoy our new baby girl.

We had made it clear at the admissions desk that we wanted to be released as soon as the pediatrician released the baby, so we were not transferred to a maternity room. They wheeled a little portable cot into the room for me to take a nap on, and they offered my partner breakfast (unidentified yellow lump, Jell-O, hot tea). I was offered nothing. It was at this moment that I most missed the birth center where our son had been born. Now that the midwife was gone, we were strictly at the mercy of hospital protocol.

But exhaustion finally overcame all discomfort, and the baby, tucked in the crook of my arm, and I fell asleep on the cot, while my partner tried to get comfortable in a short delivery bed. We had probably been asleep twenty minutes when a young and nervous aide from the hospital's social services department came and asked us to fill out the birth certificate.

She asked, "Father's name?" and we gave mine. She stared at us in disbelief and said that she would have to go ask her boss. We had no sooner gone back to sleep than the head of the social services department bustled into the room. Again, we came to.

She settled herself importantly in the chair. It was then that she saw the floor. My partner had gotten up to go to the bathroom, and the aftermath of the hemorrhaging had left a thin trail of blood leading around the end of the bed.

"What," the woman asked officiously, "happened here?" It was all that we could do to keep from laughing.

"We had a baby," we answered calmly.

She proceeded to tell us that there was absolutely no way that anyone but the father could be *the father* on the birth certificate, and no amount of suggestion or plea could get her to budge a centimeter. So the space was left blank.

Again, we had been spoiled by our first experience, as my partner is listed as the father on my son's birth certificate. Of course, we have wondered if the person who's looking at his birth certificate to give him a passport will wonder if he's met a biological wunderkind, but then life's been interesting this far, anyway.

Around five-thirty P.M., we were released. We arrived home

with an eight-hour-old baby to clean laundry, clean sheets, and a gourmet dinner. Our son barely noticed our arrival. He had been allowed to bring his tent downstairs and watch TV from inside it while sucking on a pack of Lifesavers. He was in heaven.

But he went upstairs with my partner and the baby, and the three of them lay on the bed and snuggled, while he drew pictures of his new sister.

Our guests had been busy all day getting ready for the baby's arrival, and they were as excited as we were. She was passed around and cooed over by everyone. None of them had expected to be on hand for the birth, much less see her at eight hours old. The quiet comings and goings of the household were a vivid contrast to the hospital, and we all went to sleep contentedly.

Five days later, my partner and the baby and I were back at work. The baby came to the office every day for six months. Other than showing a decided fascination with telephones, she has shown no ill effects from being the "office girl," and she and her brother are continuing to grow and thrive. There is no measure of the joy and richness they bring into our lives, and we are glad to have a chance to share their birth stories.

Elena

♡ *The woman who tells this birth story was born and raised in El Salvador. Even though she had lived in the United States for twelve consecutive years and had had four children here, she was not a legal resident of the United States when she told me this story. Her real name, therefore, is not used. I am calling her Elena.*

At the time this interview was taped, on August 16, 1990. Elena was separated from her husband (she knew she was pregnant with her fifth child when she left him) and was trying to support herself and the five children, ages twelve, eight, four, two, and three months, by baby-sitting and cooking for her neighbors. Elena was thirty-two.

I was seven months pregnant when, one night, I started having contractions. My nephew took me to the clinic and they sent me to the hospital. They give me a shot and they said, "It's too soon to have the baby." I stay two days in the hospital with pills and all that for not have the baby, because she said, "It's not ready. It's not time."

They give me pills for come back to the house. I can't have the contractions, see; I got to take the pills. I take them about every six hours. And then I think I supposed to have one at nighttime. And I forgot that one at night. I supposed to have at eleven o'clock, or maybe in the middle of the night, so I sleep and I forget about it. So, in the morning, the first thing I had is that the pain is starting. I have the same contractions—and bleeding and I feel bad.

I call the ambulance because I don't have no ride that time. And then one come over. And he said, "Well, you still walking, so I don't think you have the pain."

And I say, "Well, I have already four babies, so I know what the pain I have. If I have a pain, I call you; if I don't have a pain, I don't need to call you."

And he take me, finally, because another lady come over there and say, "She really have a pain . . ." He don't put me in the stretcher. He sit me up in the back. And then, after that, every corner . . . ooooooh. And he take me about ten o'clock in the morning and I had the baby about twelve o'clock.

I didn't take my card.[26] At that time, I didn't bring anything because I really had very big pain. I told the girl who was working at the computer, when she asked me questions, she say, "Well, what's your name?" I said, "That's the only thing I can give you is my name." And she ask me my social security number. I forgot. And so she tell me, right away, the guy, you know, he take me. The *first* day I go over there, I had papers.

[They took her to Triage, where a determination is made as to what to do with each incoming emergency patient.]

And they say, "You don't want to have early baby." And I said, "But the baby's coming. I can't do anything." Everybody's mad up there because I don't take the pill. So everybody's talking about it, but that is why nobody's paying any attention—because for the pill: "See, I give some medicine to you and you don't want to take it, so it's not our responsibility if something happen to you, because I already told you."

I don't like that. I don't like the way she acted. She was mad at me and talking bad about things like that, bitching me and everything. This part, I don't like it.

I say, "Well, but I have the pain right now. I know the baby's coming. I can't wait." And then she talk with the doctor: "She have the pain, she took the pills, and she has the pains very hard. What I have to do?"

And the doctor say, "So, try and wait for a little bit until you see what's going on. You get the injection again to stop the pains."

And she told me, "Well, I want to give you the injection again for stop the pains."

I say, "I don't need the injection. I know the baby's coming." So she check me and she tell me, the baby can't come because I have three centimeters.

So she went to get the shot for to stop the contractions, and that's what I waiting for, when she come to stop the pain. But the baby is not giving her time. The baby couldn't wait.

There were a lot of people around, a lot of nurses, lot of patients, but not with me. I call her. I say, "Nurse, my water broke," and I have very bad pains and she came right away and it was all wet around. . . . So she screamed to call the doctor and she say, "It's really true, the baby's coming."

And the doctor come to me and check me and say, "Yeah, it's time. The baby's already there."

[Elena was rushed on a stretcher to the delivery room but, while the OB was being paged to deliver the baby, the baby was born on the stretcher in the hall.]

So the doctor come and she say, "What you call me for? She already did it." She make a joke because I already had the baby. She cut the cord and take my placenta.

I like the nurses up there when I had the baby. Everybody was so nice with me.

I stay in the hospital two days. The baby stayed two weeks. She had fast breathing. She don't gain weight. She losing weight when she stayed there. So I want to keep her with me, I want to feed her. When I take her home, she gain weight.

Now, I don't want to have no more children. That's enough.

* * *

Having a Baby

Elena was scheduled to have a tubal ligation when this baby was born, had the baby been born at term. But the baby came so early and so fast that the operation was not done. The public hospital has a long waiting list of women who want tubal ligations performed. They could not fit Elena into the schedule for that day.

Elise Gunst
Houston, Texas

♡ *When I asked Elise Gunst to summarize the high points of her life for me, she responded with a sedate recital of her academic background and profession (psychotherapist) and how she met her husband, concluding with the following anecdote:*

"In the first grade I was a potato for Halloween because I forgot to tell my mother I needed a costume for school until the bus was coming so she put a big, brown paper bag over my head."

The same dry, deadpan wit keeps popping up unexpectedly in Elise's account of her pregnancy and childbirth experiences.

My first pregnancy started out picture-perfect. I was a full-time graduate student and worked part-time, living in San Antonio. As a concession to being pregnant, I cut back from a sixty-hour work week to forty hours. After all, I was pregnant, not sick. I was Macho-Woman.

At thirty-three weeks, I went into premature labor. One day everything was fine, the next I was in the hospital with IVs in my arm pumping me full of drugs to stop the labor and strapped to monitors for the contractions and the fetal heartbeat. I stayed in a labor and delivery room for five weeks.

Most people who develop premature labor can be stabilized and sent home, but, every time they reduced the drugs below a certain level, my contractions increased. I stayed through a

244

miserable Christmas and New Year's (although I did get to ride in a wheelchair, along with my tinsel-bedecked IV tree, up to the hospital's catwalk to watch the fireworks shooting over the Alamo on New Year's Eve).

With the increase in malpractice litigation, doctors and nurses were easily spooked. Some were afraid to give me too much medication. Others were afraid to give me too little. Some seemed to want to stop the contractions completely (a few an hour are normal in late pregnancy).

One of the drugs, magnesium sulfate, gave me what the nurses called the "mag blues." When my mag level had been cranked up, I was depressed. On those days, I felt like a failure. I'd been proud of how easy pregnancy had been for me; then I felt as though I couldn't do it right. I worried about the baby. What if something wrong with the baby had triggered early labor?

I was taking huge quantities of antilabor drugs, which made me retain fluid and accelerated my breathing and heart rate. They befuddled my brain: at first I couldn't think clearly enough to read or even sew. I stared into space for hours without realizing it. At least it helped pass the time.

At night I took barbiturates because, otherwise, the antilabor drugs would not have permitted me to sleep. All those months of avoiding coffee, chocolate, alcohol, even Tylenol. Now I was being prescribed barbiturates. Even without the magnesium sulfate, it was pretty depressing, but I kept a grip most of the time.

When I lost it and cried, my contraction monitor made little squiggly lines that the nurses could see from the nurses' station. So I didn't cry much, since doing so was a public affair.

The lack of privacy and the dependency were unbearable. Some days when I was having a lot of contractions, I had to use a bedpan. The worst thing about it all was *I wasn't sick*. I felt fine. Premature labor, at least for me, was not painful: the contractions were very mild. In fact, often I couldn't feel them. If it hadn't been for the monitor, no one would have known they were there and increased my medication.

Was technology my enemy? Hard to say. Sometimes I think

the staff overreacted because of the monitors. Other times I think if it *hadn't* been for the monitors, I might have lost my baby or had a preemie.

Every week, starting at thirty-six weeks, I had a sonogram, three in all, and each week for the first two weeks, an amniocentesis. The doctor wanted to be sure the baby's lungs were mature before I delivered. Each week, the verdict came back negative: not ready. I felt, and probably looked, like a turkey being tested for doneness.

Finally, at thirty-eight weeks, the contractions stopped completely. I was taken off all medication and sent home for a week, during which time I savored freedom and real food and frantically got ready for the baby.

For reasons unrelated to the premature labor, I needed to have a cesarean section. At thirty-nine weeks, the doctor decided the baby had to be ready.

There was no place I hated to go back to more than that hospital, but, at least this time, it was for a good cause. My husband stayed with me, and the baby was delivered on January 13, 1988, the morning after I checked in. I had an epidural, and my husband was in the delivery room.

After they gave me the epidural, the fire alarm went off. I had images of everybody running out and leaving me there with my legs all numb. I pointed out to everyone that I would prefer this not happen and they kindly agreed to wheel me out with them if they took off.

I later learned that my husband, who'd been told he had to wait until after the epidural to join me in the delivery room, was shut behind glass doors, alone in the prep room, when the alarm sounded.

I wouldn't have known they'd started the operation if the room hadn't gotten so quiet. A few minutes later, I heard a cough, and a little cry, and my husband saying "Oh my God, oh my God . . ." Then they handed me that little baby for whom I'd put up with so much. I still get tears in my eyes when I think of that moment. It's an unparalleled experience. None of it mattered, the weeks in the hospital, the cesarean. What mattered was looking at that little face.

Shortly thereafter, my husband tenderly announced, "My genes beat the shit out of your genes!" It's true, she did look just like his grandfather, Oscar Silverman, but, luckily, she improved greatly and is now a beautiful little girl.

Some people talk about the disappointment of having to have a cesarean. I didn't care how it got there; I just wanted the baby. I think it made a big difference that the cesarean was planned, so I never expected a natural delivery. Also, after everything else, the cesarean was almost a relief. The worrying would be over.

What did hit me hard was the baby blues. My daughter was born with a heart murmur (unrelated to anything I took), which was the last straw. I'd had to work to keep myself from being frightened for so long. Then, when I thought I could relax, they gave me the news. That, and the aftermath of surgery and the normal hormonal upheaval, all coincided, and for a few days I felt like crying all the time. Then I started feeling better, and got some sleep, and some reassurance about the murmur, and began to be able to enjoy the baby.

When my daughter was two and a half, I got pregnant again. Although I knew it was a possibility, I didn't think I'd have premature labor again. I thought stress had set it off the first time, so this time I carefully avoided overworking as much as possible. I felt fine, just like last time.

Despite my precautions, at the same time, thirty-three weeks, it happened again. I had moved and had a new doctor. This time I was put on oral antilabor medication, a kind that hadn't worked for me last time, and was sent home on limited activity and a home monitoring system—something unavailable during my first pregnancy.

I monitored for an hour, twice a day, and sent the results to the nurses on a modem, like people with pacemakers do. No IVs, no twenty-four-hour monitoring, no hospital. No mag blues.

I still had to have my mother come stay with me to help me with my daughter, but I was infinitely happier with my situation. I stayed on the couch for a month, until thirty-seven weeks, and played a lot of "Trivial Pursuit." I was not happy about my limitations with my little girl, but at least I could be with her. My worst fear had been that I would have to stay in the hospital and leave her for weeks.

At thirty-seven weeks, I was taken off the medication: no sonograms or amnioctenteses were used to make the decision. This doctor relied much less on technology. He saw no reason for me not to have a vaginal delivery after my C-section.

We waited. And waited. I began lifting heavy objects and climbing the stairs a lot.

Our childbirth instructor had told us, "If you think you might be in labor, don't eat anything you don't want to throw up later." Each night at dinner I speculated about whether I was eating something I wanted to throw up later. I never did come across anything I was really partial to throwing up, later or any other time.

At forty weeks, my doctor scheduled me for an induction the following week, since there was no indication whatsoever that I had any intention of going into labor. He said, "Those anti-labor drugs really work, don't they?" Apparently.

The day before my last checkup, and two days before the induction was scheduled, I started having contractions. Eventually, it became evident that these were different from those things I had been having for weeks, particularly when they started to hurt.

I was apprehensive about labor. I was afraid of the pain, and asked a lot of questions about when I might want an epidural. On a more primitive level, I was afraid of dying. No matter how safe they tell you it is, it remains an experience that reduces women to a primal level, beyond doctors' control. I warned my husband that, if I died and he married some floozy who wouldn't love the children, I'd haunt him.

We got to the hospital at six-thirty A.M., on June 3, 1991,

after being awake all night timing contractions. I thought they'd never get to be five minutes apart. I kissed my sleeping daughter good-bye with a lump in my throat. I knew things would never be exactly the same for us again. It felt like just as spectacular a life change this time as last time.

I was dilated to three centimeters when I got there. The nurse said, "You're going to have this baby quick. You're not going to be here all day." I'd been expecting to be there at least all day. She also said, "You're not going to need an epidural— maybe just a little Demerol." *Really?* It wasn't going to get much worse? Great!

And it didn't. Before I had time to give the epidural much more thought, I was at six centimeters. Why bother at that point? It hurt, mind you, but it just wasn't that bad. The nurse said I slept through transition. (With the help of a little Demerol.) Then, all of a sudden, she said, "In a few minutes you can start to push." Push? It was only about 9:15. But sure enough, it was time, and I pushed.

At 9:50, I delivered a nice, fat, healthy girl who let out a squawk to greet me. And this time my genes beat his genes.

Susan Vano
Brownsville, Texas

♡ *Susan Vano had wanted a second child for eight years, ever since her first was born in 1979. On Christmas Day 1987 she finally got her second child—and her third, fourth, and fifth. Susan tells her story with a lot of humor and gratitude—the two emotions that probably best helped her to cope with the joy and chaos of quadruplets.*

The miracle of Christmas has a new and special meaning for our family, as our quadruplets—Aaron Stephen, Ashley Suzanne, Ryan Joseph, and Jessica Ann—were born on December 25, 1987. Our babies were born ten weeks early with weights ranging from two pounds, five ounces to two pounds, nine ounces.

Larry and I were forty-two and thirty-five, respectively. We had almost given up hope of ever having a second child. But, instead of having one baby as our second child, we had four.

I struggled with infertility, both before and after the birth of our first baby. After seven years of marriage and two heart-breaking miscarriages, I finally gave birth to a beautiful, healthy baby girl in 1979. We named her Angela Jennifer and decided to call her Jenny. My dream of motherhood was finally realized.

In October 1986, my doctor performed a D & C after my fourth miscarriage and determined that endometriosis was making it virtually impossible for my uterus to support a pregnancy.

I was given a drug for the next six months to treat the endometriosis. Then we decided to try the fertility drug Pergonal again. The possibility of multiple births was small, and, besides, that always happens to someone else.

When the sonogram showed four sacs and I could see four little hearts beating, I felt like laughing and crying, all at the same time. We never, ever, expected four. I knew enough to know that the risks associated with multiple births are high.

When Larry came into the room and saw my face, he knew something was wrong. He was speechless when they showed him our four babies on the screen. We were in a very small room and he claims they would have had to pick him up off the floor if the wall had not been holding him up.

At ten weeks my doctor performed a cervical stitch because my cervix was already starting to dilate. By twelve weeks, I had to quit working. At fifteen weeks, I was hospitalized in Brownsville with premature labor. I was given a drug to stop the contractions. It was effective and I continued taking the drug at home every four hours.

I spent the remainder of my pregnancy in bed. During my bedrest, I prayed for a miracle. I also read every book I could find about multiple pregnancies and premature babies.

Jenny watched one of my sonograms and was excited about "seeing" her baby brothers and sisters. She helped us choose names. Jessica Ann was her first choice for a girl's name.

Fortunately, my doctor recommended that I deliver my babies in a hospital with a Level III Neonatal Intensive Care Unit. Level III facilities are equipped to care for the very premature or sick babies needing one-on-one nursing care. If I could deliver in a Level III hospital setting, my babies would not have to be transported after birth.

At twenty-four weeks I was admitted to a hospital in Houston as a precautionary measure. It was difficult for me to leave my obstetrician in Brownsville in the middle of my pregnancy. My infertility specialist in Houston referred me to a Houston OB. She graciously accepted me and my high-risk pregnancy.

Larry and Jenny came to visit me every other weekend. Being away from them was one of the hardest parts of my pregnancy. Houston is three hundred fifty miles from our hometown, Brownsville, Texas. This long-distance separation, both before and after delivery, made our experience especially difficult and expensive. But we will always believe that it meant the difference between life and death for our babies.

For the next six weeks, I didn't leave my hospital room unless I was on a stretcher. They took me down for sonograms and gave me one very quick tour of the Neonatal Intensive Care Unit (NICU).

Meanwhile, the hospital staff formed a "Quad Squad," a team of doctors and nurses who remained on call awaiting the delivery. They were prepared for my delivery at any time, but I had hoped to carry my babies at least thirty-two weeks, which would have meant mid-January. Since the lung maturity of my babies would be crucial to their survival, I was given injections of a drug to help speed up the babies' respiratory development.

At twenty-eight weeks I was as large as women are at forty-two weeks (forty weeks is considered full term). I wondered just how much bigger I would get. I wasn't terribly uncomfortable; I was just big! I gained over fifty pounds.

It became increasingly difficult for me to breathe. I couldn't lie on my back, so I rotated from side to side. When I had contractions, I felt them all the way up to my throat.

By this time, there was no such thing as sleep. The babies were very active, always kicking and waking each other up. It felt like a little foot was literally going to break through my skin. There was just no more room.

My labor-stopping drug dosage was increased to every three hours, so, even if I did fall asleep, a nurse would wake me up. Looking back, I realize this was good conditioning for those feedings every three hours, once the babies came home.

Every morning I was thankful that all five of us were still sharing the same bed. I knew that every day longer I carried these babies increased their chances for survival.

I did not feel good on Christmas Eve, but I was sure I just had the flu. I worried when I had contractions, but still didn't realize that delivery was imminent. All I could think about was seeing Larry and Jenny the next day. I thought that was going to be my best Christmas gift.

My water broke at eleven-thirty P.M. on December 24, 1987. I knew then that my babies would be born on Christmas Day. I hoped that they could wait to deliver until Larry could get there, but no such luck.

My cousin, who lives in Houston, came to hold my hand throughout the delivery. He and his wife have four children, including twin boys, and they were especially supportive throughout my pregnancy. Somehow it seemed appropriate for him to share this memorable moment with me.

The delivery room was full of people, including a team of doctors, nurses, and respiratory therapists for each baby. I was given an epidural to numb me from the waist down. I was thrilled to be able to be awake and I was comfortable during the surgery.

At two A.M. Christmas morning, all four babies were delivered by cesarean section within a span of two minutes. The doctor called out, "Boy" . . . "Girl" . . . "Boy" . . . "Girl," and she held up each baby for me to see, just for a second.

Nothing had prepared me for seeing my tiny babies. They were so small and looked so fragile. Somehow I had imagined that they would be bigger than that. I knew that they were alive and I heard their tiny cries—they sounded like little kittens. The babies were immediately taken away and hooked up to respirators.

Larry and Jenny had planned to fly to Houston Christmas afternoon to spend the weekend with me. As it turned out, Larry woke Jenny at three A.M. to tell her the good news. She was rushed in opening her gifts and getting dressed, so they could take an earlier flight to Houston. They arrived at the hospital about six hours after the babies were born.

While I was still on the delivery table, a nurse asked if it was okay to tell a local television station that I had delivered quadruplets. Actually, I hadn't given it much thought, but I said, "Yes."

My obstetrician had delivered triplets before, but this was her first set of quads. It was also the first set of quads to be born at the hospital, since their Level III NICU was relatively new. A press conference was scheduled for nine A.M., barely giving Larry time to see me before he was rushed out to reporters and photographers.

I was in no mood to be photographed, but Larry was the proudest dad you've ever seen and loved every minute of it. We were totally unprepared for the publicity and the instant celebrity status. To this day, we still draw attention wherever we go.

That day I had to get all my information from Larry and the doctors and nurses. I didn't get to see my babies again until I could get out of bed the next morning. But that night a nurse brought me Polaroid pictures of each baby. I had to look beyond all the tubes and wires connected to my babies, but I could see each one was perfectly beautiful.

Even though I couldn't carry my babies any longer, I could still provide nourishment for them with my breast milk. I began expressing milk every three hours, using an electric pump, and established an adequate milk supply for all my babies. At first, they were fed tiny amounts through a tube to their stomachs, later through a nipple, and, eventually, I was able to nurse them directly.

I was lucky. The cesarean birth and recovery were easy for me, compared to carrying the pregnancy and coping with four tiny babies in the NICU afterward. I was discharged from the hospital only six days after delivery, but it took four long months to get all four babies home. It was emotionally difficult for me to leave the hospital without my babies. I had left the hospital with empty arms too many times already.

Over the next few months, a team of highly trained doctors, nurses, and technicians monitored their heartbeats and breathing for signs of trouble. I held Aaron, Ryan, and Jessica for the first time when they were five days old. Ashley, my largest baby, was the sickest at first and was still under the oxygen hood.

Twelve days after the babies were born, Larry and Jenny went home. The babies were stable, and it was time for them to get back to work and school. I stayed in Houston until the boys were able to come home at seven weeks.

I visited the nursery daily, bringing fresh supplies of breast milk and spending as much time as possible with each baby. I spent my days touching, talking, holding, rocking, and, finally, feeding our babies.

While I was still in the hospital, Jessica, the last baby to be delivered and the smallest of our babies, was diagnosed with a congenital heart defect called a ventricular septal defect. In her case, she had a fairly large hole between two chambers of her tiny heart. It was a life-threatening condition that would require major surgery.

The cardiologists told us she would have to weigh at least twenty pounds before surgery could be considered. In the meantime, she was treated with drugs and closely monitored. She did grow ever so slowly, but life was incredibly difficult for her.

The boys had no serious setbacks and we were able to bring them home on February 15, 1988. By now they weighed almost five pounds each. Bringing our two boys home was thrilling and should have been a joyous occasion for us, but, instead, it was bittersweet. That day there were no words—only tears of joy, relief, sadness, and good-byes. My heart was torn in two different directions. I hated leaving our two tiny girls in Houston.

Ashley was able to come home five days later, but it was Jessica I worried about. Not only that, things became far more complicated, once the first babies came home. Now we had to care for three tiny babies and our older daughter at home, as well as cope with a very sick baby in Houston.

The next two months were full of stress, fear, frustration, and anxiety. Larry and I needed to be with Jessica as much as possible, and somehow we managed. Friends and relatives, especially Larry's mother, came to the rescue.

It seemed like, once we got the first three babies home, Jessica's condition began to deteriorate rapidly. By the middle of March, she was in critical condition, and it was evident that she could not live without the surgery. I cannot find the words to describe our feelings of helplessness as we watched Jessica literally fight for life.

On March 18, she was transferred to a children's hospital in Houston. On March 24, a surgeon performed an operation to close the hole in her heart. Our barely five-pound baby girl underwent open-heart surgery.

Our prayers were answered. The surgery was a complete success. On April 20, after 118 days of hospitalization, we finally brought Jessica home. She was almost four months old and weighed six pounds. Only now did I feel complete. It was such a relief to have all four babies home at last, and just in time for Mother's Day.

Our medical bills totaled almost $500,000. Much of that was covered by insurance, but our travel, telephone, and living expenses were not.

That was only the beginning. Four babies basically cost four times as much. We needed four times as many diapers and four times as much clothing. Soon we needed four cribs, four high chairs, four car seats, and even a car big enough to hold everyone, plus two double strollers.

I am a CPA and was working part-time for a local accounting firm when I got pregnant. I had planned to continue working after the birth of our second child. But plans change when you have four babies at once. Going from two incomes to one has not been easy, especially when so many expenses quadrupled for us.

Once the babies were home, it was feeding babies, changing babies, bathing babies, rocking babies, loving babies twenty-four hours a day. It was nonstop baby care all day and all night. Lights never went off at our house.

Basically, I tried to do everything I would have done for one baby—only I did it four times. A schedule was absolutely essential. At first, each baby was fed, burped, and changed at least eight times a day. With four babies, each feeding could take almost two hours. I tried to nurse at least one baby at each feeding, usually the last one to be fed. We needed at least twenty-four bottles a day and used over two hundred diapers each week.

Several friends and family members volunteered to be the extra hands we needed to care for our babies. Others cared for Larry, Jenny, and me. Friends brought meals to the house on a regular basis—every Monday, Wednesday, and Friday for four months.

One friend came over five nights a week to help Larry with the ten P.M. feeding so I could get some sleep. I took the one A.M. feeding by myself and then Larry would get up for the four A.M. feeding.

Larry is my best friend. He is also the most supportive, helpful, caring, and involved husband and father. He has always been there for me—throughout endless night feedings and diaper changes, four crying and/or screaming babies, and our older daughter's demands for love and attention.

Aaron, Ashley, Ryan, and Jessica are two years old now [in 1990]. Times have really changed, but every day continues to be a challenge for me. They are always on the go and into everything. Babyproofing takes on a whole new meaning with four toddlers in the house.

Doing anything with quadruplets is at least four times as difficult as doing it with only one child. Consequently, we didn't take them out very much.

Even now, it can take an hour or more just to get them dressed. We have four typical two-year-olds who want to do things for themselves. Before I'm finished with the last one, at least one of the others has started undressing!

We know the four have a special bond as they have shared everything from day one. We hope they will grow up to be the best of friends. Yet our goal will be to raise all of our children as individuals, rather than a single child and a set of four. Each child is special and has his or her own personality.

Jenny is an extraordinary big sister. It's not easy going from an only child to one of five overnight. Sharing Mom and Dad's time and attention has surely been the single most difficult adjustment for her. At the same time, she takes pride in her brothers' and sisters' accomplishments and enjoys them more now that they can talk and play with her. She recognizes their individuality and knows what will make each one happy.

I look at my children now and my heart is filled with gratitude. So many wonderful people have touched our lives and shared our experiences with us.

Throughout my struggle with infertility over the years, and especially in my quadruplet pregnancy, I had outstanding, caring doctors and nurses who provided much more than medical knowledge. Their genuine concern and encouragement carried me through an emotionally difficult pregnancy.

One doctor, in particular, visited me daily in the hospital, giving me pep talks. His positive attitude and optimism were contagious.

All of our efforts were rewarded and we were blessed with four precious babies. I will always be grateful for the medical technology and the dedicated doctors and nurses who helped make it possible for our tiny babies to live.

We have survived the best and the worst of times, thanks to the help of our family and many wonderful friends. Their generous response to our special needs has been nothing short of overwhelming. From the day we announced my pregnancy, they shared our worries and concerns, they prayed for all of us, and they have rejoiced in our phenomenal blessings.

Our children are alive. They can see and hear. They can walk and talk. All of them can laugh and smile, hug and kiss. Who could ask for anything more?

Final Thoughts

In *Education and Counseling for Childbirth,* Sheila Kitzinger says:

> To help women through childbirth is to share a mystery and a miracle. . . . It is also to touch life at a key point in the social system, when generation gives way to generation, when bitterness and frustration and a sense of worthlessness can be handed down to the next generation, or the opportunity taken to grow in understanding and love. There is more to having a baby than simply pushing an occipito-anterior out into the world. Birth is also implicitly an assent to life. Those who help women in childbirth have the privilege of sharing that act of assent.

If there is anything that is obvious in the stories in this book, it is that women who are having babies, if they are conscious at all, *never forget* how they were treated and *never forget* those who dispensed that treatment, whether it was good or bad or somewhere in between.

The attitude toward birth represented by Sheila Kitzinger's wise words above has been too often forgotten in the American system of childbearing. Mothers are required to call on their deepest resources when they have their children; they should be allowed to do it in a setting and under conditions that seem best to them. And, while they are involved in the world's most essential work, they should receive the maximum in support, patience, and understanding, from all those who are fortunate enough to be assisting.

Yet it is impossible to read the stories in this book without concluding that, despite some of the notable triumphs of technology—Elise Gunst's postponed preemie births, for example, or Susan Vano's quadruplets—we Americans have not done a very good job of taking care of mothers who are having babies.

In the beginning of this century we just didn't know very much about helping mothers to have babies more successfully. What the doctors sometimes did, with the best of intentions, was to cause more harm, rather than less, with the inept and casual wielding of dangerous instruments and the spreading of infection which caused devastating, recurrent childbed fever epidemics for generations. These problems continued even after most births were moved to the hospital in the name of safety and the relief of suffering.

Then medical science and the improving health of women who were no longer bearing children year after year after year really did combine to save the lives of both mothers and babies. But in the process, it seems, the sacred sense of birth—not as a disease or an injury, but as a threshold over which new living creatures pass to come into this world—was almost entirely lost.

Oh, there were always thousands of good doctors and fine nurses, whose primary concern was to give good care and support to women and their babies. Some of them are described and given credit in this book.

But it seems that the women in this book who had good childbirth experiences generally fell into one of two categories: either they were extraordinarily fortunate and just happened upon a good doctor and a positive environment for birthing—or, more likely, like Dorothy Mullenneaux, Martha McIntyre, Mary Garland, Barbara Crotty, Sherley Hollos, and Peggy Eggers, they knew what they wanted and kept looking and insisting until they found it. Too often, those who took their chances and didn't

know exactly what they were getting ended up with an experience that was frightening, painful, and bewildering—during
which they felt passive and helpless.

The problem of the passive birther still exists today. The
women I have named above should inspire all of us to do better
by our babies and ourselves. We are no longer sheltered from
knowledge about our bodies and what is going to happen to us,
if we choose to learn—but too many of us still don't really pay
attention, don't do our homework, and don't find out enough
ahead of time about the birth attendants who will help us bring
our babies into this world.

So, too many women each year still end up with cesareans—
or forceps births with big episiotomies, muttering to themselves,
"Well, the important thing is that the baby is all right," and
wondering vaguely what went wrong and whether what happened to them was really necessary.

If consumerism played a larger part in childbirth, the C-section
rate would drop. Women have already succeeded in demanding
more VBACs and ending once and for all the stern dictum
"Once a cesarean, always a cesarean."

If we began with the *first* birth, not the second—studying the
process, finding out in detail how a doctor or midwife really
conducts a birth from previous clients before we choose a birth
attendant, asking about C-section rates of doctors and hospitals,
et cetera, insisting on a more undisturbed and natural process
unless intervention is really necessary—then the system would
change. It would have to.

The important thing is not the color scheme in the lovely new
birthing suite: that's just window dressing. The important thing
is a birth attendant who *listens* as well as talks, who answers
questions honestly when they are asked, who is willing to be
flexible, who treats a mother about to have a baby as an intelligent equal—not a child or an adversary or a nuisance, and who
never, never says, "Now, honey, just don't you worry about
that. Just leave that to me."

One of the best guides a woman anticipating childbirth can

have is a Bradley instructor who teaches good nutrition during pregnancy, the details of the birthing process, and how to cope with birth effectively at every stage. The two Bradley instructors I knew were exceptionally fine and knowledgeable women, intensely committed to helping couples have good births. Probably every city of any size and many smaller communities will also have other kinds of good, independent childbirth teachers and educators who can provide similar instruction.

Even though I don't consider myself a model of any kind for parents planning natural childbirth (I didn't manage that), I think my husband and I benefited enormously from what we learned in the Bradley classes. How? I never had a C-section. I never had a forceps delivery. With the last two births I had no episiotomy—and only a small one with the first. My daughters were all in good condition from the beginning—healthy, alert.

The following advice is anathema to the true believers in natural childbirth, whom I greatly respect, but I do think that, even if a woman ends up with painkillers at the end, she still gains, and her baby gains, from putting off the drugs as long as possible. And if she can do without them entirely, so much the better.

Birth, of course, is only the beginning. Another theme that runs through this book is a concern with breastfeeding. Mother after mother says she tried it and "failed" because her milk was too "thin" or inadequate—relying on the misinformation mothers (including my own) were frequently given back in the thirties and forties. Others say they succeeded in nursing against all odds and have never forgotten the warmth and tenderness of the experience or their pride in being able to do this for their children.

It saddens me to see so many new mothers today—even some who aren't working—readily abandon the effort to nurse or not even try, when we now know it is possible for every woman, or almost every woman, to nurse her child. These days there is guidance and support available (bless those La Leche League mothers who return late-night phone calls), plus we know how important it is for that child.

It's also quite possible for a working mother to nurse success-fully part-time, morning and evening, and still have much the same sense of closeness and give the baby many of the same nutritional benefits.

Nursing is worth more than a little effort: it is the one gift you can give your baby that no one else can. Of course, no woman should force herself to nurse if she really is extremely uncomfortable with the whole idea. It does require a certain relaxation of our traditional American prudishness and sense of discomfort with the basic functions of our own bodies.

Nursing is indeed natural but it's not always easy. It requires a firm, long-term commitment to get over the hard parts—including pain sometimes, inconvenience, difficulties getting you and the baby in sync with each other, et cetera. But the baby will bloom and you and she/he will have a special relationship that is difficult to convey in words.

There is a kind of feeling when the baby is born that, although you are so glad to have her with you in person, your body almost regrets letting her go. She has been so well taken care of in the womb. Now you have to worry about a thousand things that could happen to her out in the big world. Nursing helps you make that transition, helps you remain, in a way, two in one, until you are both ready, more gently, more gradually, to separate from each other.

And finally, just a few words for first-time, about-to-be moth-ers. Don't worry that some of the bad things that are described in this book might happen to you. Your experience will be unique and unlike anyone else's, but I can almost promise you great joy—especially if you have sought knowledge, asked your-self what *you* really want, and tried earnestly to plan to make that happen. (The unexpected will always happen, too, in any birth: you have to be ready to shift ground and make a new plan if circumstances demand it.)

One of the best sources of reading material during pregnancy is the brief reading list in Susan McCutcheon-Rosegg's *Natural Childbirth the Bradley Way*. To her list I would add *A Good*

Birth, a Safe Birth by Diana Korte and Roberta Scaer; a good pregnancy exercise book like Elizabeth Noble's *Essential Exercises for the Childbearing Year;* and *Special Women: The Role of the Professional Labor Assistant*—about doulas and monitrices—by Paulina Perez and Cheryl Snedeker. A good source for books about any aspect of birth is the Birth & Life Bookstore in Seattle.

There is a wealth of fine material out there. You are so lucky. When I was first pregnant in 1969–70, the only comprehensive book I could find was *Expectant Motherhood* by Nicholson J. Eastman, which, among other things, advised women on "how to telephone the doctor" (I thought I could manage to figure that out on my own) and avoiding "bridge-table obstetrics"; in other words, don't listen to gossip from "the girls."

You are about to experience one of the greatest adventures of your life, though we tend to view it as commonplace. Ancient forces within you and the love around you will help keep you going. And, when it's over and the baby is with you, you will probably feel a euphoria that makes it hard to sleep right away, knowing that this new life is now part of yours.

This whole book has been devoted to birthing babies, but, as one of "my" mothers wrote me, "If it was as easy to raise them as it was to deliver them, I would have had a dozen!"

Birth is only the first day. Start your baby off right by nursing her/him. And when she cries, please pick her up. She will get beyond needing you much too soon as it is.

Endnotes

1. One of the women who sent me her birth story pointed out that Grantly Dick Read's last name is not hyphenated. I examined the copy I have of a letter from the doctor himself and saw that, in fact, he did not hyphenate his last name—despite the fact that many of my most respected sources do put a hyphen in it. So, I am doing without the hyphen and referring to him in the traditional American fashion as "Dr. Read." "Dr. Dick Read" with no hyphen is just too misleading.

2. The reason for tying a woman's hands down at the point of birthing was supposedly to protect the "sterile field" created around the lower part of the body with draping, cleansing, and, sometimes, the use of disinfectants. Legs were lifted, spread apart, and strapped in place in stirrups in the "lithotomy" position, to give the doctor a better view of and access to the birth. Women often found that being placed in this position and strapped down was uncomfortable and degrading— not to mention that pushing was very difficult while lying flat on one's back with legs in the air. Many doctors are no longer insisting on the lithotomy position for birthing. Before lithotomy became medically routine, the traditional position for birthing was sitting or squatting so that the force of gravity could help to bring the baby down.

3. Throughout the stories in this book the names of birth attendants and hospitals have been eliminated: The book is not intended to attack some individuals or institutions or to praise others. The problems described in most stories were not confined to a few doctors or nurses or hospitals; neither were acts of kindness and caring.

The one hospital identified (in this footnote) as the location of a birth described in this book is The University of Michigan Women's (then

"Maternity") Hospital in Ann Arbor, Michigan. Some trailblazing efforts that seem worth singling out were made there in the 1950s to bring mothers closer to their babies.

The new maternity hospital in Ann Arbor opened its doors on February 14, 1950, with an entirely unique arrangement of nurseries in relation to the mothers' rooms, planned by Hazel Avery, R.N., supervisor of nurses, with the support of Dr. Norman Miller, chief of staff. The concept was a decentralized nursery with four-bed nurseries between two semiprivate rooms for mothers, with glass partitions in between. Each mother could keep her baby with her in her room at all times or could put the baby in the adjacent nursery, where she could observe him/her through the partition. There were eleven of these small nurseries between patient rooms.

According to Nancy Rook Nelson, N '51, executive secretary of the University of Michigan School of Nursing Alumnae Association, the nurses who took care of a group of mothers also took care of the babies belonging to those mothers. At night, the babies in the small nurseries were checked by nurses every fifteen minutes. At that time, Nancy Nelson recalls, even breastfeeding mothers were not encouraged to nurse around the clock. Shades were pulled between the mothers' rooms and the nurseries and the babies were given glucose or formula at night.

Sometime during the '60s state health personnel decided that it wasn't safe for babies to remain in the smaller nurseries unattended, even though they were right next to their mothers' rooms. "But we never lost a baby," says Nancy Nelson.

Grace Puravs, librarian at the *Ann Arbor News,* recalls having a baby at the hospital in 1966 and says at that time mothers were responsible for care of the baby, if they wished, during the day and babies were returned to the central nursery at night.

4. Dr. Alice B. Stockham's *Tokology* (obstetrics), published in 1883, is a charming book, ahead of its time in many ways, that champions women and recommends that they eat whole-grain bread, walk and exercise during pregnancy, and avoid corsets throughout their lives. Stockham also insists that sexual relations should always be mutually desired, and that men should shoulder the responsibility for children to the same degree as women. On the other hand, Stockham promulgates some bogus and dated principles. Among these are her pronouncements that 1) intercourse with withdrawal causes impotence in men and sterility in women, along with "headache, defective vision, dyspepsia,

insomnia, loss of memory," and other evils, and 2) women should avoid intercourse entirely during pregnancy, because it "exhausts the mother and impairs the vitality of the child, inducing in its constitution precocious sexual development.[!]"

5. A Boston doctor, writing to the *Journal of the American Medical Association* in 1897, made the same point about using "a lady's pocket handkerchief, folded as it comes to me," to administer chloroform. (E. Chenery, letter to editor, *JAMA* 28, January 16, 1897, pp. 133–34.) Perhaps a man's handkerchief, being bigger and made of heavier material, would have absorbed too much of the chloroform and overdosed the patient.

6. From the early 1900s on, knowledgeable attendants routinely gave newborn babies drops of a 1 percent solution of silver nitrate in each eye right after birth, to prevent blindness caused by gonorrhea. Since gonorrhea often presented no symptoms in the mother and the consequences of infection in the newborn were so severe, the standard practice was to put protective drops in the eyes of *every* newborn. Because of the tendency of silver nitrate to cause temporary "chemical conjunctivitis," it is common now for attendants to use penicillin ointment (or shots), tetracycline ointment, or erythromycin ointment instead.

7. Animal bladders, rubber bags, and balloons introduced into the uterus and then inflated were used by some doctors in the first half of the 1900s to induce labor.

8. Childbed fever, or puerperal fever, was the leading cause of maternal death in the U.S. until the 1930s. A generalized infection caused by the introduction of bacteria into the woman's body during childbirth, childbed fever was more often associated with hospital births than with home births, and more often with doctors than with midwives. The cause was usually unsterile obstetric technique. Doctors carried the infection from woman to woman because they did more vaginal exams than midwives—and often went to attend laboring women directly from dissecting the corpse of a woman who had died! According to Richard and Dorothy Wertz in *Lying-In: a History of Childbirth in America,* as late as 1927 one American hospital had an epidemic of childbed fever that killed 15 percent of the patients. The dreaded disease was finally brought under control with the introduction of sulfa and penicillin.

9. Mother's Friend, a lotion intended to prevent stretch marks in pregnant women and ease the itching and dryness of stretching skin on

breasts and stomach, has quite a history. Composed of "winter-pressed" cottonseed oil, soft liquid soap, camphor, menthol, and alcohol, the product has been manufactured since 1887—according to Charles Bentley, president of Atlanta's venerable S.S.S. Company (founded in 1826). Although a cream product has been added to the line, the formula of the original product has never varied.

10. According to *Nurses Handbook of Obstetrics* by Louise Zabriskie, R.N., and Nicholson J. Eastman, M.D., the dearth of doctors, nurses, and even hospital beds during World War II forced hospitals to release new mothers after three or four days, instead of keeping them in bed for ten days or more, as had been the custom. Medical staff soon observed that, when women got up quickly, there were fewer patients who needed catheterization and fewer with constipation and abdominal distention—as well as more serious ailments like phlebitis. Thus, what began as wartime necessity finally liberated women from the tedious, uncomfortable, prolonged bedrest after childbirth, which so many women in this book found annoying.

11. Quentin was sent to China in the spring of 1948 to serve as vice-president of China National Aviation, a subsidiary of PanAm. Two months later, Frances took her three children (whom she fondly called the "pets") by freighter to join him. On December 22, 1948, he was killed when a C-54 Skymaster crashed on a journey from Shanghai to Hong Kong.

According to the Theodore Roosevelt Association, "he [Quentin] was, as we now know, in the C.I.A. in China, and sabotage is definitely suspected in his death." Frances says that flight crews calculated the flight from Shanghai to Hong Kong on foggy days, by using time and speed. The Hong Kong Chinese man who gave the crew the wrong landing time probably deliberately caused the plane to crash.

After Quentin's death, Frances continued to work as an artist and raised her children at Quentin's family home on Long Island. The oldest daughter, Alexandra, became a gifted photographer. She married anesthesiologist Ronald Dworkin in 1988 and moved to Baltimore. Daughter number two, Anna Curtenius, is an archaeologist considered to be one of the top scientists in her field, the geophysical archaeology of the Lower Amazon. In 1989 she received a MacArthur Foundation "genius" grant, $265,000 given over a five-year period, to enable her to pursue her work. The youngest child, Susan, is an attorney and teaches classes in the history of Chinese law at Harvard. She is married to William Weld, governor of Massachusetts and descendant of William Floyd, a signer of the Declaration of Independence.

12. An infectious skin disease characterized by redness, swelling, fever, and pain. It is caused by a species of group A streptococci and treated today with antibiotics.

13. Janice Gale's proud mention here of her minimal weight gain during pregnancy recalls the following important historical notes from the Wertzes' *Lying-In:* "Between 1920 and about 1975, three generations of women starved themselves during pregnancy to keep their weight gain below the recommended twenty-pound limit, thereby producing untold thousands of low-birthweight infants and possibly causing some neonatal deaths." In fact, many doctors insisted on a weight gain of *less* than twenty pounds.

This principle developed after World War I, according to *Lying-In,* because researchers discovered that the incidence of toxemia of pregnancy was reduced during the war in areas of Europe that had experienced semi-starvation. In fact, medical researchers now believe that severe restrictions in weight gain during pregnancy can lead to underweight babies—and that maternal weight gain and water retention may be *symptoms,* rather than causes, of toxemia. The doctor who is educated about nutrition is more likely now to recommend a weight gain of twenty-five to thirty-five pounds during pregnancy.

14. The use of castor oil to induce labor recurs in a number of the birth stories I received. Apparently, it was in common use for this purpose from the late 1700s until well into the present century. However, one medical school professor described it, in 1958, as a "dehydrating, debilitating, drastic drug" which "should be used on machinery only." (John Parks, quoted in G. C. Nabors' "Castor Oil as an Adjunct to Induction of Labor: Critical Reevaluation," *American Journal of Obstetrics and Gynecology* 75:1, January 1958, p. 38.)

15. The Wertzes in *Lying-In* on DES: "DES, short for the drug diethylstilbestrol, was . . . widely promoted. Between 1946 and 1977, over two million women took DES because numerous scientific journals touted its ability to provide a '96 percent normal live birthrate' for women with a history of miscarriages. Doctors began to prescribe it routinely as a preventive measure, regardless of medical indications. Only after a generation of children exposed to DES in the womb grew

up, did doctors become aware that it could cause genital cancers in girls and infertility in boys.''

This brief description of the DES disaster appears in *Lying-In* as part of a long list of other obstetrical techniques that were hailed as panaceas and used on countless women without ever being carefully tested, or that were originally intended for use in special cases, then were routinely applied to every birth, whether needed or not—and after some time were discovered to have serious, sometimes fatal, side effects. Other examples include forceps, twilight sleep, and fetal X-rays.

The Wertzes also point out that ultrasound, so widely used today, "has never undergone the large-scale, controlled clinical trials that would prove its safety. . . . Some knowledgeable observers believe that ultrasound may be the DES of the future.''

16. It is standard policy in most American hospitals today that laboring women are not allowed to eat or drink at all (they may be allowed to have ice chips)—because of the fear that they might end up in a crisis under general anesthesia and may be in danger of vomiting and then aspirating whatever is in their stomachs. They are often hooked up to an IV throughout labor, which is intended to prevent dehydration. IV solutions, of course, do nothing to relieve thirst.

Laboring women who are having their babies at home, on the other hand, are generally encouraged to drink fluids and to eat lightly, if they wish, as an aid to maintaining strength and endurance during what might be a long labor. Some hospitals are now allowing some fluid intake by mouth.

17. The book was, undoubtedly, *Six Practical Lessons for an Easier Childbirth,* published in 1967. Elizabeth Bing is a famous childbirth educator who helped to popularize the Lamaze method of natural childbirth in this country.

18. It was apparently feared that the baby had a form of jaundice, more serious than the common jaundice that often follows birth, which can result from a blood group incompatibility between mother and baby and can cause damage to the baby's nervous system and brain cells. Nursing was considered to be one more source of continuing exposure to the mother's incompatible blood. Some experts today believe that even temporarily taking the infant off the breast in cases of jaundice is not necessary—that, in most cases, the bilirubin level (orange-yellow pigment in bile, formed by the breakdown of hemoglobin in red blood

cells) will drop anyway, or treatment will cause it to drop, whether or not the baby is taken off the breast.

19. The Bradley method of husband-coached childbirth, named after Dr. Robert A. Bradley, is less well known but, I think, far more effective than the Lamaze method. There are trained Bradley instructors in most parts of the United States. They usually hold childbirth classes in their homes—not at the hospital—and put a great deal of emphasis on training for childbirth and on good nutrition during pregnancy and breastfeeding after the baby is born.

20. One of the most important benefits is avoiding bringing the baby into the world too soon because of a miscalculation of the actual duration of the pregnancy. Another possible benefit is described by Peggy Eggers as follows: "... a mother's endorphin level rises before the onset of spontaneous labor. Those endorphins act as the body's natural painkillers and mood elevators."

21. Peggy Eggers cites research that claims that, depending on indications for previous cesareans, VBAC's have a proven success rate of 73–94 percent. (See "Repeat Cesareans—Mostly Unnecessary," by Richard P. Porreco, M.D., and Paul R. Meier, M.D., in *Contemporary OB/GYN* 24, September 1984, p. 56.)

22. The doctor was present, did perineal massage to help the baby be born without an episiotomy or natural tear, delivered the head (with only a minor tear), unwrapped the cord, which was wrapped around the baby's head, and delivered the baby's arms and shoulders. Then Peter received the body.

23. Dr. Frederick Leboyer wrote *Birth Without Violence,* in which he advocated establishing a gentle environment for a newborn baby at birth, with dimmed lights, reduced noise, very sensitive and gentle handling, and a warm bath to restore the newborn to a comforting sense of the medium from which he/she has just come—the water in the uterus.

24. On June 29, 1990, and again on September 22, 1992, President George Bush vetoed a bill which would have guaranteed workers up to 12 weeks' *unpaid* leave for childbirth, adoption, or family illness. Suzanne writes that paid maternity leave in Norway has now been increased to 28 weeks—still the lowest in Scandinavia.

25. Galactosemia is an inherited recessive disorder of galactose metabo-

lism. (Galactose is a simple sugar found in lactose or milk sugar.) A baby who has the disorder rapidly shows an intolerance for milk and develops mental retardation, cataracts, and abnormal enlargement of the liver and spleen. Immediate elimination of galactose from the diet is critical.

26. The "gold card" is evidence that Elena has been properly documented and registered as someone who is eligible to receive health care services from the Harris County Hospital District. She had to prove that she was a "qualified indigent person who is a resident of Harris County" to receive the card.

Bibliography

"Advance Report of Final Natality Statistics, 1988." *Monthly Vital Statistics Report*, National Center for Health Statistics 39:4, Supplement (August 15, 1990).

Baker, S. Josephine, M.D. *Fighting for Life*. New York: Macmillan, 1939.

"Births, Marriages, Divorces, and Deaths for 1990." *Monthly Vital Statistics Report*, National Center for Health Statistics 39:12 (April 8, 1991).

Bradley, Robert A., M.D. *Husband-Coached Childbirth*, third ed. new York: Harper & Row, 1981.

Chard, Tim, and Martin Richards, eds. *Benefits and Hazards of the New Obstetrics*. Philadelphia: J. B. Lippincott, 1977.

Leavitt, Judith W. *Brought to Bed: Childbearing in America, 1750 to 1950*. New York: Oxford University Press, 1986.

Litoff, Judy B. *American Midwives: 1860 to the Present*. Westport, Connecticut: Greenwood Press, 1978.

Lull, Clifford B., M.D., and Robert A. Hingson, M.D. *Control of Pain in Childbirth: Anesthesia, Analgesia, Amnesia*. Philadelphia: J. B. Lippincott, 1944.

New York Academy of Medicine Committee on Public Health

Relations. *Maternal Mortality in New York City: a Study of All Puerperal Deaths, 1930–1932*. New York: The Commonwealth Fund, 1933.

Rich, Spencer. "Best Showing Ever: U.S. Infant Mortality Rate Still Trails Many Nations." *Washington Post*, reprinted in *Houston Chronicle*, August 31, 1990. p. 14A.

Sandelowski, Margarete. *Pain, Pleasure and American Childbirth: From the Twilight Sleep to the Read Method, 1914–1960*. Westport, Connecticut: Greenwood Press, 1984.

Shapiro, Sam, Edward R. Schlesinger, and Robert E.L. Nesbitt, Jr. *Infant, Perinatal, Maternal and Childhood Mortality in the United States*. Cambridge, Massachusetts: Harvard University Press, 1968.

Shultz, Gladys Denny. "Journal Mothers Report on Cruelty in Maternity Wards." *Ladies Home Journal*, May 1958, pp. 44–45 ff.

SoRelle, Ruth. "Infant Death Rates Split by Race: Mortality Up for Black Babies, Down for Whites, Hispanics." *Houston Chronicle*, April 12, 1991, p. 1A ff.

Stafford, Randall S., Ph.D. "The Impact of Nonclinical Factors on Repeat Cesarean Section." *Journal of the American Medical Association* (JAMA) 265: 1 (January 2, 1991), pp. 59–63.

Taffel, Selma M., B.B.A., Paul J. Placek, Ph.D., Mary Molen, M.S., and Carol L. Kosary, M.A. "1989 U.S. Cesarean Section Rate Steadies—VBAC Rate Rises to Nearly One in Five." *Birth* 18:2 (June 1991), pp. 73–77.

Tracy, Marguerite, and Mary Boyd. *Painless Childbirth: a General Survey of All Painless Methods with Special Stress on "Twilight Sleep" and Its Extension to America*. New York: Frederick A. Stokes Company, 1915.

Wertz, Richard W., and Dorothy C. Wertz. *Lying-In: A History of Childbirth in America,* expanded ed. New Haven and London: Yale University Press, 1989.

White House Conference on Child Health and Protection. *Fetal, Newborn and Maternal Morbidity and Mortality*. New York and London: D. Appleton-Century Company, 1933.

Glossary

afterbirth: Placenta and fetal membranes expelled after the baby is born.

amnesic, amnesiac: Causing total or partial loss of memory.

amniocentesis: An obstetric procedure in which a small amount of amniotic fluid is removed, usually between the sixteenth and twentieth weeks of gestation, to aid in the diagnosis of fetal abnormalities. Amniocentesis can now be performed as early as the twelfth week of pregnancy. It may also be performed near the end of pregnancy to test for fetal lung maturity (see story of Elise Gunst).

anterior vs. posterior birth: In anterior (the most common) birth the baby faces the mother's spine and comes out face-down. In a posterior birth (about 25 percent of all births) the baby moves through labor facing the front of the mother and usually turns around to the anterior position before it is born. Occasionally, a baby is born in the posterior position with face up (sometimes called "sunny side up"). A posterior labor tends to be more difficult with more backache.

Apgar score: Named after Virginia Apgar, M.D., American anesthesiologist. The evaluation of an infant's physical condition, usually performed at one minute and again at five minutes after birth. The Apgar rates the infant's heart rate, respiratory effort, muscle tone, reflex irritability, and color on a scale of 0 (low) to 2 (normal). The maximum score is 10. The five-minute score is usually higher than the one-minute score. A score of 0 to 3 indicates severe distress, a score of 4 to 7 indicates moderate distress, a score of 7 to 10 indicates an absence of difficulty in adjusting to life outside the womb. The system was developed to help identify immediately infants requiring intervention or transfer to an intensive care nursery.

Braxton-Hicks: Named after British physician John Braxton Hicks. The irregular tightening of the pregnant uterus that may occur throughout the pregnancy and increases as the birth of the baby approaches. Near term, Braxton-Hicks contractions can be strong enough that they are difficult to distinguish from the contractions of true labor.

breech birth: The baby is born feet, knees, or buttocks first, instead of in the usual position, which is head first. In about 3–4 percent of all labors, the baby is in the breech position in the uterus before birth. A breech birth is considered potentially dangerous because the body may deliver easily but the "after-coming," larger head may be trapped by an incompletely dilated cervix.

At present, according to Dr. Joseph Hanss in his article "The Efficacy of External Cephalic Version and its Impact on the Breech Experience" (*American Journal of Obstetrics and Gynecology* 162:6, June 1990, pp. 1459–64), about 90 percent of breech babies are delivered by C-section at term. Breech presentation is the second most common reason given for a C-section, according to the Taffel article in *Birth,* cited in the bibliography on the history of childbirth. The rate (about 4 percent for all deliveries) has stayed about the same, but in 1989 84 percent of breech babies were delivered by Cesarean as compared to 67 percent in 1980.

Hanss reports successful use of external cephalic version (turning the baby by external manipulation) to avoid C-sections. Hanss also maintains that breech babies born at term by C-sections don't do appreciably better than breech babies born vaginally and advocates more training of young doctors in turning babies and in the various ways of delivering breech babies. "Delivering a breech infant through an abdominal wall incision is very little different in terms of the mechanisms from delivering a breech through the vaginal canal," says Hanss. "Today many of our residents are deficient in the knowledge and skill necessary to safely extract a breech from the uterus, even through a lower uterine incision."

caudal anesthesia or caudal block: Regional anesthesia induced by an injection of a local anesthetic agent into the end of the spinal canal at the lower end of the sacrum. It is little used today because of the difficulty of controlling the level of the anesthesia, the need for large volumes of anesthetic solution, a high rate of failure (5–10 percent), frequent neurologic complications, lowered blood pressure, and reduced force of labor. It has been largely replaced by the epidural.

cesarean section: A surgical procedure in which the abdomen and uterus are cut open and the baby is delivered through the incisions.

chloroform: A nonflammable, volatile liquid that was the first inhalation anesthetic to be discovered. It can be administered with just a medicine dropper and a handkerchief face mask and is still used in underdeveloped countries where more complex equipment may not be available. It is a dangerous drug that can cause lowered blood pressure, depression of heart and breathing rates, shock, fibrillation of the heart, coma, and death. Delayed poisoning can occur, even weeks after apparent recovery. Serious damage to the eyes is also often reported.

colostrum: First fluid produced by the mother's breasts postpartum before lactation begins. Colostrum contains many important antibodies and is especially important in protecting the baby against infection for the first six months of life.

D & C: Dilatation and curettage—opening of the cervix with instruments and scraping of the lining of the uterus. This is the procedure most commonly used when an abortion is performed. It is also used for many other gynecological purposes, including removing retained material following an incomplete miscarriage.

dilatation, dilation: The opening of the cervix in labor to accommodate the passing of the baby's head. At full dilatation the diameter of the cervical opening is said to be 10 centimeters or about five fingers (each finger being about two centimeters wide).

doula: Comes from Greek words meaning "in service of." A doula is a professional labor assistant who gives physical and emotional support to the mother during labor and delivery. See also "monitrice." A study published in the *Journal of the American Medical Association* (JAMA) May 1, 1991, documented the fact that the presence of a supportive companion to help a woman in labor and delivery significantly reduced the incidence of cesareans, the use of epidurals and oxytocin, and the length of the labor.

dystocia: Difficult labor, which may be caused by an obstruction or constriction of the birth passage or an abnormal size, shape, position, or condition of the fetus. "Shoulder dystocia" is a serious complication of delivery that occurs when the head is delivered, causing the cord to be drawn into the pelvis and compressed, and then there is an arrest to the delivery of the shoulders.

epidural: Injection of a local anesthetic into the epidural space that surrounds the outermost membrane enclosing the brain and spinal cord. This is the most commonly used form of regional anesthesia in labor and delivery today. Possible side effects include accidental puncture of the membranes surrounding the spinal cord (the epidural becomes a spinal—see "spinal anesthesia"), lowered blood pressure, slowed infant heartbeat, maternal shaking and convulsions, and a reduction in the force and effec-

tiveness of contractions. Epidurals may also make pushing inef-
fective, thereby resulting in a forceps or cesarean delivery.

episiotomy: An incision made in the pelvic floor (perineum)
just prior to the baby's birth to help ease the widest part of the
baby's head through the vagina and, ostensibly, to prevent natural tearing. It is done far more commonly in the United States
than in other industrialized countries because it became customary medical practice in the early part of the century to deliver
all babies with episiotomies and outlet forceps—partly because
many women were too drugged to assist in the delivery of their
babies.

Many doctors still say that it's better to do an episiotomy and
have a neat surgical incision to repair than to try to repair a
jagged natural laceration. The fact is that many births can occur
without either incision or tear—and that natural tears are often
much smaller and easier to repair than surgical cuts. Episiotomies can result in prolonged pain and infection and can extend
into more serious tears than would occur naturally. (For a detailed discussion, see *Natural Childbirth the Bradley Way* by
Susan McCutcheon-Rosegg with Peter Rosegg.)

A recent article in *The Online Journal of Current Clinical
Trials* entitled "Does Episiotomy Prevent Perineal Trauma and
Pelvic Floor Relaxation?" supports what natual-childbirth educators have been saying for years. The authors of the research
paper conducted the first North American clinical trials testing
the usefulness of episiotomies since the introduction of the procedure in the 1920s [!] and concluded, despite the fact, they say,
that "episiotomy is one of the most common surgical procedures
in Western medicine": "We have found no evidence that liberal
or routine use of episiotomy prevents perineal trauma or pelvic
floor relaxation. Virtually all severe perineal trauma was associated with median episiotomy. Restriction of episiotomy use
among multiparous women [women who have had more than
one child] resulted in significantly more intact perineums and
less perineal suturing."

ether: A volatile liquid used as a general anesthetic. It depresses the baby and may cause uterine relaxation, postpartum hemorrhage, reduced urination, decreased tone and motility of the intestines, and brief abnormalities in liver function. It is very unpleasant for the mother, highly flammable and explosive, and often causes postoperative nausea and vomiting.

first-degree laceration: Involves the fourchet (band of mucous membranes at the posterior end of the vagina), the perineal skin, and vaginal mucous membrane—but not the underlying connective tissue or muscle.

forceps: From the Latin meaning "pair of tongs." A series of paired instruments having a handle, shank, and blade, used to assist delivery of the fetal head. Invented by Englishman Peter Chamberlen in the early 1600s and kept a family secret for more than one hundred years, the forceps was considered a great medical advance because it could free the fetus from the birth canal without killing it. Forceps are usually used today in conjunction with local or regional anesthesia and an episiotomy. High-forceps delivery, when the baby's head is not engaged in the birth canal, and mid-forceps, when the head has reached only the midplane of the mother's pelvis, are less common than cesareans these days. The use of low forceps, when the baby's head is on the pelvic floor, is still fairly common.

gas insufflation: Gas is pumped into the Fallopian tubes to open them up and remove minor obstructions.

gestational diabetes: A disorder characterized by an inability to metabolize carbohydrates, which occurs in pregnancy and usually disappears after delivery. Treatment includes a high-protein or high-fiber diet and avoidance of sugar and may require insulin injections. One of the primary dangers of gestational diabetes is the birth of an oversized infant with accompanying birth difficulties. Another danger is hypoglycemia in the newborn.

ischial spines: Two relatively sharp bony projections into the pelvic outlet from the bones that form the lower border of the pelvis.

lithotomy position: Customary posture for delivering babies in American hospitals for decades. The woman is placed flat on her back with her legs lifted, spread apart, and set in stirrups. This posture was adopted for the physician's convenience: the position makes it easy for the doctor to see what he is doing and to handle the birth of the child. It is an uncomfortable position for a pregnant woman, however, and it is very difficult for women to push a baby out in this position.

meconium: The material that collects in the intestines of a fetus and forms the first bowel movement of a newborn. The presence of meconium in the amniotic fluid during labor may indicate fetal distress.

midwife: From the Old English, meaning "with woman." A person who assists women in childbirth, as distinguished from an obstetrician who is a medical doctor specializing in childbirth. A certified nurse midwife (CNM) is a registered nurse who has also completed an extensive course of study in prenatal care, childbirth, and postpartum care approved by the American College of Nurse-Midwives. A lay midwife is a professional childbirth attendant who has not been formally certified by the American College of Nurse-Midwives. Most states in the United States outlaw midwives other than certified nurse-midwives. About eleven states license lay midwives and require that they complete a certain level of training in order to be licensed.

Through the late 1700s and much of the 1800s, a doctor who delivered babies was called a midwife and practiced midwifery. The literature is full of early criticism of male midwives, when doctors began to deliver babies, and of cries of "meddlesome midwifery," when doctors took actions that interfered with the normal physiological process. See "obstetrician."

monitrice: A professional labor assistant who not only provides nurturing and support but is also trained to assess the physical condition of mother and baby during labor and delivery. (See "doula.")

nitrous oxide (laughing gas): A gas that provides light anesthesia. It is not explosive or flammable and recovery is rapid.

obstetrician: A medical doctor specializing in the delivery of babies, often abbreviated as OB, and combined with gynecology, which concerns the health care of women. An obstetrician/gynecologist is often called an OB/GYN. The term was first used in the United States between 1820 and 1830 and means literally, from the Latin, "one who stands before." The term "obstetrics" was developed (1810–20) to dignify the formal medical study of childbirth and distinguish what doctors did from what midwives did. (See "midwife.")

paracervical block: Injection of a local anesthetic into the sides of the cervix. This method of pain relief came to be associated with abnormally slowed fetal heartbeat and is not used much anymore.

perineum: The pelvic floor—in women it is the area between the pubic arch in front and the coccyx (or tailbone) in back.

Pitocin, oxytocin: Pitocin is a trademark name for an oxytocin, a drug that stimulates the muscle of the uterus to contract—used to induce labor, to augment labor, and to contract the uterus following delivery. The most serious adverse reaction to oxytocin is very intense, sustained contractions that may cause the uterus to rupture and reduce oxygen flow to the fetus.

placenta: The organ attached to the uterine wall through which the fetus absorbs oxygen, nutrients, and other substances and excretes carbon dioxide and other wastes. The fetus is attached to the placenta through the umbilical cord. The placenta is expelled after the birth of the baby.

"Placenta previa" is a condition in which the placenta partially or completely covers the cervical opening. Even slight dilation of the opening can cause a partial detachment of the placenta from the uterus and result in bleeding.

"Abruptio placentae" is separation of the placenta from the uterus in a pregnancy of more than twenty weeks, before the fetus is born. If the placenta separates completely before the baby is born, the baby dies. Abruptio placentae can also cause severe hemorrhage and the consequent death of the mother.

postpartum depression: A psychiatric condition that occurs after childbirth, typically from three days to six weeks postpartum, characterized by symptoms ranging from mild "blues" to psychosis. Postpartum depression occurs about once in every 2,000 or 3,000 pregnancies. The cause is not proven; there may be neurochemical or psychological influences. Postpartum depression recurs in subsequent pregnancies in about 25 percent of cases.

preeclampsia, toxemia, eclampsia, PIH (pregnancy-induced hypertension): Preeclampsia or toxemia is one of the most serious complications of pregnancy, occurring in 5 to 7 percent of all pregnancies. It is characterized by acute high blood pressure after the twenty-fourth week of pregnancy. Other danger signals: the presence of large quantities of protein in the urine and swelling. Preeclampsia or toxemia can lead to eclampsia, which is characterized by grand mal convulsions that may be followed by coma and death. Other complications of toxemia include internal bleeding, cerebral hemorrhage, kidney failure, interuterine fetal growth retardation, and abruptio placentae. Maternal mortality in eclampsia is 10 percent; fetal mortality is 25 percent. The cause of preeclampsia is still not known but the incidence seems to be significantly increased in first-time mothers—especially the very young and the very mature, in malnourished pregnant women, and in women pregnant with twins.

prep: The traditional routine of shaving a woman's pubic hair and administering an enema as soon as she arrived at the hospital in labor. The ostensible purpose of the shave was to prevent infection—despite the fact that, as far back as 1922 (!), randomized, controlled tests demonstrated that pubic or perineal shaves did absolutely nothing to reduce the incidence of infection. In some tests those who *had* been shaved had a slightly higher incidence of infection. (See "Intervention and Causal Inference in Obstetric Practice" in *Benefits and Hazards of the New Obstetrics*, listed in bibliography.)

The enema was intended to give the baby more room to descend in the mother's pelvis and to reduce a woman's supposed tendency to hold back in pushing the baby out, for fear of having an accident in the delivery room. Some birth attendants also felt that an enema might intensify or shorten labor, prevent infection from a bowel movement on the delivery table, and prevent pain from a bowel movement too soon after the birth.

The consequence, however, was not only greatly enhanced discomfort during labor but also greatly enhanced discomfort after the birth—the combined effects of the standard episiotomy, prickly pubic hair growing out, and, sometimes, the irritation left over from the enema—often given with soapsuds.

Shaving is done less often these days. Enemas are still administered in hard labor all too often. Women could administer home-use enemas to themselves when labor begins, if the attending physician or midwife believes this is important.

primigravida: A woman who is pregnant for the first time.

puerperal or "childbed" fever: An infection developed shortly after childbirth that frequently resulted in kidney failure, shock, and death. Women died as a result of systemic bacterial infection most often caused by unsterile obstetric technique during childbirth. Puerperal fever was little known before hospital birth became common for poor women early in the 1800s. Epidemics swept through hospitals and killed thousands of women and their infants. Sterile technique was introduced gradually and the fever epidemics became less frequent, but childbed fever remained the most common cause of maternal death until the

1930s and was not entirely brought under control until the introduction of antibiotics. Cases of childbed fever still occur today.

saddle block: Popular term used to describe low spinal-block regional anesthesia. The term indicates that the regions anesthetized are those parts that would touch the saddle while riding, but actually a much larger area is anesthetized.

"show" or "bloody show" or "plug": The release of the thick mucus plug that accumulates in the cervical canal during pregnancy—may signal the imminent onset of labor.

spinal anesthesia: Regional anesthesia accomplished by injecting an anesthetic agent into the spinal canal. Negative consequences can include lowered blood pressure and a much-reduced placental blood flow, complete spinal blockage with respiratory paralysis, severe postpartum spinal headaches, bladder dysfunction, and urinary tract infection. The spinal is today used primarily for forceps and cesarean deliveries.

transition: The last phase of the first stage of labor, when labor proceeds from the often lengthy first-stage process of dilating or opening the cervix to the more active second or expulsive stage, during which the baby is pushed down through the birth canal and out of the mother's body.

transverse: The baby presents lying crosswise or horizontally in the mother's womb. Unless the baby turns or is turned, vaginal delivery is impossible.

Trilene: As described in Nicholson Eastman's 1963 edition of *Expectant Motherhood*, "an anesthetic liquid which resembles chloroform in smell and effects." Trilene was frequently self-administered during contractions with an inhaler and mask.

twilight sleep: A popular term used to describe the administration of a small amount of morphine and regular doses of scopolamine to mothers in labor to effect some pain relief and forgetfulness of the entire birthing experience. The drugs often had a harmful effect on the baby, who was frequently born not breathing. The scopolamine sometimes caused the mother to become delirious and hallucinate. This technique of effecting pain relief in labor is seldom used today.

VBAC: Vaginal birth after cesarean.

vernix: The "cheeselike" substance that covers the skin of the fetus and newborn infant. It acts as a protective agent during life in the womb. Rahima Baldwin in *Special Delivery* says, "vernix . . . keeps the baby from turning into a prune in the amniotic fluid. It is very good for the skin and can be rubbed in rather than washed off."

version: Turning of the baby in the womb, usually to convert a breech, transverse, or oblique presentation into a vertex. Versions are usually done externally these days by manipulating the baby through the abdominal wall.

vertex: Head-down position of the baby in the womb.

About the Author

PATRICIA BERNSTEIN grew up in Dallas and earned a Degree of Distinction in American Studies from Smith College, where she was named to Phi Beta Kappa in her junior year. For the past nineteen years she has been a publicist in Houston. In 1983 she founded her own public relations firm, which she still heads today.

For the past sixteen years or so, she has also been writing and publishing magazine articles in Houston publications and in national magazines like *Cosmopolitan, American Baby, Baby Talk,* and *Complete Woman.* Her real education for this book, however, began with the birth of her first daughter, in 1970, and continued, much later, with the births of two more daughters, in 1985 and 1988.

"Because I didn't have my babies all in a clump within a few years of each other, like many women," she says, "I saw some drastic changes in the way birth was handled over a long period of time. So birth stopped being 'just the way things are' to me and started being part of social history and change, just like any other life process. I started wanting to know how it had been for other women in other times and places." She collected dozens of birth stories; some of them are presented here.

"I also hoped other women—including my own girls," she adds, "might gain something from these wonderful tales that are angry, happy, sad, grateful, joyous—sometimes all of these things at once. These voices have a lot of wisdom to convey."